TRAUMATOLOGY OF GRIEVING

THE SERIES IN TRAUMA AND LOSS

Figley, Bride, and Mazza   *Death and Trauma: The Traumatology of Grieving*
Valent   *From Survival to Fulfillment: A Framework for the Life-Trauma Dialectic*
Zinner and Williams   *When a Community Weeps: Case Studies in Group Survivorship*
Figley   *Traumatology of Grieving: Conceptual, Theoretical, and Treatment Foundations*

ISSN 1090-9575

TRAUMATOLOGY OF GRIEVING
Conceptual, Theoretical, and Treatment Foundations

Edited by
CHARLES R. FIGLEY, Ph.D.
Psychosocial Stress Research
and Development Program
Florida State University
Tallahasee, Florida

BRUNNER/MAZEL
· Taylor & Francis Group ·

USA   Publishing Office: BRUNNER/MAZEL
A member of the Taylor & Francis Group
325 Chestnut Street
Philadelphia, PA 19106
Tel: (215) 625-8900
Fax: (215) 625-2940

Distribution Center: BRUNNER/MAZEL
A member of the Taylor & Francis Group
47 Runway Road, Suite G
Levittown, PA 19057
Tel: (215) 269-0400
Fax: (215) 269-0363

UK   BRUNNER/MAZEL
A member of the Taylor & Francis Group
1 Gunpowder Square
London EC4A 3DE
Tel: +44 171 583 0490
Fax: +44 171 583 0581

TRAUMATOLOGY OF GRIEVING: Conceptual, Theoretical, and Treatment Foundation

1   2   3   4   5   6   7   8   9   0

Printed by Edwards Brothers, Ann Arbor, MI, 1998.
Cover design by Nancy Abbott.
Cover image copyright 1997 Photo Disc, Inc.

A CIP catalog record for this book is available from the British Library.
The paper in this publication meets the requirements of the ANSI Standard Z39.48-1984 (Permanence of Paper).

Library of Congress Cataloging-in-Publication Data
Traumatology of grieving: conceptual, theoretical, and treatment foundations / edited by Charles R. Figley.
     p.   cm. – (Series in trauma and loss, ISSN 1090-9575)
Includes bibliographical references and indexes.
ISBN 0-87630-972-4 (case: alk. paper). – ISBN 0-87630-973-2 (pbk.: alk. paper)
1. Bereavement–Psychological aspects. 2. Post-traumatic stress disorder. 3. Grief therapy.
4. Post-traumatic stress disorder–Treatment. I. Figley, Charles R., 1944– . II. Series.
RC455.4.L67T7 1998   98-34143
616.85'21–dc21   CIP

0-87630-972-4 (case)
0-87630-973-2 (paper)

Contents

Contributors   ix
Editorial Note   xi
Acknowledgments   xiii
Introduction   xv

PART 1: CONCEPTUAL AND EMPIRICAL FOUNDATIONS

Chapter 1   Conceptualizing Death and Trauma:
                 A Preliminary Endeavor
                 B. Hudnall Stamm   3

                 Death as a Traumatic Stress Risk Factor   3
                 Identifying Theoretical Tools Across Death and Trauma 7
                 Identifying Contextual Risk Factors   11
                 Death as an Extreme Stressor   14
                 Conclusion   16
                 References   17

Chapter 2   Empirical Perspectives on Contextualizing Death
                 and Trauma
                 B. Hudnall Stamm   23

                 Death as a Traumatic Stress Risk Factor   23
                 Identifying Theoretical Tools Across Death and Trauma 25
                 Contemplating Contextual Risk Factors   27
                 Conclusion   32
                 References   33

Chapter 3   Factors Associated With Effective Loss
                 Accommodation
                 George A. Bonanno   37

                 The Measurement of Grief   37
                 Circumstances of the Loss Event   39
                 Personality   41

Emotion and Coping   42
The Meaning of a Loss   44
Perceived Quality of the Relationship With the Deceased   45
Conclusion   47
References   47

Chapter 4   Intersections of Grief and Trauma: Family
                          Members' Reactions to Homicide
                          M. Elizabeth Stevens-Guille   53

                          Traumatic Grief   53
                          Secondary Traumatization   54
                          Grief as a Stressful Event   54
                          Trauma Symptoms of Family Survivors   55
                          The Role of Social Support   56
                          Gender and Age Factors   57
                          Centrality of the Relationship to the Bereaved   57
                          Canadian Incidence of Homicide   57
                          The Western Canada Families of Homicide Study   58
                          Method and Procedure   58
                          Results and Discussion   62
                          Conclusion   66
                          References   67

Chapter 5   Duty-Related Deaths and Police Spouse
                          Survivors: Group Support Effects
                          John M. Violanti   71

                          The Police Culture and Surviving Spouses   71
                          A Study of Police Survivor Trauma   72
                          Method   73
                          Results   75
                          Implications for Intervention and Treatment   78
                          Conclusion   83
                          References   85

Chapter 6   Emotional Dissociation, Self-Deception, and
                          Adaptation to Loss
                          George A. Bonanno   89

                          The Traditional Grief Work Approach to Bereavement   90
                          Do Empirical Data Support the Grief Work Approach?   90
                          Alternative Psychological Approaches to Bereavement   91
                          The Adaptive Value of Emotional Dissociation and
                                Self-Deception   93
                          Limitations of the Evidence   97
                          Cross-Cultural Evidence   98

Conclusion   101
References   101

PART 2: APPLICATIONS

Chapter 7   Bereavement After Homicide: Its Assessment
              and Treatment
              E. K. Rynearson and Russell Geoffrey   109

              Historical Review: The Coconut Grove Fire Revisited   109
              The Specific Effects of Homicide   112
              Vulnerability and Resiliency   113
              A Clinical Survey of Resiliency and Vulnerability in
                  Homicidal Bereavement   115
              Assessment   119
              Preliminary Thoughts About Psychotherapy   120
              Strategies for Pacification and Partition   120
              Group Psychotherapy   121
              Case Histories   122
              Prevention   127
              Conclusion   128
              References   128

Chapter 8   The Treatment of PTSD Through Grief Work and
              Forgiveness
              Lee Hyer and Jeffrey M. Brandsma   131

              Self   132
              PTSD and Grief   134
              Growth in Grief   136
              Treatment Model   142
              Forgiveness: The Special Ingredient of Grief Therapy   145
              Conclusion   148
              References   148

Chapter 9   Relieving the Naumatic Aspects of Death with
              Naumatic Incident Resolution and EMDR
              Teresa Descilo   153

              Significance of the Stressor to the Child/Adult System   153
              Interventions for Bereavement   154
              Theoretical Perspective: Traumatic Incident Resolution   155
              Eye Movement Desensitization and Reprocessing   156
              Issues of Assessment   169
              TIR Approach Methodology   169
              Evidence of Effectiveness   178
              Conclusion   181
              References   181

Chapter 10   Death-Related Treatment Applications for the
                  Elderly
                  Michael McGee   183

                  Background   184
                  Theoretical Perspectives   185
                  Senior Developmental Activities   186
                  Developmental Activities and Major Stressors   188
                  Elder Intervention Issues   189
                  Assessment Models   189
                  Senior Trauma Methodological Approach   190
                  Senior Life Span Developmental Model for Trauma
                      Reduction   194
                  Conclusion   197
                  References   197

Chapter 11   Safety Reconnaissance for Grieving Trauma
                  Survivors
                  J. Eric Gentry and Iris M. Schmidt   201

                  Background   201
                  Procedure   203
                  Discussion   214
                  Conclusion   215
                  References   215

Name Index   217
Subject Index   227

Contributors

GEORGE A. BONANNO, PhD
The Life Cycle Institute
Department of Psychology
Catholic University of America
Washington, D.C.

JEFFREY M. BRANDSMA, PhD
Medical College of Georgia
Augusta Veterans Administration
    Medical Center
Augusta, Georgia

TERESA DESCILO, MSW
Executive Director
Victim Services Center
Miami, Florida

J. ERIC GENTRY, MA, CAC
Green Cross Projects
Florida State University
Tallahassee, Florida

RUSSELL GEOFFREY, MD
Jefferson Community Counseling
    Center
Port Townsend, Washington

LEE HYER, PhD
Medical College of Georgia
Augusta Veterans Administration
    Medical Center
Augusta, Georgia

MICHAEL McGEE, MS
The Marriage and Family Clinic
Florida State University
Tallahassee, Florida

E. K. RYNEARSON, MD
Department of Psychiatry
University of Washington
Harborview Medical Center
Seattle, Washington
Section of Psychiatry
Virginia Mason Medical Center
Seattle, Washington

B. HUDNALL STAMM, PhD
VAM National PTSD Center
Department of Psychiatry
Dartmouth Medical School
White River Junction, Vermont

M. ELIZABETH STEVENS-GUILLE, PhD
Private Practice
Edmonton, Alberta Canada

IRIS M. SCHMIDT, ACSW, MPA
Department of Psychiatry
University of West Virginia Medical School
Morgantown, Virginia

JOHN M. VIOLANTI, PhD
Department of Criminal Justice
Rochester Institute of Technology
Rochester, New York

Editorial Note

Traumatology of Grieving is the fourth book published in the Brunner/Mazel Series in Trauma and Loss. My co-editor for the series, Therese Rando, and the entire Editorial Board are very pleased with the volume, and, in this note, I would like to make several observations that place the volume in proper context.

The purpose of the series is to attract important contributions to the fields of traumatology and thanatology by drawing on both fields. The series was established in 1996, when the first book, *Death and Trauma*, was published. *Traumatology of Grieving* is, in many ways, an extension of that first volume.

Writing in the foreword to that first volume, Rando noted the gap between the two fields. She noted, for example, that practitioners working with traumatically bereaved individuals need to not only understand traumatic stress and fully comprehend the loss; they must appreciate four points. First, uncomplicated acute grief is a form of posttraumatic stress disorder. Second, practitioners must appreciate the factors that make any death circumstance traumatic. Third, death that is perceived to be traumatic by the survivor increases the likelihood of complicated mourning. Finally, traumatic elements must be treated before loss-related aspects of grief and mourning. She noted that *Death and Trauma* was the first book "devoted entirely to a conceptual and phenomenological exploration of traumatic bereavement—or, as termed on occasion herein, death-related PTSD."

This volume extends the work of *Death and Trauma* in four ways: There is a major emphasis on empirical research, such as empirically derived risk factors in bereavement. It challenges basic assumptions about bereavement, such as the requirement for "working through" and "grief work." It focuses discussion on often over-looked groups struggling with death-related trauma, such as police spouse survivors, homicide family survivors, war veterans, and the elderly. And it introduces additional treatment approaches such as traumatic incident reduction, establishing safety for clients, and the therapeutic use of forgiveness.

We hope that this volume will stimulate more like it. Indeed, the book currently in press in the series will also challenge current thinking about the role of death in trauma and the role of trauma in death and other losses in life. We are gratified by the increased interest in this new area and welcome proposals for either books or chapters.

Charles R. Figley, Editor
Tallahassee, Florida
June 1998

Acknowledgments

This book would not be possible without the contributors; their contributions are quite obvious, and I appreciate their confidence in my editorial judgments and coordination. I would like to acknowledge and thank the Series Editorial Board for their wisdom and guidance of this project. It was a challenge to give sufficient credit and incorporate fairly the best of both thanatology and traumatology in determining the content of this book. Certainly my series co-editor, Therese Rando, was a key member of this team of consultants. I would also like to acknowledge a long list of colleagues who served in one or more roles. They include Morton Bard, PhD,* American Cancer Society, Atlanta, Georgia; Ann Burgess, DNSc, University of Pennsylvania, Philadelphia; Atle Dyregrov, PhD, Director, Trauma Recovery Center (Norway); Yvette Esprey, MA, University of the Witwatersrand (South Africa); George Everly, PhD, International Critical Incident Stress Foundation, Baltimore, Maryland; Berthold P. Gersons, MD, PhD, University of Amsterdam Medical School; Bonnie L. Green, PhD, Georgetown University Medical School, Washington, D.C.; Judith L. Herman, MD, Cambridge Hospital, Cambridge, Massachusetts; Mardi Horowitz, MD, University of California, San Francisco, Medical School; Soren Buus Jensen, MD, PhD (dr.med), World Health Organization, Bosnia/Denmark; Rolf Kleber, PhD, University of Utrecht (the Netherlands); Robert Jay Lifton, MD, John Jay College of Criminal Justice, New York City; Tom Lundin, MD, Karolinska Hospital (Sweden); Jeffery Mitchell, PhD, International CIS Foundation; Frank Ochberg, MD, Michigan State University, East Lansing; Soili Poijula, PhD, Trauma Recovery Center, Oulu (Finland); Beverly Raphael, MD, Director, Center for Mental Health (Australia); Robyn Robinson, PhD, Director, Trauma Support Consultants (Australia); Gil Straker, PhD, University of the Witwatersrand (South Africa); Lars Weiseth, MD, University of Oslo Medical School (Norway); John P. Wilson, PhD, Cleveland State University, Cleveland, Ohio; Joseph Wolpe, MD,* Pepperdine University, Los Angeles, California; Frederick Lerner, DLSci, National PTSD Center; David V. Baldwin, PhD, Southern Oregon State College, Ashland, Oregon; Brian E. Bride, MSW, St. Jude's Recovery Center, Atlanta, Georgia; my colleagues at Florida State University, Nick Mazza, PhD, and Joyce L. Carbonell, PhD; Danny Brom, PhD, National Israeli Center for Psychosocial Support for Holocaust Survivors and Their Children, Jerusalem, Israel; Spencer Eth, MD, University of California, Los Angeles; Garry A. Flint, PhD, Private Practice, Vernon, British Columbia, Canada; Matthew J. Friedman, MD, PhD, National Center for PTSD, White River Junction, Vermont; Frank Gerbode, MD, Institute for Research in Metapsychology, Palo Alto, California; Dennis Grant, MD, VA Medical Center,

Phoenix, Arizona; Are Holen, MD, University of Oslo (Norway); W. Jake Jacobs, PhD, University of Southern California, Los Angeles; Steven Lazrove, MD, Yale University, New Haven, Connecticut; Gary E. May, ACSW, CCSW, University of Southern Indiana, Evansville; Kathleen Nader, PhD, Private Practice, Laguna Beach, California; Francine Shapiro, PhD, Mental Research Institute, Palo Alto, California; Jonathan Shay, MD, PhD, Tufts Medical School and VA Outpatient Clinic, Boston, Massachusetts; Zahava Solomon, PhD, University of Tel Aviv (Israel); Paul Valent, MBBS, FRANZCP, Monash Medical Center, Melbourne, Australia; Onno van der Hart, PhD, Free University (the Netherlands); Bruce H. Young, MSW, National Center for PTSD, Palo Alto, California; and William Yule, PhD, Institute of Psychiatry, University of London.

My assistant, Denise Hannon, deserves considerable credit for helping with various tasks, and my colleagues in the School of Social Work and the Interdivisional Program in Marriage and Family have always been supportive, especially the dean of the school, Dianne Montgomery. My clients, along with my graduate students (especially Janet Nambi, Mike McGee, Mike Barnes, MaryDale Salston, Eric Gentry, and Veronika Ospina-Kammerer) and their clients, taught us much about the traumatology of grieving. Finally, my family, Marilyn, Laura, and Jessica, deserve special credit for providing emotional support.

---

*Deceased.

Introduction

"The death was traumatic for us." This is a statement that is very common among people who have suffered the loss of a loved one. Yet, the professionals who study and treat those who grieve believe that death is such a normal and natural thing that it really is not traumatic. Indeed, there is a fear that combining the fields would be unwise. This was noted and addressed in the seminal volume, *Death and Trauma: The Traumatology of Loss*.

The danger, of course, is that grieving family members and mental health practitioners may then treat the bereaved no differently than others with posttraumatic stress disorder (PTSD), a mental disorder. Also, there is the possibility that "simple bereavement" may indeed trivialize PTSD, making the response so commonplace that it cannot distinguish traumatic and nontraumatic life experiences.

This is connected with another concern noted by colleague: viewing bereavement as pathology. There is even skepticism about the existence of "pathological bereavement." And if it *does* exist, there is opposition to calling it a form of PTSD or even a separate diagnostic category within the *DSM*.

We believe that all of these concerns are legitimate. Various victim rights groups generally first raised the concern about homogenization of PTSD in the 1970s. Those who worked with rape and family violence victims, for example, were quite concerned about the syndromes affecting their clients (e.g., rape trauma syndrome, battered woman syndrome) being "lumped together" with post-Vietnam syndrome, disaster stress, and others to form PTSD. That opposition seemed to all but evaporate by 1990.

The concern about "simple bereavement" is also legitimate. There has been a concerted effort over the years to distinguish traumatic stress from other types of stress and traumatic stress reactions from traumatic stress disorders. In other words, not everyone will develop PTSD following exposure to a highly stressful event. Among Vietnam war veterans for example, it is estimated that only 36% ever developed PTSD and that only slightly more than 15% still have it. This means that 64% *never* had it, although most experienced symptoms of traumatic stress. Thus, we could say that these men and women experienced a *normal reaction to an abnormally stressful situation*.

The same can be said for those who experience the death of a child or a spouse, for example. Most will be traumatized and will display traumatic stress reactions, to the surprise of few. Most will recover at a predictable rate, especially with the support of caring people. Yet, a small number will not and will require professional assistance. It is my belief that the form of this assistance could be improved or at least be informed by knowledge about the assessment and treatment of other traumatized people.

The special and unique features of death-related PTSD, along with its assessment and treatment, are the agenda of *Traumatology of Grieving*. The goal of this book is to begin the struggle for solutions to these and other issues.

Our hope is that we can contribute to the literatures of both traumatology and loss—and from them derive critical empirical axioms, concepts, and theoretical formulations that transcend both areas. As noted in the preface of the first volume in this series:

> The trauma experienced by survivors is inescapable. The challenge of the millennium for professionals who care about survivors is to work collectively toward a common goal: To gather together the most efficient and effective tools of our collective trade to ease the pain of grief and promote the natural process of bereavement. The extraordinary powerful and efficient treatment methods described in the latter section of this book are illustrations of the byproducts of cooperation.

This book builds upon and is organized in a way that is similar to *Death and Trauma*. Chapter authors followed a prescribed outline and shared a common set of elements, including case examples, drawing upon consistent concepts and definitions, and equal attention to scholarly and practical/practice concerns. The 11 chapters are divided among two parts.

PART I: CONCEPTUAL AND EMPIRICAL FOUNDATIONS

The six chapters in Part I have the most diverse structure, since each focuses on a different issue. However, each makes an effort to review and apply both the thanatology and traumatology literatures, beginning with a description of the purpose of the chapter and ending with a summary of major points.

In Chapter 1, Beth Stamm, a leading traumatologist, presents a broad-ranging, theoretical paper on death and traumatic stress. She frequently references her other chapter in this book, "Empirical Perspectives on Contextualizing Death and Trauma." Both chapters draw from theory, practice, and research to address contextual issues that can make death a predisposing risk factor for traumatic stress. At the same time, Stamm notes what makes traumatic stress a risk factor in bereavement. In this chapter, she first addresses experiencing grief as a traumatic stressor. She then identifies the theoretical tools important in the study of death and lists the empirically derived contextual risk factors for death-related psychopathology.

In Chapter 2, Stamm continues her analysis of the interface of the two areas of research by reviewing a series of studies of death and trauma organized in two areas: war and poverty and non-war related death. Although not exhaustive, her review does support and justify discussion of the structural assessment of stressful experiences study conducted by Stamm at the University of Alaska. Six statistically universal factors emerged from this study.

Stamm endorses Raphael and Martinek, who argue that the distinction between normal bereavement and traumatic bereavement is avoidance, while re-
experiencing (intrusion) symptoms are present in both PTSD and normal bereavement. The assumption here is that avoidance symptoms must be addressed before
the bereaved can grieve. The bulk of the chapter then focuses on comparing death-
related stressful experiences with other stressors. In this regard, Stamm reports a
study of 1,177 undergraduate students who completed a comprehensive survey
instrument. Among the findings is that the stressors of daily living are significantly different from both traumatic stressors and death-related stressors, which
have considerable overlap.

Women appeared more likely than men to report positive feelings regarding
reactions to coping with all types of stressors. Stamm notes that there appears
to be considerable energy expended on the part of the traumatized and bereaved
in attempting to avoid reminders of the horrible circumstances of the traumatic
death.

In Chapter 3, the first of two chapters by George Bonanno, the author identifies the flurry of new research activity in thanatology. He attributes this to a number of factors, most notably the new interest in bereavement among social psychologists and the logical extension of trauma research. The topics in the chapter
include the measurement of grief—certainly one of the most important concepts
in this book—and circumstances of the loss, including amount of forewarning,
type of loss, previous losses, perceived social support, and demographic variables. The area of personality variables is reviewed, and emotion regulation and
coping processes are discussed. Although many will find this chapter shocking in
its bluntness about the limitations of support for "grief work," such a critique is
long overdue.

In Chapter 4, "Intersections of Grief and Trauma: Family Members' Reactions to Homicide," M. Elizabeth Stevens-Guille, a pioneer in the study of family
grief patterns, reports the findings of a landmark study of families of homicide
victims. After discussing the complex of stressors associated with grief, she notes
the importance of family and social support. The study assumed that certain traumatic events such as the murder of a family member may be so overwhelming that
family members are unable to function as a social support system for each other.
In her Western Canadian study, 127 family survivors of 84 homicide victims were
investigated up to 6 years retrospectively to discover evidence of stress and grief
reactions. Stevens-Guille reports that, as expected, the stress experienced by these
families was comparable to that of body retrieval workers. Among other important
findings, the closer the victim was in relation to the research participant, the higher
the participant's current feelings of distress. Those family survivors of homicide
victims who had sought counseling had higher global severity scores and experienced more distress when they recalled past grief behavior. Yet, family members
who felt supported by their families reported higher degrees of psychopathology
and stronger feelings of current grief than those who did not feel supported by
other family members. This finding alone suggests that there is something that is

toxic in the family's support or that the investigators apparently tested the family while they were in the process of recovery.

Another contribution of the study is the discovery of gender differences. Women reported higher feelings of current grief. Young women were more likely to report stronger current grief feelings than older women. There were no differences, however, between age groups regarding the incidence of PTSD or general psychopathology. The findings suggest that younger traumatized women require more attention than older ones. Yet, these findings may reflect more of the reluctance of older women to admit feeling intense grief, that such an admission is associated with weakness and ineffectiveness.

In Chapter 5, "Duty-Related Deaths and Police Spouse Survivors: Group Support Effects," John M. Violanti reports on a study that examined the psychological distress associated with losing a police officer spouse and the subsequent effects on social interactions. Findings suggest that the distress felt was directly related to the quality of interactions and support within the police work group, as expected. However, support outside this trauma membrane of the police environment (justice system, media, community) had no apparent positive effect for these grieving spouses. This finding emphasizes more than ever the importance of building a cohesive and supportive police families system. Violanti speculates that "this may indicate that cohesiveness and a sense of belonging to the police culture somehow influence experiences of distress and trauma" among surviving police spouses. Police groups appear to promise more meaningful types of support for these grieving spouses.

Violanti suggests that police departments should be much more aware of their current policies and practices associated with the loss of a member of the department and initiate effective spouse bereavement programs informed by this study. Tangible emotional support through the entire process of grieving would last years, not months. Support should address the suddenness, violence, and gruesome circumstances of an officer's death. Other special factors for grieving police spouses are the public notice of the death, dealing with the frustrations of the criminal justice system, and the role of community antipathy toward law enforcement generally.

In Chapter 6, George Bonanno focuses on the "grief work" assumption: the adaptive value for some people of simply using avoidance to help control the dosage of emotionally draining traumatic stress. Here he expands on his work in Chapter 3 and challenges the value of mourning as the need for insight and cognitive processing. Bonanno describes the grief work assumption as a summary heuristic for contemporary beliefs about the importance of working through thoughts and emotions associated with the loss. He argues that there is considerable discrepancy between what is known about the bereavement process and what grief and trauma therapists do.

According to his review of the grief work literature, practitioners are encouraged to stress the importance of a full review and experience of the emotional meanings of loss. Yet, the evidence does not support this practice guideline. Moreover, practitioners are urged to test for maladaptive bereavement including what Bonanno believes are good coping methods. These methods include avoidance of negative material and denial. Bonanno asserts that the few empirical studies that test the working-through assumption fail to demonstrate support. In contrast, he sites his own program of research focusing on the factors that appeared to help or hinder the loss accommodation of a large group of widows living in the San Francisco Bay area. He suggests an interactionist cognitive stress perspective. According to his empirically derived model, any event, including the loss of a loved one, is stressful to the extent that it overwhelms the person and strains coping mechanisms for reducing distress. "Denial" is perceived as an initial effort to cope, as are avoidance behaviors, humor, and benign distractions. Practitioners should never force clients to do anything other than what is consistent with their own coping methods that have worked in the past. A client's natural inclinations to relieve the distress of the loss should guide therapy rather than the therapist's preconceived notions about what the client must do to "recover."

Also, sessions with a traumatologist would provide more education than therapy. According to Bonanno, these sessions should be client centered, and discussions would be determined by the interests of the client. Yet, the goals would be very clear: practicing "letting go" of the emotional pain of the loss, figuring out what to do now and in the future, discovering additional coping resources, learning how to laugh more frequently, and other self-soothing activities that will make life more tolerable.

PART II: APPLICATIONS

The five chapters in Part II, have identical structures. The specific application contexts vary greatly, however.

In Chapter 7, E. K. Rynearson and Russell Geoffrey discuss the fundamentals of helping the bereaved following a homicide, as well as their special brand of therapy. They review the evolution of thinking about bereavement and trauma and point out that, from the beginning, models of these two experiences varied in terms of focus. Bereavement models focused on the personal relationship with the deceased and the task of unconscious acceptance of the loss. Conversely, models of the traumatization and recovery process focused on impersonal effects of an overwhelming event and the conscious task of reestablishing autonomy from what had happened. Lindemann's study (1944) and the lesser known study by Adler (1943) were the first to focus on traumatic death. They came to different conclusions about the current and future functioning of the survivors. We find the same differences today.

The chapter also covers the specific effects of homicide, including Rynearson's classic "three Vs" model of traumatic dying: violence, violation, and volition. The authors present and discuss their study of 52 survivors who participated in a support project for unnatural dying that started in 1990. Among other things, the study found that those who seek treatment within the first year of homicidal bereavement present with higher levels of distress and antecedent psychiatric vulnerability than those who refuse treatment during this period. This simply confirms the importance of self-referral for treatment. Among the conclusions from the study that have implications for practitioners are that clients require considerable time for loss accommodation and that clients need some way to control their distress state during the mourning process. The authors recommend exercises that encourage relaxation (modulations) and guided imagery (diversion). The goal is to help the client modulate grief and acquire methods of stress reduction through diversion and a program to promote resiliency.

In Chapter 8, two psychologists and experts on treating war veterans with PTSD, Lee Hyer and Jeffrey M. Brandsma, discuss the disorder from the perspective of the grieving process. They point out that loss influences the development of PTSD symptoms, and, in turn, traumatic memories slow down loss accommodation. They argue that mourners suffer from self-loss, a wound to their identity (or what they call self-theory). They suggest that self-theory is a critical feature of PTSD treatment and identify eight tenets that reflect PTSD grief processes and treatment.

Hyer and Brandsma use the latter section of the chapter to present their model of treating PTSD through grief work and forgiveness, noting six overlapping stages of traumatic grief work. The last element in their treatment model, they note, is the "special ingredient of grief therapy": forgiveness. They suggest that shame and guilt are bookends to traumatic grief that are often confused and that forgiveness of self "is the ultimate act of humanity, perhaps what makes a person a person."

In Chapter 9, Teresa Descilo notes the significance of the child-adult system and the effects of the death of either person on the other. She describes two treatment approaches: traumatic incident resolution (TIR) and eye movement desensitization and reprocessing (EMDR). Both approaches are reviewed, beginning with the theoretical model on which they are based. In a synthesis of both TIR and EMDR, Descilo offers "clinical traumatology skills" to overcome the potential bias introduced by the therapist. She discusses three focusing drills to develop practitioners' effectiveness in focusing on the most critical issues and procedures of trauma work. Acknowledgment and closure drills enable practitioners to more effectively end trauma work sessions. Descilo also discusses what effective trauma treatment should look like. These end points help assure both client and therapist that the distress associated with the memories has been removed permanently. After discussing the role of emotions in processing traumatic events, the chapter focuses on TIR and then EMDR regarding assessment and treatment procedures. This is followed by a discussion of what can go wrong when applying the treatment procedures. The chapter ends with presentation and discussion of a case example.

In Chapter 10, Michael McGee presents us with a rather obvious question that seems to involve a rather complicated answer: "Do elders experience stress and loss the same way as younger adults?" He reviews the changing functional abilities of older adults (cognitive, physical, and emotional resources) and suggests that this population employs increased levels of social support. In his developmental approach, seniors pass through stages. In each of these stages, an elder's capabilities to manage stress are evaluated and a treatment plan developed. The key components are the assessment of the elder's stage of development and the degree of social support required to help alleviate the impact of the loss of a close friend's or spouse's life.

In Chapter 11, "Safety Reconnaissance for Grieving Trauma Survivors," Erick Gentry and Iris Schmidt suggest that grief is a complicated process that is complicated further by traumatic death circumstances. More than any other group, grieving clients struggling with PTSD require a therapeutic environment in which they feel safe. The authors suggest that there are at least three levels of therapeutic safety: resolution of impending environmental and interpersonal danger, amelioration of self-destructive patterns, and restructuring victim mythology into a proactive survivor identity through development and habituation of life-affirming self-care skills.

Their program, named Safety Reconnaissance, is a comprehensive way to ensure that all clients can enjoy a sense of safety. Techniques include relaxation, visualization, cognitive-behavior therapy, and systems theory. As a result of this method, the client and therapist more effectively define safety, challenge the victim mythology, and create an internal "safe place."

In summary, this second volume continues in the tradition of the first. This book and others like it help keep pace with what the general public already knows: The death of a person significant in our lives is, by definition, traumatic, and therefore both trauma and grief should be addressed simultaneously to allow better accommodation to the loss. In emphasizing the importance of grief and mourning in the traumatology of life, the book suggests that traumatic elements must be worked through before grief and loss accommodation are achieved. National experts, drawing from many years of experience, suggest that the reader consider a perspective that is informed by both research and practice over many years.

Charles R. Figley, Editor
Tallahassee, Florida
January 1998

Part One

Conceptual and Empirical Foundations

Chapter 1

Conceptualizing Death and Trauma: A Preliminary Endeavor

B. Hudnall Stamm

DEATH AS A TRAUMATIC STRESS RISK FACTOR

Internationally, the overall death rate ranges from 18 per 1,000 (West Africa) to 6 per 1,000 (East Asia), with most countries around the 9–11 per 1,000 range (figures for 1989; Aiken, 1991). In the United States and Canada, 14%–18% of pregnancies end in the spontaneous death of the fetus (Neugebauer et al., 1992). Infant mortality ranges from a low of 4.8 per 1,000 live births in the most developed countries to 161 per 1,000 in the least developed countries (World Health Organization [WHO], 1995).

Death is not a rare event. Yet, by best estimates, posttraumatic stress disorder (PTSD), the hallmark traumatic stress disorder, is not common. Nearly everyone experiences the death of a loved one. About 55% of the people in the United States are exposed to an event that would qualify as an extreme stressor according to the *Diagnostic and Statistical Manual of Mental Disorders* (*DSM-IV*; American Psychiatric Association [APA], 1994, p. 428). Yet, the estimated nonclinical population lifetime PTSD prevalence rate is only 7.8% (Kessler et al., 1995). What range of reactions might there be that could account for differences between exposure and the development of a disorder?

Posttraumatic Stress Disorder, Traumatic Stress, and Death

Until 1994, PTSD required experiencing of "an event that is outside the range of usual human experience and that would be markedly distressing to almost anyone" (APA, 1987, p. 250). This formal medical diagnosis dominated our understanding of traumatic stress for nearly two decades. However, since most people experience the death of someone with whom they were close, death per se cannot be described as "outside the range of usual human experience." Some argue it is unlikely that "ordinary" death could serve as a stressor that has the potential to produce PTSD (cf. Zisook & Schuchter, 1992). Others argue that while grief and trauma are not the same thing, the same event has the potential of producing either or both experiences (cf. Eth & Pynoos, 1985, 1994; Pynoos & Nader, 1988).

The original definitions of traumatic stress led to considerable wrangling about what events actually qualified as "traumatic" (APA, 1987). The *DSM-IV* definition of traumatic stress shifts the focus from a list of qualifying events to key elements of the event. Under the new criteria, a person must have "experienced, witnessed, or been confronted with an event or events that involve actual or threatened death or serious injury, or a threat to the physical integrity of oneself or others" (APA, 1994, p. 426). Thus, death, either as reality or threat, is the pivotal aspect of the definition. The second element—"the person's response involved intense fear, helplessness, or horror" (APA, 1994, p. 426)—opens new understandings of death as a traumatic stressor.

The event-only perspective of traumatic stress has been abandoned. Traumatic stress is an interaction between the person and the event. Because of the bifold nature of the definition, it is possible for death, even if it is sudden or violent, to be traumatic or nontraumatic based on the response of the person who is experiencing the loss. By definition, if the experience is traumatic and leads to a diagnosable pathology, the individual must have reacted with intense fear, helplessness, or horror.

Many of the experiences reported by the bereaved are similar to those that are associated with stress reactions and PTSD. Those reports can include (a) recurrent and intrusive recollections; (b) recurrent distressing dreams, flashbacks, and other dissociative experiences; (c) psychological distress at exposure to symbols of the event or the deceased, including anniversary date distress; and (d) physiological manifestations such as difficulty with sleep, irritability, and difficulty concentrating (APA, 1987, 1994; Eth & Pynoos, 1985; Glick, Weiss, & Parkes, 1974; Jacobs, 1993; Nader, Pynoos, Fairbanks, & Frederick, 1990; Rando, 1992, 1994; Trice, 1988; Trolly, 1994; Turnbull, 1986). Burnette and colleagues (1994) surveyed 77 international experts in the field of thanatology. The consensus from this group was that, even in normal bereavement, it is common to observe yearning and the need to talk about the lost person. These behaviors are accompanied by intrusive thoughts about the lost person, as well as preoccupation and distress at reminders of the person. Clearly, many of these symptoms overlap with even the most strict definition of traumatic stress (APA, 1994). Yet, the question remains, Do these symptoms mean that the person has PTSD?

As stated elsewhere (Stamm, 1995; Stamm & Friedman, in press), traumatic stress can be envisioned as a part of the larger concept of stress, which can include, but is not limited to, the mental disorders of acute stress disorder and PTSD. I suggest that stressful experiences can be conceived as an individual's experience in relation to an event, such that elements of that event in combination with that specific individual create a situation whereby the experience itself is stress producing and one's beliefs—of faith in life, in others, in self—are disorga-

Figure 1.1   Conceptualization of traumatic stress.

nized, reFstructured, or at least challenged (Stamm, 1993). The key differentiation between a traumatically stressful experience and a stressful experience is the *demand* for reorientation (Stamm, 1995; Stamm, Catherall, Terry, & McCammon, 1995). Experience-induced reorientation is stressful but may or may not cause a diagnosable traumatic stress-related mental disorder.

In fact, it is unlikely that people would change at all without some stress to act as a motivator. Positive as well as negative changes can be stressful. This raises the question as to whether stress is a single continuum ranging from minor to extreme stress or whether traumatic stress is a categorically different experience. At present, there is insufficient scientific evidence to answer this question absolutely, but ongoing biological research holds promise (e.g., Friedman, Charney, & Deutch, 1995; Perry, 1993). Figure 1.1 (Stamm, 1995) suggests the nature of this theoretical assumption.

According to the conceptualization shown in Figure 1.1, death is a stressful experience that may or may not lead to a traumatic stress disorder. Death from extreme stressors such as disaster, war, starvation, or genocide is a potent risk factor for traumatic stress responses. These kinds of events seem to demand restructuring of one's belief system (Janoff-Bulman, 1992; McCann & Pearlman, 1990; Stamm, 1995). However, even the "timely" death of another leaves those who have experienced the irrevocable physical loss in a situation in which it is virtually impossible to continue life as if no change has occurred.

This does not mean that all death experiences lead to PTSD or even traumatic stress. Some would even argue that it is possible to experience the death of another without feelings of serious distress (cf. Wortman & Silver, 1989). But some restructuring is nearly always necessary. Following a death, at the very least, someone who was previously a part of the person's life is no longer physically present. For example, after the death of a parent, a bereaved woman remarked that she had to remind herself that her grocery purchases were no longer dictated by what she thought her sick mother might be able to eat. Although this was a simple accommodation—which the woman did not consider aversive—it was nonetheless an accommodation.

In summary, this chapter proposes that death is a stressful life experience that can produce a situation ripe for a traumatic stress response that *may or may not* lead to a traumatic stress disorder. In addition, the assumption is made that stress reactions are not always ultimately injurious. Challenges to our sense of self and the world are catalysts to growth. They create opportunities for developmental enhancement unless the person-event interaction leaves the person with insufficient personal resources to meet the challenge. In this case, a pathology may develop.

This is, in fact, what the literature would suggest. For some, little or no accommodation is necessary (cf. Wortman & Silver, 1989), while others face a difficult and long-term process (cf. Corr, Martinson, & Dyer, 1985; Jacobs, 1993; Rando, 1992, 1994). Painful change is not inherently bad, and, in fact, it may ultimately bring positive maturity (Janoff-Bulman, 1992; Lazarus, 1966; Lazarus & Folkman, 1984; Stamm, 1995; Stamm, Varra, & Sandberg, 1993). Regardless of the course of the experience, death is a reality. At the very least, it signifies a change in the physical constitution of an individual's or family's psychosocial constellation (Turnbull, 1986).

Stressful Experience, Traumatic Stress Reaction, and Traumatic Stress Disorder

While no paper can ever address the full context of even a single experience, the point of this chapter is to create a window to the larger picture of death as a stressful experience and glance across the death and trauma literature. People live in a biopsychosocial context; stressful events are not isolated from the person who experiences them. The change from the *DSM-III-R* event-centered PTSD definition to the *DSM-IV* person-event interaction definition clearly recognized the importance of contextualizing stressful experiences. This chapter endeavors to raise the question of stressful experiences as an ecological, contextual issue so that we might learn to prevent the abortive growth process of PTSD and enhance the possibility of positive developmental growth in the face of the inviolate change of death.

The term *stressful experience* (Stamm, 1995; Stamm, Bieber, & Rudolph, 1996; Stamm, Varra, & Sandberg, 1993) recognizes this person-event interaction at the broadest and most encompassing level. Two other terms originated by Figley (1985, 1995) have been adapted for use here. The term *traumatic stress reaction* refers to "the natural and consequent behaviors and emotions ... [as] a set of conscious and unconscious actions and behaviors associated with dealing with the stressors" or memories of the experience (Figley, 1985, p. xix). An important underlying assumption made is that a traumatic stress reaction contains within it an element of event-induced demand for reorganization of one's belief system (Stamm, 1995). *Traumatic stress disorder* (Figley, 1985, 1995) indicates those stressful experiences that are so traumatically stressful and place such high demands on the person for change that the person's psychosocial resources are challenged sufficiently to create pathology (Stamm, 1995). Following the prevailing professional thought, pathology is defined as a diagnosable mental disorder according to criteria of the *Diagnostic and Statistical Manual of Mental Disorders*

(American Psychiatric Association) or the International Classification of Diseases system.

Traumatic Stress Other than Acute Traumatic Stress Disorder and PTSD

Traumatic stress disorders may take a variety of forms, including PTSD, which has been the focus of great attention over the past two decades. As we have come to know it better, we are more able to see the other idioms of distress (e.g., Friedman & Jaranson, 1994; Friedman & Schnurr, 1995; Kessler et al., 1995; Stamm & Friedman, in press). There is a compelling and expanding literature on these other responses. Perhaps the most developed is dissociation (Kluft, 1988; Spiegel, 1991; Steinberg, 1997; Terr, 1991). Depression is frequently seen as comorbid with PTSD and often alone following a stressful event (Kessler et al., 1995). Physical diseases and somatization are gaining recognition as well (Friedman & Schnurr, 1995; Stamm & Friedman, in press).

IDENTIFYING THEORETICAL TOOLS ACROSS DEATH AND TRAUMA

According to Lifton (1967), death is the ultimate confrontation with one's own mortality. It is, in a sense, the best material for demanding change of one's beliefs. After one confronts the possibility of death, it is no longer possible to assume invulnerability and innocence. The person must either deny the reality of the experienced death or restructure his or her world to incorporate the experienced information that human life is finite. If denial or repression is not used to keep awareness of the death at bay, the death experience requires some reorganization of one's understanding of oneself as well as the manner in which one lives in the world.

There are many useful theories that can assist us in understanding death as a medium to challenge one's beliefs, perceptions, and expectations. To that end, three theoretical perspectives are reviewed briefly here: (a) world assumption theory (Janoff-Bulman, 1992), (b) constructivist self-development theory (Mc-Cann & Pearlman, 1990a), and (c) the dimensions of grief summarized by Jacobs (1993), Stroebe and Stroebe (1987), and Turnbull (1986). These three perspectives, along with practice and research, have informed the development of the quantitatively derived Structural Conceptualization of Stressful Experiences (SCSE), designed as a metatheoretical model to address the range of stress responses, from mildly challenging to traumatically stressful (Stamm, Bieber, & Rudolph, 1996; Stamm, Varra, & Sandberg, 1993).

World Assumption Theory

World assumption theory (Janoff-Bulman, 1992) is based in clinical experience and quantitative research with general populations and trauma victims. It proposes that we have three fundamental assumptions about ourselves, the external world, and the interaction between the two. The assumptions are that (a) the world is benevolent, (b) the world is meaningful, and (c) the self is worthy (Janoff-Bulman, 1992). However, as one gains knowledge and accumulates experience, these assumptions seem naive and become increasingly illusory. Traumatic events accentuate this process. Ultimately, it becomes necessary to deny life experiences or to restructure one's assumptions along the lines of one's experiences. This requires cognitive reappraisal of the meaning of the negative event.

> Traumatic victimizations are unwanted and unchosen. Yet, the cognitive strategies used by trauma survivors attest to the possibility for some human choice even in the face of uncontrollable, unavoidable negative outcomes. These choices reside in the interpretations and reinterpretations, appraisals and reappraisals, and evaluations and reevaluations made of the traumatic experience and one's pain and suffering (Janoff-Bulman, 1992, p. 140).

Successful restructuring is a positive accomplishment. As Janoff-Bulman (1992) states, the individual "emerges somewhat sadder, but considerably wiser" (p. 175).

Constructivist Self-Development Theory

Constructivist self-development theory, a theory based in clinical experience with trauma victims and in quantitative research with trauma survivors, trauma therapists, and general population subjects, brings additional tools for understanding stressful experiences. According to this theory, one has at one's center the self, which is composed of three interrelated parts: (a) *frame of reference*, or one's overarching ways of experiencing self, others, and the world; (b) *self-capacities*, which allow one to regulate affect and maintain self-esteem; and (c) *ego resources*, which regulate interactions with the outside world (i.e., the basic cognitive schemas, both conscious and unconscious, that provide the means for interpreting experience) (McCann & Pearlman, 1990a; Pearlman & Saakvitne, 1995).

The first part, frame of reference, comprises three aspects: *identity, world view*, and *spirituality*. Identity is the experience of self in various roles, including one's experience of one's body. World view includes the notions of causality, life philosophy, moral principles, and so forth, quantitatively operationalized as experience of autonomy and experience of connection (Pearlman, MacIan, Mas, Stamm, & Bieber, 1992; Stamm, Pearlman, & Bieber, 1996). Spirituality is one's inherent human capacity for an awareness of meaning and connection with something beyond oneself, an awareness of all aspects of life, hope, and relation to the nonmaterial (Newmann & Pearlman, 1995). Subordinate to frame of reference, the theory posits five basic psychological needs that are sensitive to disruption by stressful life experiences: (a) safety, (b) trust, (c) esteem, (d) control, and (e) intimacy (McCann & Pearlman, 1990a; Pearlman & Saakvitne, 1995).

Trauma can disrupt any or all of these factors. Considering trauma from a constructivist developmental perspective, there are two posttrauma restructuring alternatives. In the first alternative, an individual has developed, in some more or less mature form, all of the basic schemas before the traumatic experience. In this case, when disruption occurs, the healing process is rehabilitative, one of restoring the disrupted structure by incorporating the traumatic material. However, if trauma occurs very early in an individual's development, the healing process is habilitative. Habilitation requires developing basic factors that enable the person to experience satisfying relationships.

Dimensions of Normal Bereavement

This section enumerates a four-dimensional pattern of grief proposed by several authors (Jacobs, 1993, Stroebe & Stroebe, 1987; Turnbull, 1986). All of these works trace a common history to Parkes (Parkes, 1972, 1985; Parkes & Weiss, 1983) and to Bowlby's attachment theory (1969/1980). The terminology used is that introduced by Raphael (1983), continued by Stroebe and Stroebe (1987), and most recently used in Burnett et al. (1994). These authors define bereavement as reaction to the loss, while grief is the emotional response (sadness, anger, guilt, etc.) to loss.

While earlier work sometimes proposed grief as occurring in linear phases, Jacobs (1993) describes grief as involving related dimensions. Jacobs contends that there is only an illusion of independent phases because of the time course of the dimensions.

The first dimension is *numbness,* which is a feeling of disbelief usually starting immediately at the death and continuing for several days. The second dimension is *separation distress* (Raphael, 1983). During separation distress, there is a pervasive desire to be with the dead person accompanied by the awareness that this is not rationally possible. Separation distress typically occurs from a few days to several weeks postdeath and reaches a peak at about 3 weeks. During this phase, the bereaved person may believe that he or she has seen or heard the deceased. Some people may engage in avoidance in an attempt to ameliorate the pain of loss. Clinically, there is also searching and protest behavior, accompanied by anxious mood (Jacobs, 1993).

The third dimension, the *mourning process* (labeled despair by Stroebe & Stroebe, 1987), is usually intermingled with separation distress. This dimension contains the depressed mood and neurovegetative symptoms commonly associated with grief. People may also experience feelings of "unreality," as if they no longer exist in any familiar world (Turnbull, 1986). Many somatic symptoms accompany this stage, including increased viral illness, listlessness, insomnia, and exhaustion. According to Turnbull (1986), this is the point at which individuals must make the transition from the old life to a new life without the physical presence of the deceased. The final dimension is *recovery*, the time during which individuals find new patterns of interactions that do not depend on the lost loved one. The recovery phase is characterized by positive coping behaviors. Jacobs (1993) includes a fifth dimension, *traumatic distress*, which is characterized by intrusion and avoidance. This typically overlaps with numbness and/or

separation distress. Similar symptoms reported by Turnbull (1986) are not seg-
regated and are assumed to be part of the process of numbness and separation
distress.

Structural Conceptualization of Stressful Experiences

SCSE is a theoretical work blending theory, practice, and research to describe the
range of experiences stressors; and "ordinary" events such as moving, divorce, or
normal death, as well as events traditionally considered "traumatic," such as rape
and natural disaster. The SCSE was designed to be applicable cross culturally but
has yet to be tested in such a manner. To date, this factor analytic-theory has been
verified in a typical college student sample, and data are being collected from
other groups (Stamm, 1993; Stamm, Bieber, & Rudolph, 1996; Stamm, Varra,
& Rudolph, 1996; Stamm, Varra, & Sandberg, 1993). Chapter 2 expands the theory and summarizes the empirical evidence on the similarities and differences
between experiences of death and other stressful life experiences.

A stressful experience occurs *to* a person in the context of an event environment. The common human response to environmental input is simply to receive
and catalogue the input unless it is contrary to one's general expectations for a
given situation. When confronted with input that is, in a sense, "larger than us,"
the taking-in process is taxed. One possible explanation of how a person can be
traumatically stressed would be that the person encounters an event with a force
greater than him- or herself and some amount of unbalancing occurs. If the resources of the person match or surpass the event, the event is absorbed, and the
individual's path continues much the same as it has been; equilibrium is present.
In theory, the more massive the event in relation to the person, the greater the
unbalancing that can potentially occur.

The SCSE attempts to understand this balance by examining the individual's
perception of his or her psychosocial resources (*resources of the person*) and the
individual's perception of the magnitude and character of the event (*magnitude of
the event*). Because neither events nor people can be described out of the context
of time and place, there is a third component of SCSE: distance, or one's perception of one's physical and psychological closeness to the event or the people
involved.

Resources of the person consist of two basic structures. The first, *place-in-
the-world*, describes an individual's perception of his or her worthiness and belonging in the environment and community. It is characterized by a feeling that
one has a place in the world, being able to make positive contributions, finding
comfort in one's beliefs, taking care of oneself, being supported by one's faith,
and not feeling like one is absent or never gets a break. The second structure,
person-to-person, describes an individual's understanding of others in relationship to him- or herself. It is characterized by an ability to adapt.

In the magnitude of the event component, the event itself is not the focus.
What is the focus is a composite of elements of the event that, if present, could

make any event sufficiently novel for it to carry the potential to change the individual's life path in either a positive or negative direction. The first element is *abrogation-of-expected-reality*, the gap between what one believes will happen and what is happening or has happened. This includes common responses such as "The event seemed too horrible to believe" and "it was like someone changed the rules." On the positive side, people often appreciate life more and remember good times. The *finiteness* element is about death: the reality of death, the desire for death, believing someone has died, and life-after-death experiences. In the case of violent or sudden death, it incorporates the grotesque. It is not dreamlike in quality, nor does it seem to have any redemptive teaching aspects. Yet, it can incorporate aspects of being able to intervene in the death process.

The final element, *person in event*, deals with the person's perceptions of his or her thoughts, feelings, and actions during the event. This is the area where the most positive attributions, or the most guilt, can accumulate. Positively, people appreciate being able to help, being able to surpass their own expectations, and being proud of what they did to help. People can also develop a sense of community, of feeling close to others and part of the group. The positive attributions that follow—realizing what was important, appreciating being alive more, appreciating people and things more, and remembering the good times—offer fertile ground for developing positive postevent attributions. Negative feelings can include not trusting what one thought was true, wanting to get away, wanting to die, feeling alone, and even being the cause of the event.

The least is known about the third component, *distance*. This includes the duration of the event, time postevent, and one's perception of one's physical and psychological closeness to the event or people in the event. This last aspect, psychological closeness to the event, is theoretically appealing because it can account for stronger or weaker reactions to the event based on the importance of the event to the person. For example, a mother's reaction to the death of her child in a far-away war might be stronger than the reaction of those much closer to the war itself. By virtue of the mother's close relationship with the child, there was little psychological distance from the war (particularly with modern news reporting), even though there might be a great physical distance.

IDENTIFYING CONTEXTUAL RISK FACTORS

Preparation Time and the Event-Resource Balance

When death is sudden and/or unexpected, such as from war, accidents, suicide, crime, or disasters, there may be little time for those in the social support network of the deceased to prepare for the loss. (Social support is defined as the "existence or availability of people on whom we can rely, people who let us know that they care about, value, and love us" [Sarason, Levine, Basham, & Sarason, 1983, p. 12].) In these cases, few resources may be available. This suddenness of loss may be exacerbated by disbelief if there is no body, as might be the case in a prenatal death or in a disaster or fire (see Chapter 4) (Hodgkinson, 1989; Rando,

1992, 1994; Smith & Borgers, 1989; Stevens-Guille, 1992). Zisook and Schuchter (1992) found differences on the Hopkins Symptom Check List when comparing sudden and unanticipated death with prolonged, anticipated death. Those who experienced the sudden, unexpected death of a loved one reported more depressive, anxiety, paniclike, and avoidant symptoms than those who had predeath preparation time.

However, having time to prepare for another's death is not, in and of itself, a fail-safe inoculation against experiencing a traumatic stress reaction. Prolonged death has its unique attendant difficulties. While there is an opportunity for the social system to engage in anticipatory grief (Friedman, 1967; Knight & Herter, 1974; Rando, 1984; Stroebe & Stroebe, 1987; van Dongen-Melman & Sanders-Woudstra, 1986), this time of preparation can create problems. For instance, complications arise in the decision-making process during the terminal phase of an individual's life. In addition, the uncertainty and lack of feelings of control associated with medical decisions and remissions may cause stress (cf. Seligman, 1975). For example, difficulties arise when a person who is expected to die is mourned but does not die (Easson, 1981; Knight & Herter, 1974; Koocher, 1984; Koocher & O'Malley, 1981; Meagher & Leff, 1990).

Certainly in first-world medicine, but also in other settings (Terry, 1995; Stamm & Stamm, 1995), the medical process itself may be potentially stress producing. Results from a controlled trial designed to improve care for dying patients have alerted us to the level of pain and distress these patients experience and question many standard first-world medical practices (Connors et al., 1995). For friends and family members, spending time with the dying person may mean viewing the person in a disfigured state (Green, 1990, 1994; Lavigne & Ryan, 1979; Shonkwiler, 1985). Moreover, some first-world modern medical treatments for terminal diseases, such as certain types of chemotherapy, may prolong life but may actually end up being the toxin from which the patient ultimately dies. At times, the quality of life that is sustained through aggressive and intrusive medical treatment is questionable, creating difficulties for those people in the social support system of the dying person in terms of making decisions that determine care (Foos-Graber, 1984; Meagher & Leff, 1990; Mindel, 1989; van Dongen-Melman & Sanders-Woudstra, 1986).

These and other experiences associated with the actual dying process may be converted into traumatic material that can fuel flashbacks, survivor guilt, the death imprint, nightmares, and concerns about personal safety (Birenbaum et al., 1990; Easson, 1981; Green, 1990, 1994; Janoff-Bulman, 1992; Hodgkinson, 1989; McCann & Pearlman, 1990a; Rando, 1992, 1994).

Potentially, it is even more difficult when choices made by the survivors either caused or are perceived to have caused the death. For example, in a city in the western United States, a child died as a result of the mother leaving the sleeping child in the family vehicle when she went to work. During the legal proceedings that followed the child's death, the death was ruled accidental; there had been confusion in the family's work schedule, and the mother thought the father had taken the child to day care. Despite the court ruling, the family will probably have a difficult time with their feelings of responsibility for their child's death. Similar feelings of responsibility have been reported in relation to disasters (cf. McCaughey, 1986) and combat (cf. Shay, 1994).

Environmental Contextual Considerations

The contextual environment in which one lives can also exacerbate or ameliorate effects of the experience of grief and trauma. Cultural norms (de Jong & van Schaik, 1994; Fabrega & Nutini, 1994; Stamm & Stamm, 1995; Terry, 1995), war status (Garbarino, Kotenly, & Dubrow, 1991; Marsella, Bornemann, Ekblad, & Orley, 1994; Stamm, Stamm, & Weine, 1994; Weine, Farley, & Munczek, 1995), geography and government, available psychosocial and medical options (Terry, 1995), age or race, and the depth of one's social support system play a role in determining the amount of personal and interpersonal resources available to individuals and their social support systems at the time of a crisis (cf. Fabrega & Nutini, 1994; Stamm, 1997; Terry, 1995).

Research on schemas and stereotypes indicates that when people are confronted with ambiguity, they are more likely to use previously devised schemas and even stereotypes to reduce perceived ambiguity (cf. Hamilton, 1987; Taylor & Crocker, 1981). In some types of deaths where situational ambiguity is high—such as in war, murder, or prolonged death—there may be an increased risk for reliance on stereotyped behavior.

Another example of stereotyped responding can be seen in families in which prolonged deaths disrupt traditional family processes (Kramer, 1987). Family members may find it necessary to assume nontraditional roles. Sex-role stereotyping, however, may make it more difficult to accommodate the needed role flexibility and may thereby add to the family's stress risks. Eagley (1987) suggests that gender roles arise from division of labor. In egalitarian groups, role taking is tied to the group's current needs (Lerner, 1989); conversely, in groups that are highly sex stereotyped, it is likely that sex-role strain will become a salient characteristic of the overall stress of the group (Garnets & Pleck, 1979). Thus, system stress may increase if previous divisions are no longer functional because of a death-related change.

System stress is particularly pernicious when members need physical caretaking, such as with children or infirm members. System stress can be direct, through factors as simple as poorer nutrition and hygiene, or indirect, through the primary caretakers' own crises (Kehle & Parsons, 1988). For children especially, disruption of the parental/caretaker system is sufficient to cause a stress reaction or even a stress disorder (McCann & Pearlman, 1990a).

Many environment factors can affect the person-event balance. When addressing a person in context, it is important to consider the biological aspects, psychosocial aspects, and sociocultural aspects of the person. Any of these areas can enhance positively or negatively the risk factors for bereavement and grief.

DEATH AS AN EXTREME STRESSOR

Even if experiencing the death of another offers opportunities to derive positive, transpersonal meaning and purpose, most people experience some level of grief-related distress following the death of another. Nevertheless, most process the death in such a way that they can meaningfully continue their life.

Yet, the possibility of pathology developing from the death experience is real (Applebaum & Burns, 1991; Easson, 1981; Green, 1990; Green, Wilson, & Lindy, 1987; Horowitz et al., 1992; Hodgkinson, 1989; Jacobs, 1993; Kastenbaum, 1969; Parkes, 1985; Rando, 1992, 1994; Raphael, 1983; Rosen, 1995; Stroebe & Stroebe, 1987). Parkes (1985) identifies four areas of potential difficulties: (a) the type of death, (b) the characteristics of the relationship between the bereaved and the lost loved one, (c) the characteristics of the survivor, and (d) social conditions. Kastenbaum (1969) as well as Neugebauer and colleagues (1992) warns that multiple deaths can cause bereavement overload.

Moreover, death by means of an extreme stressor such as murder, disaster, or war can enhance the probability of the development of pathological grief (see Chapter 4) (Eth & Pynoos, 1985), thereby making the early diagnosis and treatment of a traumatic stress response of critical importance. When pathological restructuring of one's beliefs occurs, the traumatic aspects of the loss experience become the point around which one's entire life revolves, and one's world view is thus shaped by the traumatic experience (Herman, 1992; Janoff-Bulman, 1992; McCann & Pearlman, 1990a, 1990b; Pearlman & Saakvitne, 1995; E. Rosen, 1989; H. Rosen, 1985).

According to Pynoos and Nader (1988), when one experiences a life threat or witnesses injury to another, PTSD can develop. From this perspective, if experiencing the loss of another through death brings concomitant fears of threat to one's life, pathological bereavement in the form of PTSD is not only possible, but the risk increases. As previously noted, others, including McCann and Pearlman (1990a), Lifton (1967), and Janoff-Bulman (1992), consider loss and threat to one's life as a possible precursor to stress disorders. Moreover, the very definition of PTSD (APA, 1994) calls for, in part, the perception of death or threat of death accompanied by feelings of helplessness and fear.

Green (1990, 1994) possibly makes the clearest statement of the idea of loss or threat to one's life as a precursor to traumatic stress disorders. In her article reviewing the traumatic stress literature, Green (1994) lists seven stressor dimensions that have been identified as possible precursors to PTSD. Death is a possible part of each of the seven dimensions.

Threat to life or bodily integrity is obviously related to the perception of death. This threat may come from natural or human-made disasters, from fires, transportation disasters, war, or crime. Basic reactions to these types of threats have been outlined among children (Pynoos & Nader, 1990), adults (Hodgkinson, 1989), and even families of murder victims (see Chapter 4) (Stevens-Guille, 1992; Redmund, 1992).

A second dimension outlined by Green (1990, 1994) is the experience of seeing another person disfigured, mutilated, or dead. The original cause of the disfigurement does not seem to be as important as the exposure to the grotesque element. In fact, according to some (Lavigne & Ryan, 1979; Shonkwiler, 1985), it is even possible for disfigurement from medical treatment to cause long-term stress reactions. When violent sudden loss is accompanied by seeing the person in a disfigured state, there seems to be a particularly great risk for the death imprint (cf. Hodgkinson, 1989; Lifton, 1967). According to the *DSM-IV* (APA, 1994), witnessing a dead person or being placed at risk for death may be a precursor to the requisite reaction that involves intense fear, horror, or helplessness.

While somewhat less directly related to death than seeing or handling dead bodies, experiencing physical harm or injury can also lead to pathology (Green, 1990, 1994). This dimension may have a subclass that deals with the intention of the harm. Green (1990, 1994) argues that the deliberateness of the harm may be a mitigating factor in the stressor. For example, being the recipient of harm caused with intent would be perceived as more stressful than if the harm was caused accidentally. The harm does not have to be visible to serve as a potential traumatic stressor. Simply learning of exposure to a noxious agent can serve as a dimensional precursor to traumatic stress (Green, 1990, 1994).

The final dimension discussed by Green (1990, 1994) is causing death or severe harm to another. This harm could be intentional or even job related, such as in fulfilling the role of a soldier. In fact, society does condone causing harm or the death of others in the context of war. However, even when there is societal approval, pathological complications can arise (Breslau & Davis, 1989; Hobfoll et al., 1991). When the death of another is accidental, as discussed in the case of the mother who accidentally caused the death of her child, a person can become a victim as well as the agent of the stressor event.

Responses to stressor experiences can be evoked at a primary level or at a secondary level, such as through witnessing the act, or vicariously by being told of the act (Albeck, 1994; Danieli, 1985; Figley, 1995; Green, 1991; McCann & Pearlman, 1990b; Rosenheck & Nathan, 1985; Stamm, 1995; Stamm, Bieber, & Rudolph, 1996). For example, a loved one could be diagnosed HIV positive, which serves as the original stressor. Two types of potentially traumatic stresses are present here. The person with AIDS experiences primary stress prior to his or her death. Those in the social support system of the AIDS patient may experience their own struggle at a secondary level. After the loved one dies, the social support system has the primary stress of the death comingled with the previous stress of a secondary nature.

Ultimately, pathological grief and traumatic stress disorders can arise in the context of bereavement. In fact, PTSD, under the current understanding, cannot occur without the existence of either actual or threatened death (APA, 1994). People are at particular risk for developing pathologies when the death involves elements of the grotesque, violence, or suddenness. This is negatively enhanced by the survivor's perception of helplessness, fear, or horror. These are the kinds of experiences that seem to most challenge our beliefs in the goodness and rightness of the world and thus leave us most unsettled.

CONCLUSION

While treatment recommendations are beyond the scope of this chapter, at the very least, it seems important for caregivers to be attentive to the variability of bereavement. Looking across the death and trauma literature, it is becoming increasingly clear that we must be attentive to the potential negative effects of pathological bereavement and do all that we can to enhance the positive outcome of bereavement.

Normal bereavement, stress, and traumatic stress all require some element of restructuring of an individual's belief system. This restructuring seems to focus around one's faith in life, one's understanding of others, and one's understanding of oneself (Herman, 1992; Janoff-Bulman, 1992; McCann & Pearlman, 1990a, 1990b; Stamm, 1995a, 1995b).

We do know that pathological grief occurs (cf. Jacobs, 1993; Rando, 1992, 1994; Raphael & Martinek, 1997). For most, though, normal bereavement occurs. Normal bereavement moves from a state of numbness in which restructuring is not an applicable concept, through a time of mourning and separation distress— perhaps recognition of the need for restructuring—to a state of recovery involving successful restructuring. It is in this final stage that people use positive coping behaviors to construct a new and different but positive world (Jacobs, 1993; Stroebe & Stroebe, 1987; Turnbull, 1986). This new world is one that honors the place of the lost person but is constructed with new patterns of interactions that are not dependent on the physical existence of the lost loved one.

Thus, the normal course of bereavement culminates in a positively restructured world (Gilberg, 1994; Janoff-Bulman, 1992; Turnbull, 1986; Lifton, 1993; Hodgkinson, 1989; Rando, 1984; Stamm, 1995). It is important to be aware that this normal bereavement process can be truncated or shunted by inattention to the risk factors for traumatic stress reactions. Conversely, inattention to the important aspects of normal grief and bereavement in a person struggling with traumatic stress can increase the potential risk for both a traumatic stress disorder and the development of pathological grief. By remembering that these two human phenomena are closely linked yet distinguishable by terror, perhaps we will be better able to walk the path toward positive restructuring, both in our patients' lives and in our own.

> Man by suffering shall learn.
>
> So the heart of him, again
>
> Aching with remembered pain,
>
> Bleeds and sleepeth not, until
>
> Wisdom comes against his will.
>
> (Aeschylus, *Agamemnon*)

REFERENCES

Aiken, L. R. (1991). *Dying, death and bereavement.* Boston: Allyn & Bacon.

Albeck, J. (1994). Intergenerational consequences of trauma: Reframing traps in treatment theory— A second generation perspective. In M. B. Williams & J. F. Sommer (Eds.), *Post traumatic therapy.* Westport, CT: Greenwood Press.

American Psychiatric Association. (1987). *Diagnostic and statistical manual of mental disorders* (3rd ed, rev.). Washington, DC: Author.

American Psychiatric Association. (1994). *Diagnostic and statistical manual of mental disorders* (4th ed.). Washington, DC: Author.

Applebaum, D. R., & Burns, G. L. (1991). Unexpected childhood death: Posttraumatic stress disorder in surviving siblings and parents. *Journal of Clinical and Child Psychiatry, 20,* 114–120.

Birenbaum, L., Robinson, M., Phillips, D., Stewart, B., & McCown, D. (1990). The response of children to the dying and death of a sibling. *Omega, 20,* 213–228.

Bowlby, J. (1980). *Attachment and loss.* New York: Basic Books. (Original work published 1969).

Breslau, N., & Davis, G. C. (1989). Chronic posttraumatic stress disorder in Vietnam veterans. *Harvard Medical School Mental Health Letter 5*(9), 3–5.

Burnett, P., Warwick, M., Raphel, B., Dunne, M., Moylan, A., & Martinek, N. (1994). Concepts of normal bereavement. *Journal of Traumatic Stress, 7,* 123–128.

Connors, N., et al. (1995). A controlled trial to improve care for seriously ill hospital patients: The Study to Understand Prognosis and Preferences for Outcome and Risks of Treatments (SUPPORT). *Journal of the American Medical Association, 274,* 1591–1598.

Corr, C., Martinson, I., & Dyer, K. (1985). Parental bereavement. In C. Corr & D. Corr (Eds.), *Hospice approaches to pediatric care.* New York: Springer.

Danieli, Y. (1985). The treatment and prevention of long-term effects and intergenerational transmission of victimization: A lesson from Holocaust survivors and their children. In C. R. Figley (Ed.), *Trauma and its wake: Vol. 2. The study of post-traumatic stress disorder, theory, research, and treatment.* New York: Brunner/Mazel.

de Jong, J. T., & van Schaik, M. M. (1994). Cultural and religious aspects of grief and trauma after a plane crash in the Netherlands. *Tijdschrift-voor-Psychiatrie, 36,* 291–303.

Eagley, A. (1987). *Sex Differences in Social Behavior: A Social-Role Interpretation.* Mahwah, NJ: Erlbaum.

Easson, W. (1981). *The dying child.* Springfield, IL: Charles C. Thomas.

Eth, S., & Pynoos, R. (1985). Interaction of trauma and grief in childhood. In S. Eth & R. Pynoos (Eds.), *Post-traumatic stress disorder in children.* Washington, DC: American Psychiatric Press.

Eth, S., & Pynoos, R. (1994). The child as witness to homicide. *Journal of Social Issues, 40,* 87–108.

Fabrega, H., & Nutini, H. (1994). Talxcalan constructions of acute grief. *Culture, Medicine and Psychiatry, 18,* 405–431.

Figley, C. R. (Ed.). (1985). *Trauma and its wake: Vol. 1.* New York: Brunner/Mazel.

Figley, C. R. (1995). *Compassion fatigue: Coping with secondary PTSD among those who treat the traumatized.* New York: Brunner/Mazel.

Foos-Graber, A. (1984). *Deathing: An intelligent alternative for the final moments of life.* Reading, MA: Addison-Wesley.

Friedman, M. J., Charney, D. S., & Deutch, A. Y. (Eds.). (1995). *Neurobiological and clinical consequences of stress: From normal adaptation to post-traumatic stress disorder.* Philadelphia: Lippincott-Raven.

Friedman, M. J., & Jaranson, J. M. (1994). The applicability of the posttraumatic stress disorder concept to refugees. In A. J. Marsella, T. Bornemann, S. Ekblad, & J. Orley (Eds.), *Amidst peril and pain: The mental health and well-being of the world's refugees.* Washington, DC: American Psychological Association.

Friedman, M. J., & Schnurr, P. P. (1995). The relationship between trauma, post-traumatic stress disorder and physical health. In M. J. Friedman, D. S. Charney, & A. Y. Deutch (Eds.), *Neurobi-*

ological and clinical consequences of stress: From normal adaptation to post-traumatic stress disorder. Philadelphia: Lippincott-Raven.

Friedman, S. (1967). Care of the family of the child with cancer. *Pediatrics, 40*, 498–504.

Garbarino, J., Kotenly, K., & Dubrow, N. (1991). *No place to be a child: Growing up in a war zone.* Lexington, MA: D.C. Heath.

Garnets, L., & Pleck, J. H. (1979). Sex role identity, androgyny, and sex role transcendence: A sex role strain analysis. *Psychology of Women Quarterly, 3*, 270–283.

Gilberg, A. L. (1994). The loss of my dad: An adult developmental issue. *Journal of the American Academy of Psychoanalysis, 22*, 555–558.

Glick, I., Weiss, R. S., & Parkes, C. M. (1974). *The first year of bereavement*. New York: Wiley.

Green, B. L. (1990). Defining trauma: Terminology and generic stressor dimensions. *Journal of Applied Social Psychology, 20*, 1632–1642.

Green, B. L. (1991). Evaluating the effects of disasters. *Psychological Assessment, 3*, 538–546.

Green, B. L. (1994). Identifying survivors at risk: Trauma and stressors across events. In M. B. Williams & J. F. Sommer (Eds.), *Post traumatic therapy*. Westport, CT: Greenwood Press.

Green, B. L., Wilson, J. P., & Lindy, J. D. (1987). Conceptualizing post-traumatic stress disorder: A psychosocial framework. In C. R. Figley (Ed.), *Trauma and its wake: Vol. 2*. New York: Brunner/Mazel.

Hamilton, D. L. (1987). *Social cognition analysis of stereotypes*. Paper presented at the meeting of the American Psychological Association, New York.

Herman, J. L. (1992). *Trauma and recovery*. New York: Basic Books.

Hobfoll, S. E., Spielberger, C. D., Breznitz, S., Figley, C. R., Folkman, S., Green, B. L., Meichenbaum, D., Milgram, N. A., Sandler, I. N., Sarason, I. G., Van der Kolk, B. A. (1991). War-related stress: Addressing the stress of war and other traumatic events. *American Psychologist, 46*, 848–855.

Hodgkinson, P. E. (1989). Technological disaster: Survival and bereavement. *Social Science and Medicine, 29*, 351–356.

Horowitz, M. J., Zisook, S., & Schuchter, S. R. (1992). Depression after the death of a spouse. *American Journal of Psychiatry, 11*, 579–580.

Jacobs, S. (1993). *Pathologic grief: Maladaption to loss*. Washington, DC: American Psychiatric Press.

Janoff-Bulman, R. (1992). *Shattered assumptions: Toward a new psychology of trauma*. New York: Free Press.

Kastenbaum, R. (1969). Death and bereavement in later life. In A. H. Kutsher (Ed.), *Death and bereavement*. Springfield, IL: Charles C. Thomas.

Kehle, T. J., & Parsons, J. P. (1988). Psychological and social characteristics of children of Children of Vietnam Combat vets. Paper presented at annual meeting of the National Association of School Psychologists, Chicago, IL.

Kessler, R. C., Sonnega, A., Bromet, E., Hughes, M., & Nelson, C. (1995). Posttraumatic stress disorder in the National Comorbidity Survey. *Archives of General Psychiatry, 52*, 1048–1059.

Kluft, R. P. (1988). The dissociative disorders. In J. Talbott, R. Hales, & S. Yudofsky (Eds.), *American Psychiatric Press textbook of psychiatry*. Washington, DC: American Psychiatric Press.

Knight, J. & Herter, F. (1974). Anticipatory grief. In A. Kutscher (Ed.), *Death and bereavement*. Springfield, IL: Charles C. Thomas.

Koocher, G. (1984). Terminal care and survivorship in pediatric chronic illness. *Clinical Psychology Review, 4*, 571–583.

Koocher, G., & O'Malley, J. (1981). *The Damocles syndrome: Psychosocial consequences of surviving childhood cancer*. New York: McGraw-Hill.

Kramer, R. (1987). Living with childhood cancer: Impact on the healthy siblings. In T. Krulik, B. Holaday, & I. Martinson (Eds.), *The child and family facing life-threatening illness*. Philadelphia: J.B. Lippincott.

Lavigne, J., & Ryan, M. (1979). Psychological adjustment of siblings of children with chronic illness. *Pediatrics, 63*, 616–627.

Lazarus, R. S. (1966). *Psychological stress and the coping process*. New York: McGraw-Hill.

Lazarus, R. S., & Folkman, S. (1984). *Stress, appraisal and coping*. New York: Springer.

Lerner, H. G. (1989). *The dance of anger: A woman's guide to changing patterns of intimate relationships*. New York: Harper & Row.

Lifton, R. J. (1967). *Death in life: Survivors of Hiroshima*. New York: Simon & Schuster.

Lifton, J. (1993). *The Protean self*. New York: Simon & Schuster.

Marsella, A. J., Bornemann, T., Ekblad, S., & Orley, J. (Eds.). (1994). *Amidst peril and pain: The mental health and well-being of the world's refugees*. Washington, DC: American Psychological Association.

McCann, I. L., & Pearlman, L. A. (1990a). *Psychological trauma and the adult trauma survivor: Theory, treatment and transformation*. New York: Brunner/Mazel.

McCann, I. L., & Pearlman, L. A. (1990b). Vicarious traumatization: A framework for understanding the psychological effects of working with victims. *Journal of Traumatic Stress, 3*, 131–149.

McCaughey, B. G. (1986). The psychological symptomatology of a U.S. naval disaster. *Military Medicine, 151*, 162–165.

Meagher, D., & Leff, P. (1990). In Marie's memory: The rights of the child with life-threatening or terminal illness. *Omega, 20*, 177–191.

Mindel, A. (1986). *Coma: Key to awakening*. Boston: Shambala Press.

Nader, K., Pynoos, R. S., Fairbanks, L., & Frederick, C. (1990). Childhood PTSD reactions one year after a sniper attack. *American Journal of Psychiatry, 147*, 1526–1530.

Neugebauer, R., Rabkin, J. G., Williams, J. B. W., Reimer, R. H., Goetz, R., & Gorman, J. M. (1992). Bereavement reactions among homosexual men experiencing multiple losses in the AIDS epidemic. *American Journal of Psychiatry, 11*, 253–259.

Newmann, D., & Pearlman, L. A. (1995). *Spirituality and traumatic stress*. Manuscript in preparation.

Parkes, C. M. (1972). *Bereavement: Studies in grief in adult life*. New York: International Universities Press.

Parkes, C. M., & Weiss, R. S. (1983). *Recovery from bereavement*. New York: Basic Books.

Parkes, C. (1985). Bereavement. *British Journal of Psychiatry, 146*, 11–17.

Pearlman, L. A., MacIan, P., Mas, C., Stamm, B., & Bieber, S. (1992). *Vicarious traumatization: Theory and research*. Paper presented at the Eighth Annual Meeting of the International Society for Traumatic Stress Studies, Los Angeles, CA.

Pearlman, L. A., & Saakvitne, K. W. (1995). *Trauma and the therapist: Countertransference and vicarious traumatization in psychotherapy with incest survivors*. New York: Norton.

Perry, B. D. (1993). Medicine and psychotherapy: Neurodevelopment and the neurophysiology of trauma II: Clinical work along the alarm-fear-terror continuum. *Advisor, 6*, 1, 14–20.

Pynoos, R. S., & Nader, K. (1988). Psychological first aid and treatment approach to children exposed to community violence: Research implications. *Journal of Traumatic Stress, 1*, 445–473.

Pynoos, R. S., & Nader, K. (1990). Children's exposure to violence and traumatic death. *Psychiatric Annals, 20*, 334–344.

Rando, T. A. (1984). *Grief, death & dying*. Champaign, IL: Research Press.

Rando, T. A. (1992). The increasing prevalence of complicated mourning: The onslaught is just beginning. *Omega, 26*, 43–59.

Rando, T. A. (1994). Complications in mourning traumatic death. In I. Corless, B. Germino, & M. Pitmann (Eds.), *Dying, death and bereavement: Theoretical perspectives and other ways of knowing*. Boston: Jones & Bartlett.

Raphael, B. (1983). *The anatomy of bereavement*. New York: Basic Books.

Raphael, B., & Martinek, N. (1997). Assessing traumatic bereavement and posttraumatic stress disorder. In J. P. Wilson, & T. M. Keane (Eds.), *Assessing psychological trauma and PTSD*. New York: Guilford Press.

Redmund, L. (1992). *Surviving when someone you love was murdered*. Clearwater, FL: Psychological Consultation and Educational Services.

Rosen, E. (1989). Family therapy in cases of interminable grief for the loss of a child. *Omega, 19*, 187–201.

Rosen, H. (1985). Prohibitions against mourning in childhood sibling loss. *Omega, 15*, 307–316.

Rosen, M. (1995). Delayed reaction to sibling-loss: The unmourned sibling as a block to procreation and creativity; a post-traumatic state. *Psychoanalytic Psychotherapy, 9*, 75–83.

Rosenheck, R., & Nathan, P. (1985). Secondary traumatization in children of Vietnam veterans. *Hospital and Community Psychiatry, 36*, 538–539.

Seligman, M. E. P. (1975). *Helplessness: On depression, development and death*. San Francisco: Freeman.

Shay, J. (1994). *Achilles in Viet Nam: Combat trauma and the undoing of character*. New York: Atheneum Press.

Shonkwiler, M. (1985). Sibling visits in the pediatric intensive care unit. *Pediatric Care Quarterly, 8*, 67–72.

Smith, A., & Borgers, S. (1989). Parental grief response to perinatal death. *Omega, 19*, 203–214.

Spiegel, D. (1991). Dissociation and trauma. In A. Tasman & S. Goldfinger (Eds.), *American Psychiatric Press textbook of psychiatry*. Washington, DC: American Psychiatric Press.

Stamm, B. H. (Ed.). (1995). *Secondary traumatic stress: Self-care issues for clinicians, researchers and educators*. Lutherville, MD: Sidran Press.

Stamm, B. H. (in press). *Clinical applications of telehealth in mental health care*. Professional psychology: Research and practice.

Stamm, B. H., Bieber, S. L., & Rudolph, J. M. (1996). Review of stressful experiences content analysis coding scheme. In B. H. Stamm (Ed.), *Measurement of trauma, stress and adaptation* (pp. 333–348). Lutherville, MD: Sidran Press.

Stamm, B. H., Catherall, D. R., Terry, M. J., & McCammon, S. M. (1995). *Expanding the horizons of self-care: Clinicians, researchers and educators*. Paper presented at the 11th Annual Conference of the International Society for Traumatic Stress Studies, Boston, MA.

Stamm, B. H., & Friedman, M. J. (in press). Transcultural perspectives on posttraumatic stress disorder and other reactions to extreme stress. In A. Shalev, R. Yehuda, & A. McFarlane (Eds.), *International Handbook of Human Response to Trauma*. New York: Plenum.

Stamm, B. H., Pearlman, L. A., & Bieber, S. L. (1996). Review of the TSI autonomy and connection scales. In B. H. Stamm (Ed.), *Measurement of trauma, stress and adaptation*. Lutherville, MD: Sidran Press.

Stamm, B. H., & Perednia, D. A. (1997). *Evaluating telehealth systems: Questions, frameworks and templates*. Manuscript under review.

Stamm, B. H., & Rudolph, J. M. (1997). *Preliminary report on the design theory and psychometrics of the Stressful Life Experiences Screening*. Manuscript submitted for publication.

Stamm, B. H., & Stamm, H. E. (1995). *Creating healing communities: An historical Native American perspective*. Invited presentation at the Trauma Loss and Dissociation Conference, Washington, DC.

Stamm, B. H., Stamm, H. E., & Weine, S. (1994). *Genocide and communal identity: Shoshone Indians and Bosnian Muslims*. Paper presented at the 10th Annual Conference of the International Society for Traumatic Stress Studies, Chicago, IL.

Stamm, B. H., Varra, E. M., & Rudolph, J. M. (1996). Review of Stressful Experiences Content Analysis Coding Scheme. In B. H. Stamm (Ed.), *Measurement of trauma, stress and adaptation*. Lutherville, MD: Sidran Press.

Stamm, B. H., Varra, E. M., & Sandberg, C. T. (1993). *When it happens to another: Direct and indirect trauma*. Symposium presented at the Ninth Annual Meeting of the International Society for Traumatic Stress Studies, San Antonio, TX.

Stevens-Guille, E. (1992). *PTSD in families of murder victims*. Paper presented at the Eighth Annual Meeting of the International Society for Traumatic Stress Studies, Los Angeles, CA.

Stroebe, W., & Stroebe, M. S. (1987). *Bereavement and health: The psychological and physical consequences of partner loss*. Cambridge, England: Cambridge University Press.

Taylor, S. E., & Crocker, J. (1981). Schematic bases of social information processing. In E. T. Higgins, P. Herman, & M. P. Zanna (Eds.), *The Ontario Symposium on Personality and Social Psychology*. Hillsdale, NJ: Erlbaum.

Terr, L. (1991). Childhood traumas: An outline and overview. *American Journal of Psychiatry, 148*, 357–368.

Terry, M. J. (1995). Kelengakutelleghpat: An Arctic community-based approach to trauma. In B. H. Stamm (Ed.), *Secondary traumatic stress: Self-care issues for clinicians, researchers and educators*. Lutherville, MD: Sidran Press.

Trice, A. D. (1988). Posttraumatic stress syndrome-like symptoms among AIDS caregivers. *Psychological Reports, 63*, 656–658.

Trolly, B. C. (1994). A bridge between traumatic life events and losses by death. *Omega, 28*, 285–300.

Turnbull, R. (1986). The stages of grief. In R. Trunbull (Ed.), *Terminal care*. Washington, DC: Hemisphere.

van Dongen-Melman, J., & Sanders-Woudstra, J. (1986). Psychosocial aspects of childhood cancer: A review of the literature. *Journal of Child Psychology and Psychiatry, 27*, 145–180.

Weine, S. M., Farley, M., & Munczek, D. (1995). *Trauma research as intervention in human rights violations: Prostitution, disappearance and genocide*. Paper presented at the 11th Annual Meeting of the International Society for Traumatic Stress Studies.

World Health Organization. (1995). World Health Report 1995—Executive summary (on-line). Available: http://www.who.org/programmes/whr/.back/xsum95_e.htm.

Wortman, C. B., & Silver, R. C. (1989). The myths of coping with a loss. *Journal of Consulting and Clinical Psychology, 57*, 349–357.

Zisook, S., & Schuchter, S. (1992). The first four years of widowhood. *Psychiatric Annals, 16*, 288–294.

Chapter 2

Empirical Perspectives on Contextualizing Death and Trauma

B. Hudnall Stamm

DEATH AS A TRAUMATIC STRESS RISK FACTOR

Death is a significant risk factor for traumatic stress reactions. Violent or sudden death is particularly associated with negative psychological outcomes.

War and Poverty

Some environments carry particularly high risks, most notably poverty and war. Death by poverty-related disease and war is the most important focus of public health (World Health Organization [WHO], 1995). People in the least developed (poorest) countries have a life expectancy of about 43 years, as compared with 78 years in the most developed (richest) countries (WHO, 1995). Each years, 12.2 million children under 5 years of age die in developing countries (WHO, 1995). In some areas of the world, it is impossible to find a person whose immediate family is untouched by the sudden violent death of a loved one. Many suffer posttraumatic stress disorder (PTSD) and other psychiatric disorders as a result (Friedman & Jaranson, 1994; Marsella, Friedman, Gerrity, & Scurfield, 1996).

There were an estimated 60 wars being fought in 1997 (The War Page, 1997), all of which were likely to bring negative psychiatric consequences to at least some of the people involved. Consider some of the wars that have occurred since the development of the field of traumatic stress (Figley, 1985). During the 1980–1992 civil war in El Salvador, 75,000 people died, an average of more than 6,000 per year. Many of the victims were "disappeared," or dismembered. These deaths, combined with combatlike living environment, left mourning families without access to the usual rituals associated with the death of a significant other. For some, this continues unresolved (Aron, 1988; Aron, Corne, Fursland, & Zelwer, 1991; Bowen, Carscadden, Beighle, & Fleming, 1992; Tierra Blanca, 1994). The crisis of apartheid in urban areas of South Africa is well documented (Gilbert, 1996;

Simpson, 1993a, 1993b; Tyson, 1983). Less well known is the "unofficial war," brewing since the early 1980s, that erupted in Kwazulu-Natal in 1987. Political killings, which peaked at 311 in March 1994, have shown a steady rate of decline, dropping from an average of about 60 to 20 killings per month during 1996. The recovery of this rural province, with an unemployment rate of 58%, depends on poverty relief, personal development, employment, and community development (Higson-Smith, 1997)

In Liberia, a country of 2.3 million people, 150,000 people died from massacres and malnutrition between 1990 and 1994 (Fouke, 1991; Kramer, 1995; Monrovia, 1994), and the war and death continue at an alarming rate (Bracken, Giller, & Ssekiwanuka, 1996; Save the Children, 1996), although there are signs of reconciliation. Sadly, many of the soldiers are children, which puts at increased risk the very people who would be the first generation of nonwarring people (Personal communication, David Samalou, July 1997).

Under the Pol Pot regime in Cambodia (1970–1975), nearly 10% of the country's 9 million people died, and another million died during reorganization. From 1979 to 1990, an additional 100,00 died (Garbarino, Kostelny, & Dubrow, 1991). The negative psychological effects on the living have been pervasive and long lasting (Rozee & Van Boemel, 1989; Carlson & Rosser-Hogan, 1993; Sack et al., 1994, 1995).

At least 200,000 have died and 27,000 are missing as a result of the genocide in Bosnia-Herzegovina. Moreover, the overall war in the former Yugoslavia has involved the entire population, not just soldiers (Institute for Global Communications, 1997; Weine & Laub, 1995; Stamm, Stamm, & Weine, 1994; Weine, Becker et al., 1995; Weine, Farley, & Munczek, 1995). Official estimates report 140,000 dead or missing Bosnian Muslims; the actual figure may be as high as 200,000 (Cigar, 1995). This war has had profound negative psychological effects, particularly on children (Herceg, Melamed, & Pregrad, 1996) and even relief workers (Smith, Agger, Danieli, & Weisaeth, 1996).

Non-War-Related Death

The sweep of war can be overwhelming. The consequences of the terror and genocide that can accompany war are powerful. But what about those who live in relatively politically stable areas? What is death like for these people? Without political consequences, can death be an extreme stressor? Outside of warring areas, how common is death? Perhaps more common than most realize. Consider the relatively privileged population of United States college students. In one study of 281 college students with an average age of 20 years, 49% had experienced the death of a parent, sibling, or close friend (Segal & Figley, 1988). In another study of 1,081 college students with an average age of 21 years, 23% reported a death experience as their most stressful life experience. Of the 1,830 stressful life experiences reported by these 1,081 people, 427 (23%) were death related (see Chapter 1) (Stamm, Bieber, & Rudolph, 1996). Clearly, the death of a significant other is not uncommon, even among those who are generally assumed to be insulated from death by affluence and young age.

Included in the preceding numbers are a certain percentage, as yet unclear, of deaths that were sudden and/or violent. These deaths, like those that result from the devastation of war or profound poverty, are significant risk factors for the development of traumatic stress-related disorders (e.g., Doka, 1996; Figley, Bride, & Mazza, 1997; Rando, 1992, 1994). Hodgkinson and colleagues (1995) found that those who were bereaved by disaster or other sudden death reported significantly more general psychological symptoms, denial, intrusion, and avoidance than those who expected their bereavement.

Suicide seems to be a very potent risk factor. The risk of suicide may be compounded with other known risk factors for traumatic stress, such as sexual assault and child abuse (Brand, King, Olson, Ghaziuddin, & Naylor, 1996; Davidson, Hughes, George, & Blazer, 1996; Farber, Herbert, & Reviere, 1996), disaster (Warheit, Zimmerman, Khoury, Vega, & Gill, 1996), being in combat (Farberow, Kang, & Bullman, 1990), or a chronic, life-threatening illness (Elliot, Pages, Russo, Wilson, & Roy-Byrne, 1996; Suris, Parera, & Puig, 1996). In addition, the loved ones of suicide victims are at risk for experiencing guilt, anxiety, depression, and posttraumatic stress disorder following the suicide (Brent, Moritz, Bridge, Perper, & Canobbio, 1996; Miles & Demi, 1992).

IDENTIFYING THEORETICAL TOOLS ACROSS DEATH AND TRAUMA

Identifying Factors in the Stressor Event: The Structural Assessment of Stressful Experiences Study (SASE)

What is it that makes an event stressful? What makes it terrifying to a person? Does death always contain these factors, or are there differences in the intensity of the stress related to death? The following is a description of a study that attempted to separate out the various elements of the stressor event and how it relates to the death of a loved one.

Recognizing that the stressful experience occurs *to* a person in the context of an event, the Structural Conceptualization of Stressful Experiences (SCSE) is conceived as a function of the individual's perception of his or her psychosocial resources (*resources of the person*) and the individual's perception of the magnitude and character of the event (*magnitude of the event*). Because neither events nor people can be described out of the context of time and place, there is a third part of the SCSE. This third part is *distance*, or one's perception of one's physical and psychological closeness to the event or people in the event. Unfortunately, to date, the theory has been verified only in a typical college student sample, although there are other studies in planning. While the cross-cultural generalizability of the theory is not known, the SCSE was designed to be adaptable cross culturally.

Six universal factors have been quantitatively verified in the SCSE (Stamm, Bieber, & Rudolph, 1996). (The term *universal* is not a sociocultural term. As it is used here, it is a statistical term that refers to structures that have been identified, and can be reliably reproduced, across all of the subjects in a data set. For example, for a structure to be universal to males and females in the study, it would have to appear reliably in the male and female segments of the data set. If it appeared reliably only in the male segment, it would be specific to males only. Similarly, if a structure were reproducible across all of the different classes of stressor events in the data set, it would be universal to the data set. If it appeared only in one segment of the data set, for example only among those who experienced death, it would be specific to that group.) In theory, assuming an appropriate cultural match between the reference group and the target group, a universal factor is one that can be applied regardless of the victim's sex or even the kind (class) or magnitude of the stressful experience. (Chapter 1 describes the theory of SCSE in more detail.) Briefly, two universal factors exist in regard to the resources of the person: (a) the person's conception of his or her place in the world and (b) the person's conception of others in his or her world. Three universal event magnitude factors have been identified: (a) the abrogation of one's expected reality; (b) an understanding of the finiteness of human life through experiences of death; and (c) the perception of one's thoughts, feelings, and actions during the event. One distance structure, proximity, has been identified and is described as perceived psychological and physical proximity to the event and people in the event.

The SCSE also contains specific factors applying only to a particular group. Sex-related and event-related specific factors have been identified.

Two specific factors are uniquely associated with death. The first of these two specific structures—resources of the person—refers to a paradox between the public and private experience of grief. This structure involves the social pressure that can ignore an individual's feelings and rush a person who has lost a friend or loved one "to get on with life." The other structure is associated with the event itself and is characterized by the actual details of the death and surrounding events, including the consequences of the death for the participant (e.g., if the decedent was a parent, did the child have to move to another home?).

Traumatic Versus Normal Bereavement

Raphael and Martinek (1997) noted that traumatic stress and bereavement have been confused unnecessarily by the fact that Lindemann did not separate traumatic exposure from bereavement in his original conceptualization of grief. They point out that many of those in Lindemann's study of grief were severely traumatized by their experiences. Raphael and Martinek argue that the difference between normal bereavement and traumatic bereavement can be understood in terms of *intrusion* and *avoidance*. They argue that that reexperiencing (intrusion) is present for both traumatic and normal bereavement. The difference lies in the dimension of avoidance. People experiencing normal bereavement do not avoid intrusive thoughts. In fact, such thoughts may be sought after as welcomed memories of the lost person. Those who have experienced traumatic bereavement will have intrusive images and avoidant behavior associated with the fear of threat/danger in their experiences.

If we need to learn to separate traumatic stress from loss, then it is important to examine the range of experiences that occurs and determine where death in general and traumatic death specifically fit in comparison with other stressful experiences. Is traumatic death worse than rape? How does death compare with problems in living? Are there some types of death that are more stressful than others? Are there differences based on male and female perspectives?

Looking back across the previous parts of this chapter, it would seem imperative to test these differences across different cultures and stressors. Unfortunately, cross-cultural testing is a protracted and expensive process. The study described subsequently addressed the questions raised in a college student population. The study sample was large ($n = 1,177$). Unfortunately, it suffered from the same limitations as many studies, examining young, White, intelligent, relatively privileged people. However, it did allow a relatively easily accessed first step toward understanding the dynamics of how death, particularly violent and "untimely" death, compares with other stressors.

CONTEMPLATING CONTEXTUAL RISK FACTORS

Comparing Death-Related Stressful Experiences With Other Stressful Experiences

To understand the context in which death-related trauma can occur, it is important to understand how death compares with other stressful experiences. The study described here compared death with both extreme (accidents/disasters and sexual assault) and ordinary (problems in living) stressors. The results reported were drawn from a database of college students in three regions of the United States: the Northeast ($n = 36$), the Intermountain West ($n = 1,081$), and the Pacific Northwest ($n = 51$). The appropriate institutional review boards approved the research, and all subjects were treated in accord with the ethical guidelines of the American Psychological Association. Subjects were provided with national and local information about free and low-cost mental health resources, and some received course credit for their participation.

The subjects' mean age was 21.3 years ($SD = 4.2$), and they reported an average of 13.1 years of schooling ($SD = 1.4$). There were 518 men (44%) and 658 women (56%). The largest racial group was Caucasian (85%), followed by Hispanic (3%), Black (2%), and Oriental and American Indian (each 1%). Of the 87% who reported a religious preference, 79% were Christian, and 5.5% were Atheist. Jewish, Muslim, Eastern, and pagan/occult each accounted for 1% or less. On average, men reported the importance of spiritual and religious beliefs as 5.9 ($SD = 3.2$), with women at 6.8 ($SD = 2.9$), on a scale ranging from *not at all important* (0) to *very important* (10).

Table 2.1   Distribution of Most Stressful Life Experiences

	Bad things (accident/ disaster, etc.)	Death	Problems in living	Sexual assault	Uncodable
Men	100	127	231	8	46
Women	101	172	302	52	38

Data were collected via the Impact of Events Scale (Horowitz, Wilner, & Alverez, 1979) and the SASE (Stamm, Bieber, & Rudolph, 1996; Stamm, Varra, & Rudolph, 1996). The SASE considers stressful to traumatically stressful experiences and asks about both positive and negative reactions to an event. It includes a variety of subscales designed to measure the full range of reactions to stressful experiences. The reliabilities of the scales reported here (as measured by Tucker's coefficient of congruence) range from .72 to .96 (test-retest: .72 to .82).

There are scales that apply to all of the people in the study as well as scales that are unique to male or female subjects and scales that are unique to particular types of events. The scales that apply across genders and events are discussed to show relative differences across study participants. Scales specific to male and female subjects as well as to death as a stressor are also described (as statistics are presented). The SASE was designed to measure not pathology but the range of positive and negative responses possible following stressful events. Thus, there are no established cutoff scores for pathology; scores can be understood in relation to each other. Broadly, larger positive scores are interpreted as more reported awareness and positive response to the topic of the scale. All data were analyzed via SPSS in a Sex × Event analysis of variance followed by Bonferroni-adjusted post hoc tests.

Classification of Stressful Experiences

The protocol outlined in Stamm, Varra, and Rudolph (1996) was used to classify subjects' experiences into five categories of stressful experiences based on a content analysis of 1,177 people's self-selected most stressful life experiences (see Table 2.1).

Two exploratory, post hoc subdivisions of the death category were used. Data from the SASE were analyzed by suicidal death ($n = 28$) and nonsuicidal death ($n = 204$; largely nonviolent deaths due to old age) (see Table 2.2).

As a means of examining the small group of "untimely" deaths, data were categorized into three groups: (a) violent, (b) accident or disaster, and (c) illness (see Table 2.3). Because of the small sample size, data were compared only on the Impact of Event Scale, which has only 15 items (the SASE includes nearly 200 items).

Table 2.2 Distribution of Suicide Versus Nonsuicidal Deaths

	Suicide	Nonsuicide
Men	9	90
Women	19	114

Table 2.3 Distribution of "Nonnormal" Deaths

	Violent (self- or other inflicted)	Accident/ disaster	Illness
Men	17	24	6
Women	16	14	25

Psychosocial Resources

The study subjects were not different in terms of the way they reported their beliefs concerning their understandings of others in relation to themselves (Person to Person scale) or their understanding of themselves in relation to others and their place in the world (Place in the World scale). It appears that the general psychosocial resources available to these people were not different either in type or in magnitude across the five classes of stressful experiences.

The way women who had experienced death ($M = 31.6$) adapted was not different from those who had experienced accidents/disasters ($M = 31.4$), problems in living ($M = 32.1$), or emotional support provision ($M = 34.9$). However, all of these women reported making significantly fewer accommodations to the stressor than did those women who had been sexually assaulted ($M = 36.6$) (Feminine Situational Adaptation scale), $F(4, 547) = 3.88$, $p < .01$. This suggests that, at least in female adaptation, death is more similar to the other classes of stressful experiences than it is to sexual assault.

Male and female subjects were not different in the aspect of using personal resources to cope with the public and private aspects of death-related loss. They responded similarly to what has been reported in the clinical literature as "putting up a brave front in public" (Public Coping/Private Pain scale) while feeling empty inside (Rando, 1984; Turnbull, 1986).

Magnitude of the Event

Interestingly, the scale that addresses the actual aspects of death, the reality of death, desire for death, believing someone has died, and life-after-death experiences (Details of Death scale) was experienced as similar by all of the study subjects. Death is death, it would seem, regardless of one's experiences.

However, it does seem that the experience of death brings about differential perceptions in other areas. For example, in terms of the shattering of one's assumptions about life (Abrogation of Expected Reality scale), death ($M = -209.6$) is more like accidents and disasters ($M = -198.6$) and sexual assault ($M = -236.2$) than the group of everyday stressful events encountered as problems in living ($M = -186.4$), $F(4, 889) = 13.2$, $p < .01$.

Understanding of the finality of death, as measured by the Finiteness scale, seemed to be similar across the different classes of stressful experiences. However, there was a difference in the way male and female subjects reported their perceptions of the finiteness of death. Women ($M = 39.2$) reported a stronger understanding of the finality of death than men ($M = 33.5$), $F(1, 889) = 9.93$, $p < .01$. Moreover, when a post hoc analysis was done comparing the differences between death by suicide ($M = 27.7$) and death by a more "normal" process ($M = 40.7$), awareness of the finality of death was perceived in a more negative light for suicide than for "normal" death, $F(2, 292) = 5.0$, $p < .01$, and more positively by women ($M = 40.0$) than by men ($M = 32.8$) $F(1, 292) = 5.7$, $p = .02$.

In regard to an individual's perception of his or her thoughts, feelings, and beliefs (Person in Event scale) during a stressful experience, it would seem that believing that one is able to help provides more opportunities for positive appraisals. Those who had experienced death ($M = 58.8$) were more likely to have positive appraisals of their behavior during the event than those who had experienced accidents/disasters ($M = 42.0$), sexual assault ($M = 11.9$), or even problems in living ($M = 37.5$), $F(4, 889) = 21.79$, $p < .01$. There were no significant differences between those who experienced suicide and nonsuicidal deaths.

There are two sex-specific subscales in the event section of the SASE. The Protection within the Collective scale, a female scale, is characterized by feeling victimized by people or circumstances yet being protected by membership in a community. The magnitude of protection was statistically different from all of the other stressors and highest for those women who were in the death category, $F(4, 534) = 22.8$, $p < .01$. This suggests again that, for women, positive appraisal may be obtained from being with—and a part of—others.

In sum, people seem to be operating with similar schemas, or belief factors, about their psychosocial resources and about the experience of potentially stressful events. When comparing the magnitude of disruption on these schemas as a result of different categories of stressful experiences, those who experience death are generally more like those who have experienced traditionally defined traumatic stressor events than they are like those who experience problems in daily living. However, very broadly, experiencing the death of another does seem to offer peculiar opportunities for deriving positive, transpersonal meaning and purpose from the stressor experience.

Table 2.4   Impact of Events Scale Intrusion and Avoidance Subscales Across Types of Death

	Violence				Accident/disaster				Illness			
	Men		Women		Men		Women		Men		Women	
	M	SD	M	SD	M	SD	M	SD	M	SD	M	SD
Intrusion	3.4	1.6	2.2	1.7	2.3	1.6	2.8	1.7	1.6	1.8	2.3	1.7
Avoidance	2.7	1.5	2.2	1.5	1.7	1.3	2.4	1.4	1.6	1.4	1.7	1.4

Impact of Events Scale

Data on the Impact of Events Scale are particularly interesting given the previously discussed theoretical distinction made by Raphael and Martinek (1997). Specifically, Raphael and Martinek suggest that reexperiencing (intrusion) is present for both traumatic bereavement and normal bereavement but that they differ profoundly on the dimension of avoidance. As mentioned earlier, people experiencing normal bereavement will not avoid intrusive thoughts, and they may seek such thoughts as welcomed memories of the lost person. Those who have experienced traumatic bereavement will have intrusive images and avoidant behavior associated with the fear of threat or danger in their experiences. Thus, the expectation is that all who experience death will respond similarly to the intrusion scale but that those who experience death associated with an extreme event will endorse more avoidance items than those who experience more "normal" death.

As in previous sections of this chapter, the first analysis compared those who experienced death and those who experienced the other stressors (bad things, problems in living, and sexual assault), and a similar pattern emerged. There were no statistical differences by sex or among the four groups on the intrusion scale. However, on the avoidance scale, $F(3, 1015) = 12.34$, $p < .001$, those who were sexually assaulted were the most avoidant ($M = 2.6$) and were significantly different from all others. Those who had experienced death ($M = 1.9$) were also significantly different from the other groups (i.e, lower than the sexual assault group and higher than the bad things [1.6] and problems in living [1.7] groups). This begs the question as to whether the distinction between traumatic death, with intrusion and avoidance, and normal death, with intrusion and no avoidance, is buried in the results.

As a means of addressing this question, the death sample was further subdivided. Unfortunately, it was only possible to extract complete Impact of Events Scale data on 89 people. Even so, the data support the hypothesis that people with bereavements that are likely to be traumatic have similar scores on intrusion but higher scores on avoidance than those who are "normally" bereaved. As predicted by the theory, people did not differ by sex or intrusion (see Table 2.4). There was a significant difference between the groups on avoidance, $F(2, 83) = 3.33$,

$p = .04$. Post hoc tests (joint Bonferroni) indicated that violent death was different from death by either accident or illness. However, death by accident/disaster was not different from death by illness.

CONCLUSION

Violent death is a potent risk factor for the development of traumatic stress disorders. When the violent death occurs because of war or war-related poverty, particularly in the context of genocidal war, there is a very high potential for the development of a stress response that may linger for many years. Death of a violent or sudden nature that is not war related can also be a potent risk factor for development of traumatic stress responses. This is particularly true for suicide and homicide. In the case of the former, guilt over not preventing the death can linger for many years. In the latter, anger at the person causing the death, supported by the ongoing complications of the legal process, can fuel the traumatic stress.

Even among relatively privileged United States college students, death can have far-reaching effects. For college women, accommodating death was more like accommodating disasters, accidents, and problems in living than like accommodating sexual assault. Both men and women endorsed feeling differently in private than they acted in public (often dubbed "putting up a brave front"). The actual aspects of understanding death and its finiteness were similar across different classes of stressors, but women seemed to be stronger in their understanding of death than men. Death by suicide was perceived more negatively than nonsuicidal death. Again, women reported being clearer about the implications of the finality of the death than men.

One of the most interesting differences between death and other stressor classes was that those who experienced death were more likely to have positive appraisals of their actions during the event than those who experienced accidents/disasters, sexual assault, or even problems in living. A possible reason is that people find more opportunities to help at the time of the death of another than with other stressors and thus have more "redemptive" opportunities. While it is impossible to determine whether it reflects a cultural gender bias, a reporting bias, or a reflection of gender differences, women are more likely to report positive feelings than men.

It is important that the nature of death be more closely differentiated. The data from the Impact of Events Scale suggest that memories of the dead arise in the minds of most people. What seems to be different is the amount of energy spent removing those memories. Those who experience violent deaths are more likely to try to avoid reminders than those who experience the loss of another by illness or old age.

Looking across the range of stressors reported here, the people who are most likely to make positive reappraisals after stressful life experiences are those who have death-related stressful experiences. This is hopeful. Even though most people do not spend a great deal of time thinking about death, death as a concept—in and of itself—does not break the social contract of expected reality. Violent, unexpected death does break this contract. It would seem that the key lies in supporting people's ability to participate meaningfully in the death process even in the face of abject fear.

> To this we've come: that men withhold the world from men.
>
> No ships nor shore for him who drowns at sea.
>
> No home nor grave for him who dies on land.
>
> To this we've come: that man be born a stranger upon God's earth,
>
> That he be chosen without a chance for choice,
>
> That he be hunted without the hope of refuge.

> Is there one, any one behind those doors to whom the heart can still be explained?. . .
>
> What shall I tell you to make you understand?
>
> My child is dead. John's mother is dying, My own life is in danger. . .
>
> Look at my eyes, they are afraid to sleep.
>
> I ask you for your help and all you give me is papers.
>
> What will your papers do?
>
> They cannot stop the clock
>
> They are too thin an armor against a bullet. . . .

> Oh, that day will come, I know.
>
> When our hearts aflame will burn your paper chains
>
> That day, neither ink nor seal shall cage our souls!
>
> That day will come, that day will come!

> (Magda's Aria, from
>
> *The Consul* by Gian Carlo Menotti)

REFERENCES

Aron, A. (1988). Refugees without sanctuary: Salvadorans in the United States. In A. Aron (Ed.), *Flight, exile, and return: Mental health and the refugee.* San Francisco: Committee for Health Rights in Central America.

Aron, A., Corne, S., Fursland, A., & Zelwer, B. (1991). The gender-specific terror of El Salvador and Guatemala: Post-traumatic stress disorder in Central American refugee women. *Women's Studies International Forum, 14,* 37–47.

Bowen, D. J., Carscadden, L., Beighle, K., & Fleming, I. (1992). Post-traumatic stress disorder among Salvadoran women: Empirical evidence and description of treatment. In E. Cole, O. M. Espin, E. D. Rothblum (Eds.), *Refugee women and their mental health: Shattered societies, shattered lives.* New York: Harrington Park Press.

Bracken, P. J., Giller, J. E., & Ssekiwanuka, J. K. (1996). The rehabilitation of child soldiers: Defining needs and appropriate responses. *Medicine, Conflict and Survival, 12*, 114–125.

Brand, E. F., King, C. A., Olson, E., Ghaziuddin, N., & Naylor, M. (1996). Depressed adolesents with a history of sexual abuse: Diagnostic comorbidity and suicidality. *Journal of the American Academy of Child and Adolescent Psychiatry, 35*, 34–41.

Brent, D. A., Moritz, G., Bridge, J., Perper, J. A., & Canobbio, R. (1996). Long-term impact of exposure to suicide: A three year controlled follow-up. *Journal of the American Academy of Child and Adolescent Psychiatry, 35*, 646–653.

Carlson, E. B., & Rosser-Hogan, R. (1993). Mental health status of Cambodian refugees ten years after leaving their homes. *American Journal of Orthopsychiatry, 63*, 223–231.

Cigar, N. (1995). *Genocide in Bosnia: The policy of "ethnic cleansing."* College Station: Texas A&M Press.

Davidson, J. R. T., Hughes, D. C., George, L. K., & Blazer, D. G. (1996). The association of sexual assault and attempted suicide within the community. *Archives of General Psychiatry, 53*, 550–555.

Doka, K. J. (1996). *Living with grief after sudden loss: Suicide, homicide, accident, heart attack, or stroke.* Washington, DC: Hospice Foundation of America.

Elliot, A. J., Pages, K. P., Russo, J., Wilson, L. G., & Roy-Byrne, P. P. (1996). A profile of medically serious suicide attempts. *Journal of Clinical Psychiatry, 57*, 567–571.

Farber, E. W., Herbert, S. E., & Reviere, S. L. (1996). Childhood abuse and suicidality in obstetrics patients in a hospital-based urban prenatal clinic. *General Hospital Psychiatry, 18*, 56–60.

Farberow, N. L., Kang, H. K., & Bullman, T. A. (1990). Major depression or uncomplicated bereavement?: A follow-up of youth exposed to suicide. *Journal of the American Academy of Adolescent Psychiatry, 33*, 231–239.

Figley, C. R. (Ed.). (1985). *Trauma and its wake: Vol. 1.* New York: Brunner/Mazel.

Figley, C. R., Bride, B. E., & Mazza, N. (Eds.). (1997). *Death and trauma: The traumatology of grieving.* Philadelphia: Taylor & Francis.

Fouke, C. J. (1991). Churches bring relief to devastated Liberia. *Christian Century, 108*, 853–859.

Friedman, M. J., & Jaranson, J. M. (1994). The applicability of the posttraumatic stress disorder concept to refugees. In A. J. Marsella, T. Bornemann, S. Ekblad, & J. Orley (Eds.), *Amidst peril and pain: The mental health and well-being of the world's refugees.* Washington, DC: American Psychological Association.

Garbarino, J., Kostelny, K., & Dubrow, N. (1991). *No place to be a child: Growing up in a war zone.* Lexington, MA: D.C. Heath.

Gilbert, L. (1996). Urban violence and health: South Africa 1995. *Social Science and Medicine, 43*, 873–886.

Herceg, M. S., Melamed, B. G., & Pregrad, J. (1996). Effects of war on refugee and non-refugee children from Croatia and Bosnia-Herzegovina. *Croatian Medical Journal, 37*, 111–114.

Higson-Smith, C. (1997). *Background to Kwazulu-Natal, South Africa* [On-line]. Available: http://www.goecities.com/HotSprings/Spa/3028/webdoc1.htm.

Hodgkinson, P. E., Joseph, S. A., Yule, W., & Williams, R. M. (1995). Measuring grief after sudden, violent death: Zeebruggee bereaved at 30 months. *Personality and Individual Differences, 18*, 805–808.

Horowitz, M. J., Wilner, N., & Alverez, W. (1979). Impact of Events Scale: A measure of subjective stress. *Psychosomatic Medicine, 41*, 209–218.

Kramer, R. (1995). *Liberia: A casualty of the Cold War's end* [On-line]. Available: www.africanews.org/usaf/liberia.html.

Miles, M. S., & Demi, A. S. (1992). A comparison of guilt in bereaved parents whose children died by suicide, accident, or chronic disease. *Omega, 24*, 203–215.

Monrovia. (1994, March 19). *Syracuse Post-Standard* A-1.

Nader, K., Pynoos, R. S., Fairbanks, L., & Frederick, C. J. (1990). Childhood PTSD reactions one year after a sniper attack. *American Journal of Psychiatry, 147*, 1526–1530.

Rando, T. A. (1984). *Grief, death and dying*. Champaign, IL: Research Press.

Rando, T. A. (1992). The increasing prevalence of complicated mourning: The onslaught is just beginning. *Omega, 26*, 43–59.

Rando, T. A. (1994). Complications in mourning traumatic death. In I. Corless, B. Germino, & M. Pitmann (Eds.), *Dying, death and bereavement: Theoretical perspectives and other ways of knowing*. Boston: Jones & Bartlett.

Raphael, B., & Martinek, N. (1997). Assessing traumatic bereavement and posttraumatic stress disorder. In J. P. Wilson & T. M. Keane (Eds.) *Assessing psychological trauma and PTSD* (pp. 373–395). New York: Guilford.

Rozee, P. D., & Van Boemel, G. B. (1989). The psychological effects of war trauma and abuse on older Cambodian refugee women. *Women and Therapy, 8*, 23–50.

Sack, W. H., Clarke, G. N., Kinney, R., Belestos, G., Him, C., & Seeley, J. R. (1995). The Khmer adolescent project: II. Functional capacities in two generations of Cambodian refugees. *Journal of Nervous and Mental Disease, 183*, 177–181.

Sack, W. H., McSharry, S., Clarke, G. N., Kinney, R., Seeley, J. R., & Lewinsohn, P. (1994). The Khmer adolescent project: I. Epidemiologic findings in two generations of Cambodian refugees. *Journal of Nervous and Mental Disease, 182*, 387–395.

Save the Children. (1996). *Calls for action to end liberian refugee misery* [On-line]. Available: oneworld.org/scf/press/may14.html.

Segal, S. A., & Figley, C. R. (1988). Stressful events. *Hospital and Community Psychiatry, 39*, 998.

Simpson, M. A. (1993a). Bitter waters: Effects on children of the stresses of unrest and oppression. In J. P. Wilson, & B. Raphael (Eds.), *International handbook of traumatic stress syndromes*. New York: Plenum.

Simpson, M. A. (1993b). Traumatic stress and the bruising of the soul: The effects of torture and coercive interrogation. In J. P. Wilson, & B. Raphael (Eds.), *International handbook of traumatic stress syndromes*. New York: Plenum.

Smith, B., Agger, I., Danieli, Y., & Weisaeth, L. (1996). Health activities across traumatized populations: Emotional responses of international humanitarian aid workers: The contribution of nongovernmental organizations. In Y. Danieli, N. S. Rodley, & L. Weisaeth (Eds.), *International responses to traumatic stress: Humanitarian, human rights, justice, peace and development contributions, collaborative actions and future initiatives*. Amityville, NY: Baywood.

Stamm, B. H., Bieber, S. L., & Rudolph, J. M. (1996). Review of stressful experiences content analysis coding scheme. In B. H. Stamm (Ed.), *Measurement of trauma, stress and adaptation* (pp. 333–348). Lutherville, MD: Sidran Press.

Stamm, B. H., Stamm, H. E., & Weine, S. (1994). *Genocide and communal identity: Shoshone Indians and Bosnian Muslims*. Paper presented at the 10th Annual Conference of the International Society for Traumatic Stress Studies, Chicago, IL.

Stamm, B. H., Varra, E. M., & Rudolph, J. M. (1996). Psychometric review of Stressful Events Content Analysis Coding Scheme (SECACS). In B. H. Stamm (Ed.), *Measurement of trauma, stress and adaptation*. Lutherville, MD: Sidran Press.

Suris, J., Parere, N., & Puig, C. (1996). Chronic illness and emotional distress in adolescents. *Journal of Adolescent Health, 19*, 153–156.

The War Page. (1997). *1997 has about 60 wars in progress* [On-line]. Available: www/aloha.net/ fritzbee/pagesix.htm#61.

Tierra Blanca. (1994, March 19). *Syracuse Post-Standard* C-1.

Turnbull, R. (1986). The stages of grief. In R. Turnbull (Ed.), *Terminal care*. Washington, DC: Hemisphere.

Tyson, G. A. (1983). Stress and detention. *South African Medical Journal, 64*, 858–859.

Warheit, G. J., Zimmerman, R. S., Khoury, E. L., Vega, W. A., & Gil, A. G. (1996). Disaster related stresses, depressive signs and symptoms, and suicidal ideation among a multi-racial/ethnic sample of adolescents: A longitudinal analysis. *Journal of Child Psychology and Psychiatry and Allied Disciplines, 37*, 435–444.

Weine, S., Becker, D., McGlashan, T., Vojvoda, D., Hartmen, S., & Robbins, J. (1995). The psychiatric consequences of "ethnic cleansing:" Clinical assessments and testimony of Bosnian refugees recently resettled in America. *American Journal of Psychiatry, 152*, 536–542.

Weine, S. M., Farley, M., & Munczek, D. (1995). *Trauma research as intervention in human rights violations: Prostitution, disappearance and genocide.* Paper presented at the 11th Annual Meeting of the International Society for Traumatic Stress Studies, Boston, MA.

Weine, S. M., & Laub, D. (1995). Narrative constructions of historical realities in testimony with Bosnian survivors of "ethnic cleansing". *Psychiatry, 58*, 246–260.

World Health Organization. (1995). *World Health Report 1995—Executive summary* [On-line]. Available: http://www.who.org/programmes/whr/.back/xsum95_e.htm.

Chapter 3

Factors Associated With Effective Loss Accommodation

George A. Bonanno

The pain of losing a loved one is an almost unavoidable human experience. Coping with such a loss is generally considered to be one of the most demanding human endeavors (Holmes & Rahe, 1967). Yet, until recently there has been remarkably little in the way of empirical research on the bereavement process or the factors that might predict grief course. In the absence of empirical data, clinical accounts of bereavement have remained for the most part uncritically rooted in Freud's (1917/1957) original concept of the "work" of mourning. The vast majority of professionals in contact with the bereaved have tended to endorse the view that psychological health or "resolution" during bereavement is possible only after a concerted period of "grief work," i.e., review and expression of the cognitive and emotional meanings of the loss (W. Stroebe & Stroebe, 1987).

In recent years, however, the bereavement field appears to have undergone somewhat of an empirical renaissance. A range of new empirical findings and methods have appeared. The growth of interest in bereavement research is attributable to a number of sources, among them the increasing interest in the topic among social psychologists, the widespread growth in the general study of traumatic experience, and the new, multiple-measure approaches to stress and coping. Here I review some of these recent empirical advances, including methods and findings from a recent longitudinal study of midlife conjugal bereavement in which I have been involved. This review is not intended to be exhaustive. Rather, I limit my discussion to what appears to be the most relevant new findings so that I might also highlight those questions that have yet to benefit from empirical examination or that have received some empirical attention but continue to remain relatively unresolved.

THE MEASUREMENT OF GRIEF

The logical place to start when considering potential predictors of grief severity and course is with the question of how grief outcome might be measured.

Research in bereavement has suffered from an absence of clear operational definitions of grief and grief resolution. A major criticism of much of the extant research on this topic is that most studies typically employ self-report measures of depression or related constructs but fail to measure symptoms and difficulties specific to the experience of loss (Wortman, Silver, & Kessler, 1993). Studies using grief-specific measures have reported adequate internal consistency (e.g., Faschingbauer, Zisook, & Devaul, 1987) but have generally failed to demonstrate the validity of the measures. Furthermore, while there appears to be at least some overlap among grief, depression (Zisook & Schuster, 1991; Zisook et al., 1994), and trauma reactions (Bagge & Brandsma, 1994; Rynearson & McCreery, 1993), a systematic empirical assessment of these different symptom types, how they might overlap across stressor events, and how they may be unique to specific stressors has yet to be conducted. Establishing the convergent and discriminant validity of a grief-specific assessment instrument will greatly advance knowledge about the parameters of grief and grief course. This advance, in turn, will facilitate attempts to empirically identify predictors of grief course. Such data will also allow for important comparisons with the findings of related research on the predictors and course of depression and trauma reactions.

My colleagues and I recently reported the preliminary findings from a research program aimed at the development of a psychometrically sound interview measure of the disruption in functioning caused by grief (Bonanno, Keltner, Holen, & Horowitz, 1995; Bonanno & Keltner, 1997). In developing this interview measure, we began with a broad range of grief-related complaints and problems described in the bereavement literature. Candidate items were then pilot tested with a small, recently bereaved sample. A preliminary set of 30 items was selected for use in subsequent research, such that each item represented an interference in the bereaved participant's daily functioning that was directly attributable to the loss of a loved one. Among the items were distressing, intrusive experiences related to the deceased or to the loss (e.g., unbidden memories of the deceased); behaviors that represent difficulties accepting the finality of the loss (e.g., an inability to part with the deceased's possessions); and general troubles adapting to the loss (e.g., feeling "in limbo" or that life has come to a standstill, unusual irritability, or difficulty being emotionally available in significant relationships).

As a means of establishing the reliability of the 30-item set, interviews were conducted by clinical interviewers who had no knowledge of the goals and hypotheses of the study. The interviews were videotaped and recoded by a second interviewer, producing an acceptable level of interrater reliability ($\kappa = .78$). Although the internal consistency alpha coefficient for the initial 30-item set was satisfactory (.53), subsequent item analyses and item reduction have increased this value (.70; Field, Bonanno, Williams, & Horowitz, 1996). In addition, because a broad range of symptoms were included in the initial set of items, more detailed item analyses are possible and are anticipated as additional data become available. For example, a recent, preliminary psychometric analysis of the 30 items composing the grief score suggested that complicated grief reactions show some overlap with trauma reactions and more general depressive symptoms but also have unique features not shared by these other types of stress response (Horowitz et al., in press).

The validity of the interviewer-rated grief score was supported by high correlations with related self-report instruments such as the Texas Revised Inventory of Grief (Faschingbauer, 1981; $r = .64$); grief-specific intrusion, as measured by the Impact of Event Scale (Horowitz, Wilner, & Alvarez, 1979; $r = .59$); and depression on the Beck Depression Inventory (Beck & Steer, 1987; $r = .60$). Importantly, the interviewer-rated grief score also correlated highly with ratings of grief severity made blindly in independent interviews conducted by experienced psychotherapists ($r = .67$; Bonanno et al., 1995).

CIRCUMSTANCES OF THE LOSS EVENT

Forewarning

Sudden, unexpected losses are generally considered to result in a more difficult and prolonged grief course. There is some evidence for this assumption (Lundin, 1984; Parkes & Weiss, 1983; Sanders, 1993), but there are also published studies that have not shown effects related to degree of forewarning (Bonanno et al., 1995; Bornstein et al., 1973; Maddison & Walker, 1967). These types of contradictory findings might be explained by the interaction of forewarning with personality variables. For example, W. Stroebe and Stroebe (1993) recently suggested that unexpected losses might be more difficult for individuals low in internal locus of control (see personality findings described later).

Type of Loss

The loss of a child is widely believed to be the most severe loss a person can endure. Interestingly, however, Holmes and Rahe (1967) ranked the death of a spouse as the most demanding of all stressor events. An initial empirical study appeared to support the view that child loss produces more severe grief reactions than other types of loss (Sanders, 1980). This study, however, failed to control for important confounding factors such as sample differences in age or degree of forewarning (M. Stroebe, Hansson, & Stroebe, 1993). Furthermore, in a more recent study that did control for these variables, the opposite result was observed; in some outcome domains, conjugal loss appeared to produce greater long-term difficulties than child loss (Lehman, Wortman, & Williams, 1987).

In the specific context of child loss, an important but understudied question pertains to the possible relationship between grief severity and the age of the deceased child. For example, consider a recent and quite compelling study of anticipatory (hypothetical) grief (Crawford, Salter, & Jang, 1989) that used Fisher's (1930) concept of *reproductive value*, or the number of potential offspring an individual may produce. While reproductive value varies across cultures, it generally rises soon after birth and peaks at approximately 15 to 17 years of age. As the individual reaches his or her mid-20s, reproductive value drops fairly dramatically. Crawford et al. asked respondents to rate how much grief they anticipated experiencing to a series of hypothetical child losses and then compared the hypothetical child's chronological age with its reproductive value. Reproductive value, it turned out, was a more accurate predictor of anticipated grief severity than was the deceased's chronological age.

Demographic Variables

Poorer adjustment to loss has been found typically in younger participants (Jacobs et al., 1989; W. Stroebe & Stroebe, 1987; Wortman & Bolger, 1988; Zisook & Shuchter, 1991; Zisook, Schneider, & Schuster, 1990) and among males (M. Stroebe & Stroebe, 1983; W. Stroebe & Stroebe, 1987; Windholz, Marmar, & Horowitz, 1985). However, several studies have failed to observe either or both of these effects (Bonanno et al., 1995; Jacobs et al., 1991; Lund, Caserta, & Dimond, 1989). Financial hardship has also been associated with poorer adjustment in most (Sanders, 1993; Zisook et al., 1990) but not all (Lund et al., 1986) studies. Again, the inconsistencies in these predictors may be due in part to the influence across studies of unaccounted for—and as yet unknown—moderator variables (Sanders, 1993).

Previous Losses and Level of Adjustment

Increases in grief-related symptoms have been linked to various a priori life events and circumstances. Examples of such a priori life events include a past history of depression or anxiety (Jacobs et al., 1990; Zisook & Schuster, 1991), greater incidence of stressful life events prior to the loss (Parkes, 1970), and previous losses (Raphael et al., 1993). At present, little is known about the ways in which these various risk variables might interact with ongoing coping behaviors during bereavement or with the type of bereavement.

Perceived Social Support

Preliminary investigations of the role of social support during bereavement appeared to indicate that perceived availability of support from friends and relatives is an important buffering resource in adjustment to loss (Bonanno & Eddins, 1997; Gallagher, 1986; Sanders, 1993; W. Stroebe & Stroebe, 1987). However, the findings of a recent, well-controlled study challenged this view (W. Stroebe, Stroebe, Abakoumkin, & Schut, 1996). In this study, matched groups of bereaved and married individuals were compared over time by means of several different outcome measures. Perceived social support was linked to fewer depressive and somatic symptoms overall but did not show effects specific to bereavement. In other words, perceived support was generally associated with better functioning but did not evidence the anticipated, bereavement-specific buffering effect.

PERSONALITY

Individual differences in personality disposition are often cited among the most likely predictors of grief severity (Horowitz, Bonanno, & Holen, 1993; Sanders, 1993; W. Stroebe & Stroebe, 1987). Despite this common assumption, however, there has been remarkably little in the way of systematic research on the role of personality in bereavement.

One personality variable that recently has been found to predict grief outcome is the repressor personality style. Repressors are defined as individuals who report low levels of trait anxiety but, in contrast to other "low anxious" individuals, have high scores on indirect measures of defensiveness (Weinberger, Schwartz, & Davidson, 1979). Repressors have been characterized by their use of a relatively automatic or habitual "perceptual avoidance schema" (Bonanno & Singer, 1990) that allows them to ignore or to discretely process threatening information. As a consequence, repressors appear to experience genuinely reduced levels of distress, even though they simultaneously exhibit elevated basal salivary cortisol levels (Brown et al., 1996) and, during stressful tasks, show elevations in physiological arousal (Asendorpf & Scherer, 1983; Newton & Contrada, 1992; Weinberger et al., 1979). Repressors have also demonstrated a greater ability than other participants to ignore specified information (Bonanno, Davis, Singer, & Schwartz, 1991), and they have shown genuine deficits in memory for emotional material (Davis & Schwartz, 1987; Davis, Singer, Bonanno, & Schwartz, 1988; Hansen & Hansen, 1988).

In a recent bereavement study, repressors were rated by clinical interviewers as having fewer grief symptoms and showed an earlier reduction in grief symptoms relative to all other participants (Bonanno, Siddique, Keltner, & Horowitz, 1996). Repressors in that study also scored highest on a related trait measure of self-deceptive enhancement (Paulhus, 1984, 1991), and this measure, in turn, was linked to a similar healthy bereavement profile. Importantly, these personality effects were evidenced even when the general propensity toward reporting low distress or "negative affectivity" was controlled. Repressors showed an earlier reduction in grief than did a so-called "true low anxious" group of participants, and the self-deceptive enhancement measure predicted less grief and distress and better perceived health even when initial scores on these variables were statistically controlled. In contrast, the related personality variable of impression management, which measures the habitual tendency to self-present in a manner that will appear positively to others, was unrelated to outcome once initial scores on the outcome measures were controlled. Thus, the repressor and self-deceptive enhancement dimensions predicted a better bereavement outcome over and above the general association of these dimensions with low distress, while the propensity to self-report in a favorable manner was not related to outcome when adjusted for its general association with low distress. Additional data relating the avoidance or minimization of emotion to grief course are described in Chapter 6.

In another recent study from the same longitudinal project, Gunzerath and Bonanno (1997) collected several different measures of borderline personality disorder (BPD) and assessed their relationship to grief outcome. Based on previous studies, BPD was assessed via (a) the five-factor model of personality (Costa & McCrae, 1992), specifically defined as a profile of high neuroticism, low conscientiousness, and low agreeableness (Widiger & Costa, 1994); (b) the Defensive Styles Questionnaire (Bond, Gardner, Christian, & Sigal, 1983), specifically defined as a profile of high use of maladaptive and image-distorting defenses and low use of adaptive defenses (Bond, Paris, & Zweig-Frank, 1994); (c) a cluster of items selected to approximate the nine items composing the *Diagnostic and Statistical Manual of Mental Disorders* (4th edition; *DSM-IV*; American Psychiatric Association, 1994) diagnosis for borderline functioning; and (d) borderline subtypes based on the *DSM* items, which resulted in a dominant factor (self-destructive unpredictability) and two additional factors (volatility and identity disturbance) (Rusch, Guastello, & Mason, 1992). As expected, these various BPD measures showed considerable convergence. Each measure also showed some relation to initial grief and distress. However, when initial grief and distress were controlled through regression analyses, only the *DSM* borderline subtypes evidenced a predictive relationship to later grief or distress. The self-destructive unpredictability subtype, consisting of affective instability and suicidality, was a reliable predictor of later grief even when initial grief was statistically controlled. The volatility subtype was a reliable predictor of later distress even when initial distress was statistically controlled.

Preliminary evidence is also available from another longitudinal study to suggest the possible moderating influence of several additional personality variables. Highly neurotic individuals reported increased depression during the early assessments after a loss (W. Stroebe & Stroebe, 1987), but this effect disappeared at later assessments (W. Stroebe & Stroebe, 1993). In a related finding from the same study, dispositional beliefs about locus of control did not produce main effects on grief course but were found to interact with the relative forewarning of the loss. Specifically, individuals who believed that they could do little to control the course of events in their lives (low internal control) and who suffered an unexpected loss reported increased depression and increased somatic complaints across the 2-year period covered by the study (W. Stroebe & Stroebe, 1993).

EMOTION AND COPING

Emotional Experience and Expression

It has long been assumed that experiencing and expressing emotion associated with a loss are essential for recovery. The hypothesized benefit of prolonged and intensive emotional processing or "grief work" during bereavement has generally been confined to negative emotion (Bowlby, 1980; Lazare, 1989; Osterweis et al., 1984), particularly anger (Bowlby, 1980; Belitsky & Jacobs, 1986; Cerney & Buskirk, 1991). The experience and expression of positive emotion have been commonly interpreted as diagnostic of a maladaptive denial of the loss and have been assumed to contribute to chronic (Bowlby, 1980; Horowitz et al., 1993) or delayed (Deutsch, 1937; Sanders, 1993) mourning.

Several theorists have noted recently, however, that there is little empirical evidence to support the assumed necessity of intense emotional processing of the loss (Bonanno, in press; W. Stroebe & Stroebe, 1987; Wortman & Silver, 1989). Indeed, early levels of distress are consistently among the strongest predictors of later grief severity (Bornstein et al., 1973; Vachon et al., 1982; Wortman & Silver, 1989; Zisook & Schuster, 1991). Furthermore, recent evidence has convincingly associated a better or less symptomatic grief course with the reduced experience and expression of negative emotion and with the increased expression of positive emotion during the early phases of bereavement (Bonanno et al., 1995; Bonanno & Keltner, 1997). In addition, Keltner and Bonanno (1997) have recently provided empirical evidence of the advantages of laughter during bereavement. The findings pertaining to emotion and grief course are discussed further in Chapter 6.

Appraisal and Coping Processes

The absence of empirical evidence on the relative efficacy or inefficacy of various overt coping behaviors during bereavement has been identified elsewhere as a central concern for future empirical studies (M. Stroebe et al., 1993). The need for data on basic appraisal and coping processes during bereavement is pointed to by the fact that such data would provide an important context from which to evaluate existing theoretical positions. For example, traditional "grief work" theorists have emphasized the importance of direct, confrontative, emotion-focused coping processes (Raphael, 1983). In contrast, an interactionist stress perspective suggests the importance of appraisal and predicts that reduced emotional distress will likely free up personal resources for adaptive, problem-focused coping (Bonanno et al., 1995; Nolen-Hoeksema, 1993), which in turn should help ameliorate the longer term disruptive effects of conjugal loss (e.g., financial concerns, changes in family configuration) (W. Stroebe & Stroebe, 1987; Schuster & Zisook, 1993). The longitudinal examination of these variables would greatly enhance knowledge of both the interrelation of emotion and coping and the components that inform long-term adjustment during bereavement.

Preliminary data on the relationship between self-reported coping behaviors and grief severity have recently become available from a longitudinal study of bereavement among gay men who had recently lost their partners to AIDS (Folkman et al., 1996). In this study, increased depressive mood from baseline (measured prior to the loss) to 7 months postloss was associated with self-reported distancing (e.g., "didn't let it get to me—refused to think about it too much") and self-blame. The link between self-reported distancing and increased depression is of particular interest in light of the recent finding, discussed earlier, that emotional dissociation and the reduced experience and expression of emotion predict a less severe grief course (Bonanno et al., 1995). These results highlight the crucial importance of multidimensional measurements that can distinguish between relatively automated behaviors (e.g., verbal-autonomic response dissociation) that appear to occur with little or no awareness (Weinberger & Davidson, 1994) and more deliberate and reportable coping behaviors (e.g., those measured by the self-report items) related to distancing. In the context of this distinction, it is interesting to note that verbal-autonomic response dissociation during bereavement has been found to correlate inversely with a global, self-report measure of avoidant behaviors pertaining specifically to the loss (Bonanno et al., 1995). Furthermore, consistent with Folkman et al.'s (1996) findings, the deliberate avoidance measure used in this study was also predictive of increased grief symptoms (Bonanno et al., 1995). Thus, deliberate avoidant coping behaviors and relatively automatic repressive or dissociative behaviors represent distinct responses to the pain of bereavement that require different types of measurement and that predict different—and, in fact, opposite—outcomes.

Folkman et al.'s (1996) demonstration of an association between increased grief symptoms and the coping behavior of self-blame received additional support in another recent study. In contrast to Folkman et al.'s (1996) use of self-reported coping behaviors, Field and colleagues assessed self-blame, blaming the deceased, and helplessness by coding bereaved participants' statements from transcripts, obtained 6 months after a conjugal loss, of an imaginary monologue with the deceased (Field et al., 1996). In this case, self-blame was predictive of decreased perceived health and increases in several categories of interviewer-rated grief symptoms over time. Statements related to blaming the deceased predicted increased interviewer-rated grief and increased anxiety as well. Interestingly, this study also produced the intriguing finding that statements indicative of helplessness predicted increased grief symptoms but also increased perceived health over time. Thus, a sense of helplessness after the loss of a spouse increases the psychological disruption of the loss but has some adaptive advantages in terms of improved perceptions of health. Further exploration of this finding is needed to fully understand these relationships.

THE MEANING OF A LOSS

The dimensions through which people create and maintain personal meaning have emerged as an important but, until recently, relatively neglected area of psychological inquiry (Baumeister, 1989; Baumeister & Newman, 1994). In a related vein, recent models of stress responsivity and trauma reactions have emphasized the importance of maintaining basic assumptions that the world is benevolent and meaningful and that the self is worthy (Janoff-Bulman, 1989). In this view, severe trauma reactions result in a weakening or "shattering" of these assumptions, while recovery is predicated on the resolution of the pre- and posttrauma interpretations of reality and an eventual reconstitution of the core assumptions (Janoff-Bulman, 1992).

Frequent references have similarly been made to the important role of personal meaning and understanding in the recovery process during bereavement

(Bowlby, 1980; Parkes & Weiss, 1983; Raphael, 1983; Wortman et al., 1993). Preliminary research on meaning and bereavement has been promising (Lehman et al., 1987). However, the parameters of meaning during bereavement, and their relationship to other basic process and outcome measures, have not yet been systematically examined in an empirical study.

PERCEIVED QUALITY OF THE RELATIONSHIP WITH THE DECEASED

It is widely believed that ambivalent or conflicted relationships lead to greater problems in adjustment during bereavement (Freud, 1917/1957; Horowitz et al., 1993; Lindemann, 1944; Parkes & Weiss, 1983; Raphael, 1983; Sanders, 1993). However, several recent controlled studies of conjugal loss using different methodologies have not supported this assumption.

One approach to this question is to measure the quality of the conjugal relationship prior to the loss and assess its predictive relationship to grief symptoms after the loss. Preliminary findings from a national prospective survey that used this approach showed that individuals who had reported troubled marriages (low marital satisfaction, high conflict) prior to the loss of their spouse actually had less depression during bereavement (Wortman et al., 1993). In contrast, individuals whose marriages were characterized by high levels of satisfaction and low reported conflict showed the greatest distress after the loss. Thus, contrary to traditional theory, these findings suggest that losing a partner from a healthy, functional relationship is more of a clear "loss" and results in more severe grief. Losing a partner from a troubled marriage, while not necessarily a desirable outcome, may nonetheless be less of a clear loss and thus less of a stressor.

A second approach is to examine retrospective perceptions or evaluations of the conjugal relationship during bereavement, after the relationship has already been lost. This approach is predicted on the fact that, regardless of the preloss quality of the conjugal relationship, how the relationship is perceived or recalled during bereavement will best inform the survivor's grief experience. My colleagues and I used this approach recently in an attempt to test several hypotheses from the bereavement literature regarding the causal relationship between ambivalence toward the deceased and grief severity (Bonanno, Notarius, Gunzerath, Keltner, & Horowitz, in press). Previous studies of this question have suffered from the absence of a valid and clearly operationalized measure of ambivalence. For this study, we created the Semantic Representations of Others Scale (SROS) based on an approach, frequently used by social psychologists, for the measurement of ambivalent attitudes (Kaplan, 1972; Scott, 1966). Accordingly, conjugally bereaved participants were asked to rate adjectives pertaining to either the positive or the negative aspects of their representations of the deceased. The adjectives were grouped by valence so that participants first rated the deceased on only one dimension (e.g., positive aspects), while ignoring the other dimension (e.g., negative aspects), and then repeated this procedure on a separate rating form by rating only the previously ignored dimension (e.g., negative aspects). The mean negative and positive ratings for each participant were then combined in an algorithmic computation of ambivalence.

Ambivalence toward another person, as measured by the SROS, was thus operationally defined as simultaneous positive and negative representations of that person experienced with equal strength and not easily reconciled. As convergent support of this definition, the SROS score for ambivalent representations of the deceased was found to correlate significantly with both emotional instability, as measured by neuroticism, and the total score from the Inventory of Interpersonal Problems, which assessed distress in the particular sphere of interpersonal relationships (L. Horowitz et al., 1988). In addition, SROS ambivalence toward the deceased correlated with facial expressions of both anger and sadness when discussing the deceased.

To assess outcome, we administered the SROS at several points during bereavement and also obtained similar scores from a nonbereaved, comparison sample. In the nonbereaved sample, ambivalent representations of the current partner correlated positively with self-reported distress and correlated inversely with perceived health. Ambivalent representations of the deceased spouse at 6 months postloss were also correlated with distress and inversely correlated with perceived health. In addition, ambivalence toward the deceased was correlated with the more objective, interviewer-rated grief score. Importantly, however, when initial levels of grief, distress, and health were statistically controlled via regression analyses, ambivalent representations of the deceased spouse were not predictive of long-term outcome. Thus, these findings suggested that ambivalence toward a partner, whether alive or deceased, is a correlate of distress and poor perceived health but does not interact with the stress of loss and does not influence later outcome.

Somewhat surprisingly, however, when we examined the opposite causal configuration—initial levels of symptoms and distress in comparison with later ambivalence scores—the predictive relationship was significant. High levels of interviewer-rated grief and self-reported distress predicted increased ambivalence toward the deceased spouse 8 months later. Furthermore, this relationship was still meaningful when initial levels of ambivalence were statistically controlled. A similar pattern of findings was obtained in this same study with a standardized measure of relationship adjustment, the Dyadic Adjustment Scale (Spanier, 1976). Initial grief and distress predicted increasingly negative or less well-adjusted evaluations of the lost relationship at later assessments.

These findings clearly illustrate the importance of repeated assessments of the perceived quality of the conjugal relationship and how that relationship may change in bereaved individuals over time as they struggle with the pain of their loss. Bonanno, Notarius, Gunzerath, Keltner, and Horowitz (in press) suggested a number of alternative theoretical interpretations for these findings. However, additional research evidence will need to be obtained before findings of this type can be fully evaluated.

CONCLUSION

Although this has by no means been an exhaustive review of the empirical research on predictors of grief course and grief severity, the studies considered amply illustrate the new directions and new ideas that have recently appeared in the bereavement field. In contrast to traditional approaches that have been dominated primarily by Freud's early theorizing and the psychoanalytic perspective on loss, more recent approaches suggest a clear influence of social psychology, the burgeoning interest in trauma research, and the multiple-measure approach to stress and coping. The range of new findings that have become available present a marked challenge to traditional theory in bereavement and highlight interesting new directions for further research.

REFERENCES

American Psychiatric Association. (1994). *Diagnostic and statistical manual of mental disorders* (4th ed.). Washington, DC: Author.

Asendorpf, J. B., & Scherer, K. R. (1983). The discrepant repressor: Differentiation between low anxiety, high anxiety, and repression of anxiety by autonomic-facial-verbal patterns of behavior. *Journal of Personality and Social Psychology, 45*, 1334–1346.

Bagge, R. W., & Brandsma, J. M. (1994). PTSD and bereavement: Traumatic grief. In L. Hyer (Ed.), *Trauma victim: Theoretical issues and practical suggestions* (pp. 569–585). Muncie, IN: Accelerated Development.

Baumeister, R. (1989). The problem of life's meaning. In D. M. Buss & N. Cantor (Eds.), *Personality psychology: Recent trends and emerging directions* (pp. 138–148). New York: Springer-Verlag.

Baumeister, R. F., & Newman, L. S. (1994). How stories make sense of personal experiences: Motives that shape autobiographical narratives. *Personality and Social Psychology Bulletin, 20*, 676–690.

Beck, A. T., & Steer, R. A. (1987). *Manual for the Beck Depression Inventory*. New York: Harcourt Brace Jovanovich.

Belitsky, R., & Jacobs, S. (1986). Bereavement, attachment theory, and mental disorders. *Psychiatric Annals, 16*, 276–280.

Bonanno, G. A. (in press). The concept of "working through" loss: A critical evaluation of the cultural, historical, and empirical evidence. In A. Maercker, M. Schuetzwohl, & Z. Solomon (Eds.), *Posttraumatic stress disorder: Vulnerability and resilience in the life-span*. Seattle, WA: Hogrefe & Huber.

Bonanno, G. A., Davis, P. J., Singer, J. L., & Schwartz, G. E. (1991). The repressor personality and avoidant information processing: A dichotic listening study. *Journal of Research in Personality, 25*, 386–401.

Bonanno, G. A., & Eddins, C. (1997). *Talking about the loss of a spouse: Dimensions of verbal disclosure and the prediction of long-term bereavement outcome*. Manuscript submitted for publication.

Bonanno, G. A., Notarius, C., Gunzerath, L., Keltner, D., & Horowitz, M. J. (in press). Interpersonal ambivalence, perceived dyadic adjustment, and conjugal loss. *Journal of Consulting and Clinical Psychology*.

Bonanno, G. A., & Keltner, D. (1997). Facial expressions of emotion and the course of conjugal bereavement. *Journal of Abnormal Psychology, 106*, 126–137.

Bonanno, G. A., Keltner, D., Holen, A., & Horowitz, M. J. (1995). When avoiding unpleasant emotion might not be such a bad thing: Verbal-autonomic response dissociation and midlife conjugal bereavement. *Journal of Personality and Social Psychology, 46*, 975–989.

Bonanno, G. A., Siddique, H., Keltner, D., & Horowitz, M. J. (1996). *Correlates and consequences of dispositional repression and self-deception following the loss of a spouse.* Manuscript submitted for publication.

Bonanno, G. A., & Singer, J. L. (1990). Repressive personality style: Theoretical and methodological implications for health and pathology. In J. L. Singer (Ed.), *Repression and dissociation* (pp. 435–470). Chicago: University of Chicago Press.

Bond, M., Gardner, S. T., Christian, J., & Sigal, J. J. (1983). Empirical study of self-rated defense styles. *Archives of General Psychiatry, 40,* 333–338.

Bond, M., Paris, J., & Zweig-Frank, H. (1994). Defense styles and borderline personality disorder. *Journal of Personality Disorders, 8,* 28–31.

Bornstein, P. E., Clayton, P. J., Halikas, J. A., Maurice, W. L., & Robins, E. (1973). The depression of widowhood after thirteen months. *British Journal of Psychiatry, 122,* 561–566.

Bowlby, J. (1980). *Loss: Sadness and depression.* New York: Basic Books.

Brown, L. L., Tomarken, A. J., Orth, D. N., Loosen, P. T., Kalin, N. H., & Davidson, R. J. (1996). Individual differences in repressive-defensiveness predict basal salivary cortisol levels. *Journal of Personality and Social Psychology, 70,* 362–371.

Cerney, M. W., & Buskirk, J. R. (1991). Anger: The hidden part of grief. *Bulletin of the Menninger Clinic, 55,* 228–237.

Costa, P. T., & McCrae, R. R. (1992). *Revised NEO Personality Inventory (NEO-PIR) and NEO Five-Factor Inventory (NEO-FFI) professional manual.* Odessa, FL: Psychological Assessment Resources.

Crawford, C. B., Salter, B. E., & Jang, K. L. (1989). Human grief: Is its intensity related to the reproductive value of the deceased? *Ethology and Sociobiology, 10,* 297–307.

Davis, P. J., & Schwartz, G. E. (1987). Repression and the inaccessibility of affective memories. *Journal of Personality and Social Psychology, 52,* 155–163.

Davis, P. J., Singer, J. L., Bonanno, G. A., & Schwartz, G. E. (1988). Repressor personality style and response bias during an affective memory recognition task: A signal detection analysis. *Australian Journal of Psychology, 40,* 147–157.

Dawkins, K., & Furnham, A. (1989). The color naming of emotional words. *British Journal of Psychology, 80,* 383–389.

Deutsch, H. (1937). Absence of grief. *Psychoanalytic Quarterly, 6,* 12–22.

Downey, G., Silver, R. C., & Wortman, C. B. (1990). Reconsidering the attribution-adjustment relationship following a major negative event: Coping with the loss of a child. *Journal of Personality and Social Psychology, 59,* 925–940.

Dyregove, A., & Matthiesen, S. B. (1991). Parental grief following the death of an infant: A follow-up over one year. *Scandinavian Journal of Psychology, 32,* 193–207.

Faschingbauer, T. R. (1981). *The Texas Revised Inventory of Grief manual.* Houston, TX: Honeycomb.

Faschingbauer, T. R., Zisook, S., & Devaul, R. D. (1987). The Texas Revised Inventory of Grief. In S. Zisook (Ed.), *Biopsychosocial aspects of bereavement* (pp. 111–124). Washington, DC: American Psychiatric Press.

Field, N., Bonanno, G. A., Williams, P., & Horowitz, M. J. (1996). *Applying an empty-chair monologue paradigm to examine appraisals of conjugal loss.* Manuscript submitted for publication.

Fisher, R. A. (1930). *The genetical theory of natural selection.* New York: Dover.

Folkman, S., Chesney, M., Collette, L., Boccellari, A., & Cooke, M. (1996). Postbereavement depressive mood and its prebereavement predictors in HIV+ and HIV− gay men. *Journal of Personality and Social Psychology, 70,* 336–348.

Freud, S. (1957). Mourning and melancholia. In J. Strachey (Ed.), *The standard edition of the complete psychological works of Sigmund Freud* (Vol. 14, pp. 152–170). London: Hogarth Press. (Original work published 1917).

Gallagher, D. (1986). Therapeutic issues in the treatment of spousal bereavement reactions in the elderly. In F. J. Pirozzato & G. J. Maletta (Eds.), *Assessment and treatment of the elderly neuropsychiatric patient* (pp. 215–240). New York: Praeger.

Gunzerath, L., & Bonanno, G. A. (1997). Personality and bereavement: Borderline tendancies as a predictor of chronic grief. Unpublished manuscript, Catholic University of America.

Hansen, R. D., & Hansen, C. H. (1988). Repression of emotionally tagged memories: The architecture of less complex emotions. *Journal of Personality and Social Psychology, 55*, 811–818.

Holmes, T., & Rahe, R. (1967). The Social Readjustment Scale. *Journal of Psychosomatic Research, 11*, 213–218.

Horowitz, L. M., Rosenberg, S. E., Baer, B. A., Ureño, G., & Villaseñor, V. S. (1988). Inventory of Interpersonal Problems: Psychometric properties and clinical applications. *Journal of Consulting and Clinical Psychology, 56*, 885–892.

Horowitz, M. J., Bonanno, G. A., & Holen, A. (1993). Pathological grief: Diagnosis and explanations. *Psychosomatic Medicine, 55*, 260–273.

Horowitz, M. J., Siegel, B., Holen, A., Bonanno, G. A., Milbrath, C., & Stinson, C. H. (in press). Diagnostic criteria for complicated grief disorders. *American Journal of Psychiatry*.

Horowitz, M. J., Wilner, N., & Alvarez, M. A. (1979). Impact of Events Scale: A measure of subjective distress. *Psychosomatic Medicine, 41*, 209–218.

Jacobs, S., Hansen, F., Berkman, L., Kasl, S., & Ostfeld, A. (1989). Depressions of bereavement. *Comprehensive Psychiatry, 30*, 218–224.

Jacobs, S., Hansen, F., Kasl, S., Ostfeld, A., Berkman, L., & Kim, K. (1990). Anxiety disorders during acute bereavement: Risk and risk factors. *Journal of Clinical Psychiatry, 51*, 269–274.

Janoff-Bulman, R. (1989). Assumptive worlds and the stress of traumatic events: Applications of the schema construct. *Social Cognition, 7*, 113–136.

Janoff-Bulman, R. (1992). *Shattered assumptions: Toward a new psychology of trauma*. New York: Free Press.

Kaplan, K. J. (1972). On the ambivalence-indifference problem in attitude theory and measurement: A suggested modification of the semantic differential technique. *Psychological Bulletin, 77*, 361–372.

Keltner, D., & Bonanno, G. A. (1997). A study of laughter and dissociation: Distinct correlates of laughter and smiling during bereavement. *Journal of Personality and Social Psychology, 73*, 687–702.

Lazare, A. (1989). Bereavement and unresolved grief. In A. Lazare (Ed.), *Outpatient psychiatry: Diagnosis and treatment* (2nd ed.) (pp. 381–397). Baltimore: Williams & Wilkins.

Lehman, D. R., Wortman, C. B., & Williams, A. F. (1987). Long-term effects of losing a spouse or child in a motor vehicle crash. *Journal of Personality and Social Psychology, 52*, 218–231.

Lindemann, E. (1944). The symptomatology and management of acute grief. *American Journal of Psychiatry, 101*, 141–148.

Lund, D. A., Casserta, M. S., & Dimond, M. F. (1989). Impact of spousal bereavement on the subjective well-being of older adults. In D. A. Lund (Ed.), *Older bereaved spouses: Research with practical applications* (pp. 3–15). New York: Hemisphere.

Lundin, T. (1984). Long-term outcome of bereavement. *British Journal of Psychiatry, 145*, 428–434.

Maddison, D., & Walker, W. L. (1967). Factors affecting the outcome of conjugal bereavement. *International Journal of Psychiatry, 113*, 1057–1067.

Newton, T. L., & Contrada, R. J. (1992). Repressive coping and verbal-autonomic response dissociation: The influence of social context. *Journal of Personality and Social Psychology, 62*, 159–167.

Nolen-Hoeksema, S. (1993). Sex differences in control of depression. In D. M. Wegner & J. W. Pennebaker (Eds.), *Handbook of mental control* (pp. 306–324). New York: Prentice Hall.

Osterweis, M., Solomon, F., & Green, F. (Eds.). (1984). *Bereavement: Reactions, consequences, and care*. Washington, DC: National Academy Press.

Parkes, C. M. (1970). The first year of bereavement: A longitudinal study of the reaction of London widows to the death of their husbands. *Psychiatry, 33*, 444–467.

Parkes, C. M., & Weiss, R. S. (1983). *Recovery from bereavement*. New York: Basic Books.

Paulhus, D. L. (1984). Two-component models of socially desirable responding. *Journal of Personality and Social Psychology, 46*, 598–609.

Paulhus, D. L. (1991). *Assessing self-deception and impression management in self-reports: The Balanced Inventory of Desirable Responding, Version 6.* Unpublished manual, University of British Columbia.

Raphael, B. (1983). *The anatomy of bereavement.* New York: Basic Books.

Raphael, B., Middleton, W., Martinek, N., & Misso, V. (1993). Counseling and therapy of the bereaved. In M. S. Stroebe, W. Stroebe, & R. O. Hansson (Eds.), *Handbook of bereavement: Theory, research, and intervention* (pp. 427–456). Cambridge, England: Cambridge University Press.

Rusch, K. M., Guastello, S. J., & Mason, P. T. (1992). Differentiating symptom clusters of borderline personality disorder. *Journal of Clinical Psychology, 48,* 730–738.

Rynearson, E. K., & McCreery, J. M. (1993). Bereavement after homicide: A synergism of trauma loss. *American Journal of Psychiatry, 150,* 258–261.

Sanders, C. M. (1980). A comparison of adult bereavement in the death of a spouse, child, and parent. *Omega, 10,* 303–322.

Sanders, C. M. (1993). Risk factors in bereavement outcome. In M. S. Stroebe, W. Stroebe, & R. O. Hansson (Eds.), *Handbook of bereavement: Theory, research, and intervention* (pp. 255–270). Cambridge, England: Cambridge University Press.

Scott, W. A. (1966). Measures of cognitive structure. *Multivariate Behavioral Research, 1,* 391–395.

Schuster, S. R., & Zisook, S. (1993). The course of normal grief. In M. S. Stroebe, W. Stroebe, & R. O. Hansson (Eds.), *Handbook of bereavement: Theory, research, and intervention* (pp. 23–43). Cambridge, England: Cambridge University Press.

Spanier, G. B. (1976). Measuring dyadic adjustment: New scales for assessing the quality of marriage and similar dyads. *Journal of Marriage and the Family, 38,* 15–28.

Stroebe, M. S., Hansson, R. O., & Stroebe, W. (1993). Contemporary themes and controversies in bereavement research. In M. S. Stroebe, W. Stroebe, & R. O. Hansson (Eds.), *Handbook of bereavement: Theory, research, and intervention* (pp. 457–476). Cambridge, England: Cambridge University Press.

Stroebe, M. S., & Stroebe, W. (1993). The mortality of bereavement. In M. S. Stroebe, W. Stroebe, & R. O. Hansen (Eds.), *Handbook of bereavement: Theory, research, and intervention* (pp. 175–195). Cambridge, England: Cambridge University Press.

Stroebe, W., & Stroebe, M. S. (1987). *Bereavement and health: The psychological and physical consequences of partner loss.* Cambridge, England: Cambridge University Press.

Stroebe, W., & Stroebe, M. S. (1993). Determinants of adjustment to bereavement in younger widows and widowers. In M. S. Stroebe, W. Stroebe, & R. O. Hansson (Eds.), *Handbook of bereavement: Theory, research, and intervention* (pp. 208–226). Cambridge, England: Cambridge University Press.

Stroebe, W., Stroebe, M. S., Abakoumkin, G., & Schut, H. (1996). The role of loneliness and social support in adjustment to loss: A test of attachment versus stress theory. *Journal of Personality and Social Psychology, 70,* 1241–1249.

Vachon, M. L. S., Rogers, J., Lyall, W. A. L., Lancee, W. J., Sheldon, A. R., & Freeman, S. J. J. (1982). Predictors and correlates of adaptation to conjugal bereavement. *American Journal of Psychiatry, 139,* 998–1002.

Weinberger, D. A., & Davidson, M. N. (1994). Styles of inhibiting emotional expression: Distinguishing repressive coping from impression management. *Journal of Personality, 62,* 587–613.

Weinberger, D. A., Schwartz, G. E., & Davidson, J. R. (1979). Low-anxious and repressive coping styles: Psychometric patterns of behavioral and physiological responses to stress. *Journal of Abnormal Psychology, 88,* 369–380.

Widiger, T. A., & Costa, P. T. (1994). Personality and personality disorders. *Journal of Abnormal Psychology, 103,* 78–91.

Windholz, M. J., Marmar, C. R., & Horowitz, M. J. (1985). A review of research on conjugal bereavement: Impact on health and efficacy of intervention. *Comprehensive Psychiatry, 26,* 433–447.

Wortman, C. B., & Bolger, N. (1988). *Life course timing, degree of forewarning, and adjustment in widowhood.* Paper presented at the 41st Annual Meeting of the Gerontological Society of America, San Francisco.

Wortman, C. B., & Silver, R. C. (1989). The myths of coping with loss. *Journal of Personality and Social Psychology, 57,* 349–357.

Wortman, C. B., Silver, R. C., & Kessler, R. C. (1993). The meaning of loss and adjustment to bereavement. In M. S. Stroebe, W. Stroebe, & R. O. Hansson (Eds.), *Handbook of bereavement: Theory, research, and intervention* (pp. 349–366). Cambridge, England: Cambridge University Press.

Zisook, S., Schneider, D., & Schuster, S. R. (1990). Anxiety and bereavement. *Psychiatric Medicine, 8,* 83–96.

Zisook, S., & Schuster, S. R. (1991). Depression through the first year after the death of a spouse. *American Journal of Psychiatry, 148,* 1346–1352.

Zisook, S., Schuster, S. R., Irwin, M., Darko, D. F., Sledge, P., & Rosovsky, K. (1994). Bereavement, depression, and immune function. *Psychiatric Research, 52,* 1–10.

Chapter 4

Intersections of Grief and Trauma: Family Members' Reactions to Homicide

M. Elizabeth Stevens-Guille[1]

Research that identifies intersections in the fields of death and trauma has burgeoned into a separate area of study (e.g., Figley, Bride, & Mazza, 1997). This chapter outlines initial results from a Western Canadian study that focused on stress and grief reactions of family survivors of homicide victims. A brief theoretical overview discusses grief as a stress factor and emphasizes the role of social support, centrality of the relationship, and gender differences in surviving family members who have been bereaved by homicide.

TRAUMATIC GRIEF

The grief experienced by families of homicide victims is at once the same and different from that experienced by most bereaved individuals. It is the same in that grief must be fully experienced if the family is to come to terms with the loss (Worden, 1982). It is different in that the manner of death forces conditions upon family survivors that may be overwhelming. When the death of a loved one is due to homicide, grief reactions of the survivors are thought to be the most severe and enduring (Rinear, 1988; Rando, 1990). Although the first task of grieving is to accept that the person is dead (Worden, 1982), families of homicide victims must also come to terms with the idea that there is nothing they can do to restore their loved one's life (McCann & Pearlman, 1990). Families of survivors, as well as the survivors themselves, are susceptible to posttrauma reactions, including posttraumatic stress disorder (Figley, 1986; Danieli, 1994). Family members experiencing deep empathy for the plight of a loved one may be prone to evolving real personal distress.

[1] Dr. B. Hudnall Stamm provided valuable feedback on the technical clarity and organization of this chapter.

The process of experiencing grief is complicated by the manner of death, the amount of suffering the loved one is likely to have experienced, and the intensity of interest that surrounds a forbidden act (Rinear, 1988). In addition, surviving family members must endure police investigations and the experience of being spectators in the eyes of the court. Some may also endure the public's intrusion into their grief should the case spark the interest of the press. They may become victims of the media as details of their family life become available for public examination. People may avoid family members because they do not know what to say precisely when friendship is most necessary. Raphael and Middleton (1987) theorize that homicidal and other violent deaths are likely to lead to posttraumatic stress disorder, intense anger, helplessness, and grief.

SECONDARY TRAUMATIZATION

It is becoming accepted that family survivors of trauma victims in general (Figley, 1986, 1995; Pearlman, MacIan, Mas, Stamm, & Bieber, 1992), and homicide victims in particular (Rinear, 1984, 1988; Amick-McMullen, Kilpatrick, Veronen, & Smith, 1989; Rynearson & McCreery, 1993), experience posttraumatic stress reactions in addition to the shock of unanticipated grief (Rando, 1994). Lehman, Wortman, and Williams stated unequivocally that "the death of a spouse or child is one of the most stressful events that a person can experience during the course of his or her life" (1987, p. 218). Pynoos and Eth (1984) studied a group of children who had witnessed the homicide of a parent and were then compelled to participate in criminal justice proceedings. They found that these children often exhibited symptoms of posttraumatic stress disorder as well as a wide range of grief reactions. In her pioneering study with parents of murdered children, Rinear found that symptoms and reactions of parents of murdered children do not fully conform to currently existing models of grief and mourning. She noted that the symptoms more closely approximate those cited as criteria for posttraumatic stress disorder. Applebaum and Burns (1991) also reported posttraumatic stress disorder in surviving siblings and parents of children who died unexpectedly.

Secondary traumatization has been documented in wives of war veterans (Mikulincer, Florian, & Solomon, 1995; Solomon, 1992), families of rape victims (Figley, 1986), and nurses following disaster debriefing (Pickett et al., 1994).

Stamm (see Chapters 1 and 2) suggests that the terms outlining primary and secondary trauma reactions should be clarified. Stamm suggests that when the event happens to the person, it is primary trauma; if the person encounters distress while empathizing for another who has been affected by an event, it is secondary. In many cases, particularly with the death of another, both primary and secondary trauma may be present. For family survivors of homicide, although the empathy is for the predicament of a dying loved one, the trauma is ultimately experienced directly, since the loss happens to the family.

GRIEF AS A STRESSFUL EVENT

There is convincing epidemiological evidence that the loss of a close family member can be a traumatically stressful event in any culture (Holmes & Masuda, 1974; Glick, Weiss, & Parkes, 1974; Parkes & Weiss, 1983). Stamm (Chapter 1) suggests that all deaths are stressful experiences. Yet far from all deaths are traumatically stressful. The differentiation between a stressful experience and a diagnosable traumatic stress-related disorder is tied to the intensity of the demand that people reorient their world to accommodate the event. As well, bereavement can be the cause of physical and mental illness (Stroebe & Stroebe, 1983; Kim & Jacobs, 1995; Kaprio, Koskenvico, & Rita, 1987). Parkes (1972) views loss as a principal form of stress encountered by organisms.

Based on Bowlby's attachment theory (1969) and the "grief work" theory proposed by Lindemann (1944), Parkes (1970) posited three phases of grief prior to the resolution phase that clearly show death as a stressful event for the bereaved. First, on a biological level, an individual in the initial stage of alarm retreats into a state of shock and alertness. Parkes speculates that the shock reaction arms the survivors as a form of protection from whatever danger that exists. In the second stage of grief, the survivor searches for the lost love object. In the animal world, this procedure often results in a successful reunion. This may be the first attempt at a solution to the stress of the loss. The third phase is disorganization, when the bereaved find it difficult to function as they accept the reality of the death. Mitigation, the final stage proposed by Parkes, is a healthy adaptation to the reality of the death of the loved attachment object and an ability to reinvest in another. Perhaps because Parkes's major studies were of spousal bereavement, he viewed, intimacy as a signal of grief resolution.

Grief theory, at least in part, has its foundations in trauma. Consider the following.

The picture of grief or bereavement reactions and trauma was inevitably complicated by Lindemann's (1944) classic clinical description of the symptomatology and management of acute grief. This was derived from his work with the bereaved survivors of the Coconut Grove nightclub fire in Boston, and many of those people had themselves not only been bereaved, but also severely traumatized. Lindemann made no effort to dissect out these separate phenomena.

(Raphael & Martinek, 1997, p. 374).

TRAUMA SYMPTOMS OF FAMILY SURVIVORS

Perhaps one of the most obvious conditions necessitating a blending of trauma and bereavement is that among families who have sustained the murder of one of their members. The depth of emotional reactions for loved ones of a murder victim is overwhelming and cannot be overstated. Trauma has been found most difficult to resolve when the traumatic event is thought to be deliberately caused by another human (Creamer, Burgess, Buckingham, & Pattison, 1993). The symptoms of traumatic loss center on recurrent terrifying images of the victim's death (Eth & Pynoos, 1985; Rynearson, 1984, 1995; Rynearson & McCreery, 1993). These images intrude upon waking life as flashbacks and disturb sleep with nightmares (Van der Hart, Brown, & Turco, 1990). They are accompanied by fears of death and dying and by feelings of helplessness and shame familiar to traumatologists (Lindy et al., 1983). Survivors try to avoid reminders of the loss and death in general, often by moving from one location to another.

It is impossible for others to understand that an obsessive review of the circumstances surrounding the murder is necessary for the survivors. This preoccupation is what Parkes (1972) called searching behavior. The living engage in it before they are able to put away the notion that loved ones will reappear. When the hope that the loved one will reappear is abandoned and the death accepted, grieving begins. Grief is complicated by an overwhelming sense of rage and guilt. Rage is often directed at institutions represented by the court system and the perpetrator (Rinear, 1984; Getzel & Masters, 1984; Bard & Sangrey, 1979). The intensity of emotions previously noted is layered with an overpowering desire to be with the loved one (Rinear, 1984), eliciting suicide ideation for many clients. In recent work, Parkes (1993) noted a high incidence of psychiatric conditions in surviving family members of homicide victims.

A disproportionate number of pathological grief reactions have been reported anecdotally. These reactions include anxiety attacks, existential crises resulting in suicide ideation, and overwhelming rage triggered by trivialities (Masters, Friedman, & Getzel, 1988), phobic avoidance of homicide-related stimuli, and increased self-protective behavior (Burgess, 1975; Rynearson, 1984). Poussaint (1984) has observed a tendency to try to hunt for the killer. Thus, posttraumatic reactions prevent grief work; they mask, inhibit, and delay the mourning process (Van der Hart et al., 1990). Family survivors of homicide victims often become withdrawn, and frequently friends become uncomfortable. As time passes, friends and relatives withdraw (Getzel & Masters, 1984).

THE ROLE OF SOCIAL SUPPORT

Intuitively, people react with horror to murder. Society's inability to acknowledge or understand the length of time necessary for crisis resolution and lack of knowledge regarding how to respond leave survivors isolated. Many friends avoid people as if their peril were contagious (Sprang, McNeil, & Wright, 1989). For some people diagnosed with posttraumatic stress disorder, a perception of strong social support seems to reduce trauma reactions, while those with a social network of equivalent size but less support report a higher incidence of distress (Davidson, Hughes, Blazer, & George, 1991). Parkes (1972) found that widows who were the most angry experienced the highest degree of social isolation. Klass (1988) concluded that the social support system for grieving parents is central to the quality of resolution. Lyons (1991) found that the quality of the network interaction is more important than the size of the social support group.

GENDER AND AGE FACTORS

Many bereavement studies (Parkes, 1972; Maddison & Walker, 1967) are based on the participation of women. It may be that women are at risk for greater distress. Perhaps women have been socialized to be more expressive of their emotions or, as the caretakers of society, to seek appropriate treatment, which makes them more visible to researchers. There may also be biological reasons for perceived differences. Recent studies have found that women become more aroused in response to stressful conditions (Adler, 1993). In addition, Jacobs (1993) found that younger adults are more at risk of developing secondary bereavement reactions. Regardless of their origins, there does seem to be evidence to support differential bereavement responses among men and women and among younger and older adults.

CENTRALITY OF THE RELATIONSHIP TO THE BEREAVED

Without consideration of the gender or age of the bereaved, there is speculation that reactions to the death of a family member depend on the centrality of the relationship to the bereaved (Bugen, 1977). The centrality does not necessarily depend on the familial relationship, but on the emotional attachment of the bereaved to the deceased. Bugen theorized that the centrality of the relationship was directly related to the extent and duration of grief. Bereavement in this study encompassed the first 6 years after death.

CANADIAN INCIDENCE OF HOMICIDE

In 1995, 656 homicides occurred in Canada, one fourth that of the United States. The data here focus on Western Canada, since it has historically evidenced higher rates of murder than other areas of the country. In 1995, Alberta reported a homicide rate of 2.15 per 100,000; Saskatchewan, 2.07; Manitoba, 2.37; and British Columbia, 3.19. The homicide rate in major metropolitan areas was only slightly higher (63%) than the national average. Homicide continues to represent less than 1% of all violent crimes reported in Canada. The homicide trend has remained relatively stable over the last 10 years but has fallen slightly since the 1970s (Statistics Canada, 1995).

In this period, 95% of homicide incidents involved a single victim. Slightly more deaths were caused by stabbing (31%) than by firearms (30%). Males accounted for two thirds of the victims and 9 of the 10 accused. Almost half of the victims were killed in their own residence, and a stranger committed only one of every six murders (Statistics Canada, 1995). When the statistics are examined, it is not surprising that little information is available regarding the effects of homicide on family members.

Canadian distances are wide, and mental health services are diminishing. Expertise in terms of specialized groups, such as family survivors of homicide victims or other violent deaths, is uneven, particularly in less well-populated areas of the country, and yet the need for expertise is equivalent across all of Canada. Rural surviving family members, who represent nearly half of the victims, are less likely to have access to bereavement groups or to feel that their experience is understood.

Although empirical research in North America is growing (Thompson, Norris, & Ruback, 1998; Rynearson, 1995; Rynearson & McCreery, 1993; Bard, 1982), research in the area of homicide is limited. Two empirical studies (Amick-McMullen, Kilpatrick, Vernoen, & Smith, 1989; Rinear, 1984, 1989) provided the foundation for this study. Rinear's larger 1984 study examined grief reactions of parents who had lost a child by homicide. The parents were all members of a national support group called Parents of Murdered Children. In Canada, an equivalent group does not exist, nor has any research been conducted.

THE WESTERN CANADA FAMILIES OF HOMICIDE STUDY

The present study was an investigation into emotional reactions of all family members—rather than just parents—to the murder of one or more of their own. Thus, the investigation examined grief reactions and stress reactions. As shown earlier, it is very difficult to separate traumatic stress from bereavement in families of murder victims. In fact, it is probably not possible or even helpful to find pure examples of bereavement or trauma in this population. Thus, in this exploratory study, I tried to address important facets of both bereavement and traumatic stress. The study focused on levels of posttraumatic reactions, who experienced traumatic stress and who experienced grief, and whether traumatic stress and grief are related to perceived social support. Specifically, the following questions were addressed: (a) Is closeness to the victim related to grief and pathology following the murder? (b) Is there a relationship between overall social support and grief and pathology? (c) Are particular types of social support related to particular types of postevent distress? and (d) Are there differences based on gender, and are younger women more at risk than older women?

METHOD AND PROCEDURE

As a means of locating next of kin as potential participants, a record review was conducted (up to 6 years retrospectively; death occurred between 1986 and 1992) on all of the homicide files in four Western Canadian provinces (British Columbia, Alberta, Saskatchewan, and Manitoba). In Saskatchewan, next of kin are not routinely recorded, so searches were conducted by the chief coroner's staff and police. Coroner's files are not routinely accessed, and considerable care was taken to respect local customs and the feelings of the next of kin.

Following the provincial coroners and medical examiners guidelines, a letter explaining the research proposal was sent to the homicide victim's next of kin using the addresses found in each file. A letter from the chief coroner or medical examiner of each province indicating support for the project accompanied a letter of inquiry from the researcher.

The research was guided by the ethical principles of the American Psychological Association (1992) and approved by the University of Alberta's Institutional Review Board. Given the potentially disturbing nature of the questions asked, I assumed that some people might experience psychological distress while recalling their experiences. Therefore, individual provincial resources for psychological services were detailed, and a hotline number accompanied the survey package forwarded to those willing to participate in the study.

Characteristics of Respondents

Multiple generations were represented by those who responded to the survey; ages ranged from 17–78 years. The mean age was 43 years, and the median was 42 years, although there were a number of respondents in their 20s. Given that the mean age of the person who died was 30 years (median = 26.5, mode of = 19), the age of respondents was consistent with the age of parents and siblings. As could be expected based on the participation rate in other studies (Maddison & Walker, 1967; Stroebe & Stroebe, 1983), twice as many women (66%) as men (33%) responded. Also similar to other studies, it was not possible to determine whether this difference stemmed from social or epidemiological reasons, or perhaps both. It is difficult to explain the higher response rate for women than for men. Perhaps women are more socialized to respond, or maybe women responded symbolically on behalf of the family. Perhaps the reason is that there are more women survivors. Or there may be some entirely different reason. Most likely, it is a combination of these reasons.

The responses represented 89 unique homicide victims. In some cases, more than one member of a family responded. This chapter reports on the individual's responses. Additional analyses considering the data in a familywise manner are in progress. Consistent with the young age of the murder victims, 32 people identified their brother or son as the deceased person. Twenty people said that they had lost their daughter, and 16 identified their sister as having been murdered. Only 7 people had lost their husband; 5, their father; and 4, their mother. Nine people identified an extended family member as the murder victim; 3 lost an aunt, 1 a grandson, and 1 a niece, and 4 were other relations.

In terms of age, the 89 victims ranged from infants to 82 years old. Victims were most commonly in the 19–27-year group. The mean age of victims was 30 years, and the, median was 26.

Of the 127 people who replied, 122 identified themselves as Caucasian and 5 identified themselves as of other ethnicities. Protestants composed 42.5% of the sample, while Catholics represented 39%; the remaining 18.5% reported no religious affiliation or unique other affiliations. Those who responded to the survey tended to have completed high school (mean: 12.7 years), with the educational level of respondents ranging from 6 to 25 years. This level of education is likely to indicate a comfort level with the format of a written survey as a research tool but should not be taken to be representative of the education level of all families of homicide victims.

Instruments

The following instruments were used: Symptom Checklist 90–Revised (SCL-90-R; Derogatis, 1979, 1983), Texas Revised Grief Inventory (TRIG; Faschingbauer, 1981), and Purdue Post-Traumatic Disorder Scale (PPTDS; Hartsough, 1986).

Symptom Checklist 90–Revised   This instrument is a self-report inventory designed to assess the psychological symptoms of psychiatric and medical patients. Subjects were asked to rate their experience in the previous 7 days in terms of each of 90 symptoms. Ratings were made on a 0–4 Likert scale. The inventory measures somatization, obsessive-compulsive symptoms, interpersonal sensitivity, depression, anxiety, phobic anxiety, psychoticism, paranoid ideation, and hostility. One of three global indexes of distress, the General Severity Index (GSI), was used to indicate the level of distress of participants in this study. The SCL-90-R has been used to measure responses to stressful life events or chronic strains in nonpatient samples, and it has been used to examine psychiatric symptomatology in other studies of people experiencing loss, trauma, and death. Elevated symptom scores have been shown for women seeking abortions, spouses of chronic pain patients, parents of children who have died in traffic accidents, people grieving the death of a parent, survivors of catastrophic fire, and relatives of suicide and rape victims. Crime-related posttraumatic stress reactions among women have been assessed with the SCL-90-R (Saunders, Arata, & Kilpatrick, 1990), and war-related PTSD diagnosis has been developed through a set of items from the that scale (Weathers et al., 1996). Because of the differences between these scales, a specific PTSD scale was used to assess PTSD symptoms in this study.

Texas Revised Grief Inventory   This inventory, composed of 21 items, is used to measure absence of grief, delayed grief, prolonged grief, and acute unresolved grief. A 5-point Likert scale (completely false, mostly false, true and false, mostly true, and completely true) is used in rating items. High scores indicate a higher level of grief. The TRIG has two parts. Part 1 includes dependency and grief, along with funeral attendance and grief, while Part 2 measures time, gender, and degree of relatedness. Split-half reliability for Part 1 is .74, and the alpha coefficient is .77. Split-half reliability for Part 2 is .88, and the alpha coefficient is .86.

Sprang, McNeil, and Wright (1993) have begun to develop a causal model of grief specific to family survivors of homicide victims based on this instrument. Rynearson and McCreery (1993) discovered higher levels of intensity in family survivors of homicide than in normal bereaved subjects via scores on the inventory.

Purdue Post-Traumatic Disorder Scale   This instrument is designed to measure PTSD symptoms during the previous week in survivors of a potentially traumatic incident. The scale asks participants to report their degree of endorsement in terms of 15 items rated on a 5-point scale ranging from 1 (*least bothered*) to 5 (*most bothered*). Thirteen of the items reflect specific symptoms of PTSD as described in the criteria, and 2 questions ask about respondents' levels of general distress. The scale correlated .89 with judges' ratings of posttraumatic stress based on interviews. There are currently no norms for the scale. In a validation study of rescue workers, the average score was 29.08.

Scale Intercorrelation

As stated previously, distinctions among loss and grief, trauma, and psychopathology are not clear. The scales used were chosen with the awareness that there would be some intercorrelation between them. However, it is important that the variables not completely replicate each other. Table 4.1 presents the correlations between the scales. The SCL-90-R and the TRIG were moderately correlated, sharing about one fifth to one third of their variance. Consistent with reports by Hartsough (1986, 1996), the PPTDS was more highly correlated with the general measure of psychopathology but still shared just over one half (57%) of the variance. The PPTDS and the TRIG scales shared just over a third (36%). Thus, each of the instruments contributed uniquely to the measurement of postevent reactions.

Table 4.1   Dependent Measure Scale Intercorrelations

	GSI	PPTDS	TRIG (current)	TRIG (past)
GSI	1.00			
PPTDS	.75	1.00		
TRIG (current)	.40	.61	1.00	
TRIG (past)	.59	.59	.42	1.00

Data Analysis

All data were analyzed with SPSS-PC for Windows. In recognition of the potentially negative effect of collinearity, regression analysis was used to partial out the unique contribution of each of the instruments.

Because this was the first study of its kind and it was exploratory in nature, a liberal approach to data analysis was used. This was done to provide as much information as possible for future studies. For example, the multiple regressions involved variables that theoretically should work together (rather than variable reduction techniques such as stepwise regression). Similarly, no adjustments were made for multiple tests.

RESULTS AND DISCUSSION

Overall, the participants in this study reported levels of grief and pathology that exceeded norms for general or even inpatient psychiatric populations. More than half of the participants (56%) had lost their family member more than 2 years previously, and at least a full year had passed for 90% of the participants. Even so, their feelings regarding the murder ran deep. There were powerful differences in this sample's reports of their current feelings on the TRIG as compared with the TRIG norms, $t(82) = 33.2$, $p < .05$. Less strong but similar feelings were reported on the past behavior scale of the TRIG, $t(82) = 8.35$, $p < .05$. Scores on the GSI exceeded significantly those reported by nonpatient samples, psychiatric outpatients, and even psychiatric inpatients, $t(82) = 11.9$, $p < .05$. Similar differences were seen on the PPTDS, with scores of the present sample exceeding the scores of general rescue workers and those assigned to body removal following a disaster, $t(82) = 5.75$, $p < .05$. Table 4.2 shows the means and standard deviations of the most extreme comparison groups and the current sample for each scale.

In considering that these results are well above averages for other significantly impaired groups, it seems evident that, on average, family survivors of

Table 4.2 Comparisons of Study Results and Scale Norms

| | Homicide sample | | Norm sample | |
	M	SD	M	SD
GSI (psychiatric inpatients)	1.97	0.70	1.3	0.82
PPTDS (body removal)	2.85	0.73	2.42	Unknown
TRIG (current)	3.87	0.8	1.28	0.7
TRIG (past)	3.14	1.0	2.22	0.8

homicide victims experience extreme grief and posttrauma reactions. The results bring into question the types of trauma reactions involved. The correlation between the SCL-90-R and the PPTDS suggests that stress reactions involve the traumatic nature of the death and that the level of grief is profound. Just as the kind of grief is unknown, the kinds of stress reactions are unknown. The responses call into question whether the reactions represent primary or secondary traumatization. It could be that the difference in type of traumatization is one of degree, given that the criteria for secondary trauma reactions are the same as for all posttraumatic stress reactions.

Closeness to the Victim as a Risk Factor for Developing Pathology

The first issue regarding closeness to the victim involves whether those who report being closer to the victim are more at risk for prolonged or intense grief and pathology following the murder. A multiple regression was conducted to address this question (see Table 4.3). The overall test indicated that there was a significant relationship between the measures of grief and pathology and feelings of closeness, $F(4, 119) = 4.7$, $p < .001$, adjusted $R^2 = .11$. However, inspection of the partial regression coefficients indicated that the important variable in the equation was (TRIG) current feelings, $\beta = .23$; $t(119) = -2.1$, $p = .04$. None of the other variables (GSI, PPTDS, or TRIG past behaviors) made a significant unique contribution to the regression equation. Reported feelings of current distress were predictive of feeling close to the victim.

Current feelings of grief are based on memory and, as such, are predictive of people remembering the relationship as being close. The relationship may have, in fact, been close, or it may have been difficult. Difficult relationships are often invested with emotion, which could also precipitate great feelings of distress. Perhaps feelings of grief helped people remember their relationship as being close, even if it had not been close at all. The act of remembering fosters a feeling of closeness that may bring increased comfort to the bereaved.

Table 4.3 Coefficients for Multiple Regression on Closeness to the Victim

Variable	B	SE B	β	T	Significance of T
GSI	−.15	.20	−.10	−.79	.43
PPTDS	.02	.01	.20	1.3	.19
TRIG (current)	.28	.13	.23	2.1	.04
TRIG (past)	.09	.11	.09	.77	.44

Social Support as a Risk Factor for Developing Pathology

The PPTDS and the two TRIG scales were not significant predictors of social support. Probably because the variable used to estimate social support was rather weakly constructed (the sum of five discrete items rated yes or no). Thus, the items were investigated individually, and specific elements of social support, including friends, peer support groups, professional counselors, family members, and helping professionals (e.g., police, lawyers, social workers, and doctors), were examined.

There were no significant differences between those who received support from their friends and those who did not on any of the four scales. Similarly, there were no significant differences on any of the four scales (GSI, PPTDS, TRIG (current), and TRIG (past)) between those who participated in peer support groups and those who did not.

There were no significant differences on any of the four scales when those who felt supported by professionals such as police, lawyers, social workers, and doctors were compared with those who did not feel supported by these professionals.

There were mixed results for those who sought professional counseling and those who did not. Those who did seek counseling had significantly higher scores on the GSI (counseling $M = 2.0$, $SD = 0.65$; no counseling $M = 1.73$, $SD = 0.57$), $F(1, 121) = 4.1$, $p < .05$. There were also differences between these two groups on the TRIG past behavior scale, with those seeking counseling reporting more distress in their past behavior ($M = 3.2$, $SD = 0.88$) than those not seeking counseling ($M = 2.8$, $SD = 0.93$), $F(1, 121) = 4.1$, $p < .05$.

There were no significant differences on the GSI and the TRIG past behavior scale when those who felt supported by their families were compared with those who did not feel supported by their families. There was a significant difference in comparisons involving perceived familial support on the PPTDS. Those who felt family support ($M = 2.9$, $SD = 0.66$) reported higher levels of PTSD symptomology than those who did not feel supported ($M = 2.5$, $SD = 0.83$), $F(1, 121) = 5.9$, $p < .01$.

Those who reported having the support of their families also reported stronger current feelings of grief (TRIG) ($M = 3.8$, $SD = 0.72$) than those who did not have the support of their family ($M = 3.5$, $SD = 0.89$), $F(1, 121) = 4.2$, $p < .04$.

Rynearson (1995) has also documented the heightened degree of distress exhibited by family survivors of homicide victims who seek treatment. Results that indicate strong feelings of past grief as well as heightened symptomology demonstrate that the members of counseling group struggled from the onset and were probably aware that they were experiencing unmanageable emotions (hence their effort to find appropriate treatment).

The finding that family support was significantly different on a measure of pathology (PPTDS) from lack of support could be due to a number of causes. People who reported feeling unsupported by their family may have focused more on their own emotions or on their anger at feeling unsupported. Thus, they may have focused less on the imagery connected with thoughts of a dying loved one, which often attends more serious symptoms. It is also possible that if families were not close, the emotions were not strong. Conversely, families who were closely connected probably felt that the death inflicted on one of their own had been inflicted on themselves. They would have focused on the experience of the loved one rather than on their own reactions. Another explanation could be that close families often have a more intimate degree of interpersonal communication within their circle, and self-expression is encouraged. If the family, by its communication style, is unable to break out of the traumatic cycle, the pathology would interfere with grief and become entrenched. In addition, families without expectations or experience of violence may be forced by other factors, such as media attention, to draw together, reinforcing their trauma by discussions with each other. Alternately, families may have gathered together for support due to public disapproval of the victim so that the trauma becomes the public disapprobation. It may also be that some families admit to higher levels of grief than others do.

Gender Differences

There are two important issues to be addressed regarding gender differences. The first is whether or not there is a difference between the experience of grief and posthomicide pathology in men and women. Analysis of variance results comparing male scores and female scores on the four scales fell just outside significant differences. Because the lack of significant results was most likely caused by the small and uneven sample size, exploratory correlations were run between gender and the four scales. Spearman correlations were used, with sex coded 0 for male subjects and 1 for female subjects. This allowed a clear indication of the relationship without a need to reduce the power of the small sample size. The data showed that higher scores on the GSI and the TRIG current feelings (more distress) were correlated with higher scores on gender (being female) ($r = .18$, $p = .04$, and $r = .19$, $p = .03$, respectively). While this was clearly a proxy analysis, it does suggest that future studies should investigate the possibility of gender differences.

The second question stems from work by Jacobs (1993), who suggested that younger adults are more at risk for bereavement reactions than their older counterparts. In addressing this question, data from the women were considered. All four scales were used to predict age. The results indicated that age was, in fact, a significant risk factor for the presence of distress, $F(4, 78) = 5.1$, $p < .01$, adjusted $R^2 = .17$. The regression coefficients revealed that, together, the issues tapped by the two TRIG scales predicted age. Younger women seem more at risk for grief reactions but not for PTSD or general psychopathology (see Table 4.4).

Results of the gender investigation supported Jacobs's (1993) finding that younger adults are more likely to experience bereavement difficulties. The reasons

Table 4.4 Coefficients for Multiple Regression on Female Age

Variable	B	$SE\ B$	β	T	Significance of T
GSI	−.15	.20	−.10	−.79	.43
PPTDS	.02	.01	.20	1.3	.19
TRIG (current)	.28	.13	.23	2.1	.04
TRIG (past)	.09	.11	.09	.77	.44

for these phenomena are unclear. One reason may be that, developmentally, young adults have difficulty understanding the permanence of death until their mid-20s. Higher grief scores for young women possibly reflect a coming to terms with the prematurity of the death rather than centering on the way their loved one died.

CONCLUSION

Surviving family members of homicide victims record grief and posttrauma reactions that exceed those of psychiatric inpatients and body retrieval workers. Those with the highest scores had sought psychological intervention. People who felt supported by family members recorded significant differences from those surviving family members who did not feel supported. As expected, closeness of the relationship to the deceased predicted more intense grief reactions. Women were more significantly affected by posttraumatic reactions than men, and young women experienced higher feelings of grief than older women. With scores on measures of grief and posttrauma reactions exceeding the highest rates of impaired samples, clinicians must recognize that people who present for counseling after the homicidal death of a family member are probably significantly affected.

Clinically, trauma issues must be addressed and contained in order to approach the grief. Clinicians without trauma experience may not be prepared for the severity or intensity of the grief and stress reactions confirmed by this study. If the primary task of a trauma therapist is to act as a witness (Herman, 1992) and the primary task of a thanatologist is to recognize that no one can walk into death and walk back out the same person (Rosenthal, 1973), then the intersections of the experience must be understood. Six years after the murder of her 2-year-old daughter, one mother reported: "I still need a lot of help." Another expressed the following (Stevens-Guille, 1992):

Each day is living in a form, but special occasions,

songs, a person walking down the street who is tall

with long hair, the same walk as my daughter brings

back memories. I know that I will live with this

until the day I die.

REFERENCES

Adler, T. (1993). Men and women affected by stress but differently. *APA Monitor, 24*, 8–9.

American Psychological Association. (1992). Ethical principles of psychologists and code of conduct. *American Psychologist, 47*, 1597–1611.

Amick-McMullen, A., Kilpatrick, D. G., Veronen, L. J., & Smith, S. (1989). Family survivors of homicide victims: Theoretical perspectives and an exploratory study. *Journal of Traumatic Stress, 2*, 21–35.

Applebaum, D. R., & Burns, G. L. (1991). Unexpected childhood death: Posttraumatic stress disorder in surviving siblings and parents. *Journal of Clinical and Child Psychiatry, 20*, 114–120.

Bard, M. (1982). *A retrospective study of homicide survivor adaptation* (Final Repot, Grant R01 MH31685). Bethesda, MD: National Institute of Mental Health.

Bard, M., & Sangrey, D. (1979). *The crime victim's book*. New York: Basic Books.

Bowlby, J. (1969). *Attachment and loss: Vol 1. Attachment*. New York: Basic Books.

Bowlby, J. (1980). *Attachment and loss*. New York: Basic Books. (Original work published 1969).

Bugen, L. A. (1977). Human grief: A model for prediction and intervention. *American Journal of Orthopsychiatry, 27*, 196–206.

Burgess, A. W. (1975). Family reaction to homicide. *American Journal of Orthopsychiatry, 45*, 391–398.

Creamer, M., Burgess, P. Y., Buckingham, W., & Pattison, P. (1993). Posttrauma reactions following a multiple shooting: A retrospective study and methodological inquiry. In J. P. Wilson & B. Raphael (Eds.), *International handbook of traumatic stress syndromes* (pp. 201–212). New York: Plenum.

Danieli, Y. (1984). The treatment and prevention of long-term effects and intergenerational transmission of victimization: A lesson from Holocaust survivors and their children. In C. R. Figley (Ed.), *Trauma and its wake: Vol. 2. The study of post-traumatic stress disorder, theory, research, and treatment*. New York: Brunner/Mazel.

Danieli, Y. (1994). Countertransference and trauma: Self healing and training issues. In M. B. Williams & J. F. Sommer, Jr. (Eds.), *Handbook of post-traumatic therapy* (pp. 540–550). Westport, CT: Greenwood Press.

Davidson, J. T., Hughes, D., Blazer, D. G., & George, L. K. (1991). Post-traumatic stress disorder in the community: An epidemiological study. *Psychological Medicine, 21*, 713–721.

Derogatis, L. R. (1979). *SCL-90 norms*. Towson, MD: Clinical Psychometric Research.

Derogatis, L. R. (1983). *SCL-90-R: Administration, scoring and procedure manual–II for the revised version*. Baltimore: Johns Hopkins University School of Medicine.

Eth, S., & Pynoos, R. (1985). Interaction of trauma and grief in childhood. In S. Eth & R. Pynoos (Eds.), *Post-traumatic stress disorder in children*. Washington, DC: American Psychiatric Press.

Faschingbauer, T. R. (1981). *Texas Revised Inventory of Grief: Manual*. Houston, TX: Honeycomb.

Figley, C. R. (Ed.). (1986). *Trauma and its wake* (Vol. 2). New York: Brunner/Mazel.

Figley, C. R. (1995). *Compassion fatigue: Coping with secondary PTSD among those who treat the traumatized*. New York: Brunner/Mazel.

Figley, C. R., Bride, B. E., & Mazza, N. (Eds.). (1997). *Death and trauma: The traumatology of grieving*. Philadelphia: Taylor & Francis.

Getzel, G. S., & Masters, R. (1984). Serving families who survive homicide. *Social Casework: The Journal of Contemporary Social Work, 4*, 138–144.

Glick, I., Weiss, R. S., & Parkes, C. M. (1974). *The first year of bereavement*. New York: Wiley.

Hartsough, D. M. (1986). *Variables affecting duty-related stress after an air crash disaster*. Unpublished manuscript, University of Colorado.

Hartsough, D. M. (1996). Review of Purdue PTSD Scale. In B. H. Stamm (Ed.), *Measurement of stress, trauma and adaptation*. Lutherville, MD: Sidran Press.

Herman, J. L. (1992). *Trauma and recovery*. New York: Basic Books.

Holmes, T., & Masuda, M. (1974). Life change and illness susceptibility. In B. S. Dohrenwend &
    B. P. Dohrenwend (Eds.), *Stressful life events: Their nature and effects*. New York: Wiley.
Jacobs, S. (1993). *Pathologic grief: Maladaption to loss*. Washington, DC: American Psychiatric
    Press.
Kaprio, J., Koskenvico, M., & Rita, H. (1987). Mortality after bereavement: A prospective study of
    95,647 widowed persons. *American Journal of Public Health, 77,* 283–287.
Kim, K., & Jacobs, S. C. (1995). Stress of bereavement and consequent psychiatric illness. In C. M.
    Mazure (Ed.), *Does Stress Cause Psychiatric Illness?* Washington, DC: American Psychiatric
    Press.
Klass, D. (1988). *Parental grief: Solace and resolution*. New York: Springer.
Lehman, D. R., Wortman, C. B., & Williams, A. F. (1987). Long-term effects of losing a spouse or a
    child in a motor vehicle crash. *Journal of Personality and Social Psychology, 52,* 218–231.
Lindemann, E. (1944). Symptomatology and management of acute grief. *American Journal of Psychi-
    atry, 101,* 141–148.
Lindy, J. D., Grego, B. C., Grace, M. C., & Titchener, J. D. (1983). Psychotherapy with survivors of
    the Beverly Hills Club fire. *American Journal of Psychotherapy, 27,* 593–610.
Lyons, J. A. (1991). Strategies for assessing the potential for positive adjustment following trauma.
    Journal of Traumatic Stress, 4, 93–111.
Maddison, D. C., & Walker, W. L. (1967). Factors affecting outcomes of conjugal bereavement. *British
    Journal of Psychiatry, 13,* 1057–1067.
Masters, R., Friedman, L., & Getzel, G. (1988). Helping families of homicide victims: A multidimen-
    sional approach. *Journal of Traumatic Stress, 1,* 101–125.
McCann, I. D., & Pearlman, L. A. (1990). *Psychological trauma and the adult survivor: Theory,
    therapy and transformation*. New York: Brunner/Mazel.
Mikulincer, M., Florian, V., & Solomon, Z. (1995). Marital intimacy, family support and secondary
    traumatization: A study of wives of veterans with combat stress reaction. *Anxiety Stress and
    Coping, 8,* 203–213.
Parkes, C. M. (1970). The first year of bereavement: A longitudinal study of the reaction of London
    widows to the death of their husband. *Psychiatry, 4,* 444–467.
Parkes, C. M. (1972). *Bereavement—Studies of grief in adult life*. London: Pelican Books.
Parkes, C. M. (1993). Psychiatric problems following bereavement by murder or manslaughter. *British
    Journal of Psychiatry, 162,* 49–54.
Parkes, C. M., & Weiss, R. S. (1983). *Recovery from bereavement*. New York: Basic Books.
Pearlman, L. A., MacIan, P., Mas, C., Stamm, B., & Bieber, S. (1992). *Vicarious traumatization:
    Theory and research*. Paper presented at the Eighth Annual Meeting of the International Society
    for Traumatic Stress Studies, Los Angeles, CA.
Pickett, M., Brennan, A. M. W., Greenberg, H. S., Leicht, L., & Worrell, J. D. (1994). Use of debriefing
    techniques to prevent compassion fatigue in research teams. *Nursing Research, 43,* 250–252.
Poussaint, A. F. (1984). *The grief response following a homicide*. Paper presented at the annual meet-
    ing of the American Psychological Association, Toronto, Ontario, Canada.
Pynoos, R. S., & Eth, S. (1984). The child as witness to homicide. *Journal of Social Issues, 40,* 87–107.
Rando, T. A. (1990). Foreword. In L. M. Redmond (Ed.), *Surviving: When someone you love was
    murdered* (pp. ix–xiii). Clearwater, FL: Psychological Consultation and Education Services.
Raphael, B., & Martinek, N. (1997). Assessing traumatic bereavement and posttraumatic stress dis-
    order. In T. M. Keane & J. P. Wilson (Eds.), *Assessing psychological trauma and PTSD*. New
    York: Guilford Press.
Raphael, B., & Middleton, W. (1987). Current state of research in the field of bereavement. *Journal of
    Related Science, 24,* 1–2.
Rinear, E. E. (1984). Parental response to child murder: An exploratory study. *Dissertation Abstracts
    International, 46,* 1001.
Rinear, E. E. (1988). Psychosocial aspects of parental response patterns to the death of a child by
    homicide. *Journal of Traumatic Stress, 1(3),* 305–322.

Rosenthal, J. (1973). *How could I not be among you?* New York: George Braziller.

Rynearson, E. K. (1984). Bereavement after homicide. *American Journal of Psychiatry, 141,* 1452–1454.

Rynearson, E. K. (1995). Bereavement after homicide: A comparison of treatment seekers and refusers. *British Journal of Psychiatry, 166,* 507–510.

Rynearson, E. K., & McCreery, J. M. (1993). Bereavement after homicide: A synergism of trauma and loss. *American Journal of Psychiatry, 150,* 258–261.

Saunders, B. E., Arata, C. M., & Kilpatrick, D. G. (1990). Development of a crime related post-traumatic stress disorder scale for women within the Symptom Checklist-90-Revised. *Journal of Traumatic Stress, 3,* 439–448.

Sprang, V. M., McNeil, J. S., & Wright, R. (1989, March). Psychological changes after the murder of a significant other. *Social Casework: The Journal of Contemporary Social Work,* pp. 159–164.

Sprang, V. M., McNeil, J. S., & Wright, R. (1993). Grief among surviving family members of homicide victims: A causal approach. *Omega, 26,* 145–160.

Statistics Canada. (1995). *Juristat Service Bulletin.* Ottawa: Publication Division, Statistics Canada.

Stevens-Guille, M. E. (1992). *Grief and stress reactions in family survivors of homicide victims.* Unpublished doctoral dissertation, University of Alberta, Edmonton, Alberta, Canada.

Stroebe, M. S., & Stroebe, W. (1983). Who suffers more in sex differences in health: Risk of the widowed. *Psychological Bulletin, 93,* 279–301.

Stroebe, W., & Stroebe, M. S. (1987). *Bereavement and health: The psychological and physical consequences of partner loss.* Cambridge, England: Cambridge University Press.

Thompson, M. P., Norris, F. H., & Ruback, R. B. (1998). Comparative distress levels of inner-city family members of homicide victims. *Journal of Traumatic Stress, 11(2),* 223–242.

Van der Hart, O., Brown, P., & Turco, R. M. (1990). Hypnotherapy for traumatic grief: Janetian and modern approaches integrated. *American Journal of Clinical Hypnosis, 32,* 263–271.

Weathers, F. W., Litz, B. T., Keane, T. M., Herman, D. S., Steinberg, H. R., Huska, J. A., & Kreamer, H. C. (1996). The utility of the SCL-90-R for the diagnosis of war.

Worden, J. W. (1982). *Grief counseling and grief therapy: A handbook for the mental health practitioner.* New York: Springer.

Chapter 5

Duty-Related Deaths and Police Spouse Survivors: Group Support Effects

John M. Violanti

The duty-related death of a police officer is a traumatic event for family members and other officers (Violanti, 1996; Green, Lindy, Grace, & Glaser, 1989; Green, Wilson, & Lindy, 1985; Kroes, Margolis, & Hurrell, 1974). Police officers consistently rate duty-related death as the most distressful event in their work (Violanti & Aron, 1994). Parkes (1993) found that murder of a loved one is often associated with anxiety states, panic syndromes, and depression.

Raymond (1988) found that intrusive memories of violent death very often trigger psychological difficulties in survivors. Survivors of line-of-duty military deaths often report psychological distress and trauma (Kirschner, 1982; Tyler & Gifford, 1991). Amick-McMullin, Kilpatrick, Veronen, and Smith (1989) found that 66% of homicide survivors had increased levels of psychiatric distress, prompted by dissatisfaction with the criminal justice system. Bard, Arnone, and Nemiroff (1985) found that trauma symptoms existed among surviving family members of a homicide. Rynearson and McCreery (1984) found increased trauma symptoms in their sample of homicide survivors.

Police officers are frequently exposed to traumatic events in their work (Solomon & Horn, 1986). Approximately 1 million police officers have been assaulted since 1960, and these assaults have resulted in the murder of 2,129 police officers and injury to 328,000 others. In some 631,000 other incidents, officers suffered attacks without physical injury. Within the last decade, 801 police officers have been feloniously murdered and 713 killed in duty-related accidents (Federal Bureau of Investigation, 1989). Since 1990, 915 officers have been killed in the line of duty (Concerns of Police Survivors, 1997).

THE POLICE CULTURE AND SURVIVING SPOUSES

Police officers and their families are enmeshed in a cohesive work culture. Officers often mistrust those who are not police, socialize only with other officers, and express the feeling that only other officers can fully understand them. Group cohesion is bolstered by aversive reactions of the community, media, and the criminal justice system (Bonafacio, 1991). Finister (1994) defined the police as a "psychosocial group" in which both officers and their families are psychologically aware of each other, interact with one another, and perceive themselves as a whole.

If an officer is killed in the line of duty, the surviving spouse may rely upon other officers, the police agency, and police benevolent groups to provide understanding and support (Williams, 1987; Reiser & Geiger, 1984). The police work culture may thus provide familiar structure, leadership, companionship, and motivation for grief recovery (Figley, 1988b).

Significant interaction within cohesive groups after a traumatic event may reduce psychological trauma and distress (Green et al., 1985; Green, 1993). Lindy, Grace, and Green (1981) first described this function as the "trauma membrane" effect, where a network of trusted, close persons serves to protect the traumatized individual from further distress. For the most part, protective action emerges from a group to which victims see themselves as belonging (Cohen, Mermelstein, Kamarck, and Hoberman (1985). Lin, Woelfel, and Light (1985) found that strong social ties, resulting from association with others of similar characteristics, lifestyles, and attitudes, are successful in ameliorating distress. Kazak (1991) found that near-group social context is an important element in recovery from distress. Boman (1979) found that a cohesive social network helps to reduce the effects of trauma stress. Tyler and Gifford (1991) found that cohesive military units facilitate trauma resolution in soldiers and their families.

Conversely, psychological distress appears to increase when close group ties are absent after trauma. Ottenberg (1987) suggested that members of dissimilar groups who experience trauma do not feel a sense of connectedness and therefore do not cope well with the traumatic event. Young and Erickson (1988) concluded that victims isolated from strong cultural ties have increased vulnerability to traumatic stress disorders. Matsakis (1988) found that Vietnam military wives who experienced isolation from military life often did not cope well with emotional distress. Ursano, Holloway, Jones, Rodriguez, and Belenky (1989) reported that military families who experience prolonged absences of spouses, frequent moves, isolation from the civilian community, and potential loss of a family member to war do not cope well with trauma.

A STUDY OF POLICE SURVIVOR TRAUMA

Despite the magnitude of violence exposure in police work, few studies have examined the effects of duty-related police deaths on surviving spouses. An early investigation by Danto (1975) involved a small descriptive study of widows of police officers from Detroit and found reported weight loss, sleep difficulties, loss of interest in activities, and suicidal thoughts among these survivors. Niederhoffer and Niederhoffer (1978) commented that a lack of understanding by those outside the police profession contributes to problems experienced by surviving spouses of slain police officers. Shaw (1986a) noted that the successful recovery of the police spouse and family is directly related to events that follow the death; emotional and tangible support were essential for survivors. Shaw (1986b) described the difficulties that police widows must face, such as public scrutiny, military-style funerals, the hesitancy of other officers in talking, and misperceptions of their vulnerability. Stillman (1986a) commented that the psychological impact of death on the officer's family has been neglected by police administrators, mental health professionals, and society in general. Police officers, as well as their families, are expected to be invulnerable to psychological harm. Mitchell (1994) described obligations of critical incident support teams to police survivors, including funeral preparations, immediate psychological support, safe places for survivors to go, follow-up services, and possible psychological referral.

Stillman (1986b) was among the first to empirically measure psychological distress and trauma in police spouse survivors. She initially found that 58% of survivors met the criteria of a measure assessing posttraumatic stress disorder (PTSD) after the death of their husband. On a psychological symptomatology measure, surviving spouses demonstrated greater levels of depression, anxiety, hostility, and guilt.

The focus of Stillman's investigation was the relationship between the type of death and psychological symptoms. No significant differences in measures of PTSD or negative psychological symptoms existed between spouses of officers killed accidentally and spouses of officers killed feloniously. The suddenness of the death appeared to make no difference; spouses exhibited similar high levels of negative psychological symptoms whether the death was sudden or extended.

Although Stillman adequately described the impact of the police culture on surviving spouses, she did not empirically measure this relationship. To add to Stillman's findings, I conducted a secondary analysis to determine the impact of social interaction on psychological distress and trauma following a duty-related police death. It was hypothesized that social interactions with and responses of cohesive police groups after the death of a police officer would affect trauma and distress in surviving spouses.

METHOD

Data Source

Stillman's data, from her work titled *Concerns of Police Survivors*, were obtained through the Inter-University Consortium for Political and Social Research (1990). The sample consisted of all police widows who applied for death compensation benefits through the federal Justice Department from November 1982 to February 1985. The mean age of respondents was 40.1 years; 99% were female, 85% were Caucasian, 6% were African American, 4% were Hispanic, and 6% were classified as other. Respondents had been married a mean length of 11.8 years at the time of their spouse's death, and 76% had been married only one time. The mean length of time since the officer's death was 2.4 years. One hundred sixty-two of 260 spouses responded to Stillman's survey (62% response rate).

Measures

Psychological Distress   As a measure of symptomatic psychological distress, Stillman used an earlier version of the revised Symptom Checklist 90 (SCL-90-R; Derogatis, 1975). The SCL-90-R has passed rigorous tests of reliability and validity, as reported by Derogatis (1983), and has been widely used in studies of distress and psychopathology resulting from traumatic events (Horowitz, Wilner, Kaltreider, & Alverez, 1980; Horowitz, 1986).

Trauma   The Trauma Reaction Index (Frederick, 1985) was used by Stillman to assess PTSD criteria in surviving spouses. The scale has been previously used to assess PTSD in normal persons involved in traumas such as airline crashes, combat, battering, personal injury, and natural disasters (Frederick, 1980).

Change in Social Interaction After Traumatic Death   With an indicator of change in social interaction, I hoped to measure support in terms of a sense of group belonging, as described by Cohen et al. (1985). Belonging is most often provided by interpersonal relationships in close-knit groups and has been hypothesized to produce an elevated mood (Cohen & McKay, 1984). Lack of such support may indicate loneliness and isolation and result in depressive symptoms. Since belonging may be present in both pre- and posttraumatic incident groups (Hartsough, 1988; Wojcik, 1987), I attempted to measure the change of frequency of this support before and after the officer's death.

In her original survey, Stillman (1986a) did not provide a clear measure of social interaction. However, she did provide survey items that indicated possible changes in the quality of interaction due to the officer's death: (a) "*Before* the officer's death, how often did you consider the relationship with the following to be an enjoyable one?" and (b) "*Since* the officer's death, how often did you consider the relationship with the following to be an enjoyable one?" Spouses responded to these items, on a 5-point scale ranging from *never* (1) to always (5), as they applied to police friends, nonpolice friends, coworkers, relatives, children, in-laws, and parents. To develop a change in the quality of interaction score, I subtracted interaction scores before the officer's death from those after the officer's death for each person mentioned (police friends, nonpolice friends, coworkers, relatives, children, in-laws, and parents) (Hartsough, 1990). It was hypothesized that a positive change in interaction with those in the police group would significantly decrease psychological distress and trauma.

A second dimension of social interaction concerned satisfaction with various groups after the officer's death. The item asked "To what extent were you satisfied with the treatment or response you received from the following groups?" The groups included were police agencies, police fraternal organizations, and groups outside the police (criminal justice system, the media, and members of the community). Spouses' scores were determined from a 5-point scale ranging from *very dissatisfied* (1) to *very satisfied* (5). Using these scores as independent variables, one can test relationships of satisfaction with police and nonpolice groups and psychological distress.

RESULTS

In sum, findings indicated that police survivors experienced increased levels of psychological distress and trauma following the death of their spouse. Global distress levels were higher in police survivors than in other nonpatient women, and in some categories these levels were higher than those of psychiatric outpatients. Trauma scores remained elevated and even increased as time since the death increased. Perceptions of support and positive interaction with police groups were statistically associated with a decrease in overall distress and trauma scores. The same was not true for interaction with groups outside the police (community, criminal justice system, media). A detailed explanation of the results follows.

Responses to the SCL-90-R

Figure 5.1 illustrates SCL-90-R scores for police survivors as compared with norms established by Derogatis (1983). Police spouse survivor global scores ($M = 1.25$; $SD = 0.79$) were in close proximity to psychiatric outpatient norms

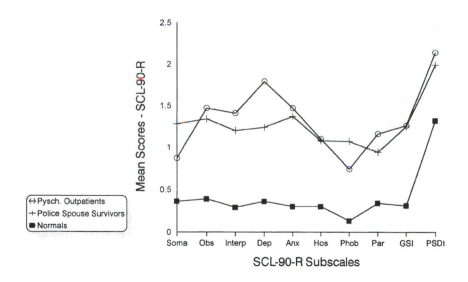

Figure 5.1 Comparison of SCL-90-R mean scores: police spouse survivors, normal subjects, and psychiatric outpatients.

and well elevated in terms of female nonpatient norms ($M = 0.30$). Survivors scored approximately the same as psychiatric outpatients on hostility and anxiety and scored higher on phobic reactions.

Group Interaction as a Predictor of Symptomatology

Regression analysis was used to examine the impact of change in quality of social interaction as well as satisfaction with the responses of others to the death. Two regression equations were used, with SCL-90-R GSI (genenor symptom inventory) scores serving as the dependent variable in one equation and global Trauma Reaction Index scores serving as the dependent variable in the second. In addition to social interaction variables, number of months since the officer's death was entered into each equation as an independent variable to control for the effect of the "decay curve" (Drabek, 1986) associated with time past since a traumatic event. Table 5.1 displays the results of this analysis.

As the change in quality of interaction with police friends became more positive following the officer's death, GSI scores decreased significantly ($\beta = -.287$, $p < .008$). Trauma Reaction Index scores also decreased, but not significantly, for those reporting increased positive interaction. Spouses who reported increased satisfaction with police agencies and fraternal groups also reported decreased symptomatology scores. Satisfaction with police agencies appeared to have a stronger negative association with GSI and Trauma Reaction Index scores than

Table 5.1   Regression Analysis of Social Interactions and Satisfaction With Group Responses on Psychological Distress and Trauma

	SCL-90-R GSI scores[a] ($N = 162$)		Trauma Reaction Index global scores[b] ($N = 162$)	
	β	p	β	p
Change in quality of interaction after death				
Police friends	−.287	.008**	−.157	.086
Relatives	−.012	.883	−.029	.741
Satisfaction with responses of groups after death				
Police agencies	−.254	.0009**	−.336	.001**
Police fraternal groups	−.227	.016*	−.115	.243
Outside community	.157	.075	.212	.017*
Months since death of officer	−.170	.045*	−.155	.088

[a]$R^2 = .229$, $F = 5.61$, $p < .0001$.
[b]$R^2 = .220$, $F = 5.36$, $p < .0001$.
*$p < .05$; **$p < .001$.

satisfaction with other groups. Spouses who reported increased satisfaction with responses to the officer's death by groups outside the police environment (justice system, media, and members of the community) had higher SCL-90-R symptomatology scores and Trauma Reaction Index scores. Regardless of reported positive interactions with outside groups, distress and trauma did not decrease in police survivors. An increase in the number of months since the officer's death predicted a significant reduction in GSI scores ($\beta = -.170$, $p < .045$) and a near significant reduction in Trauma Reaction Index scores ($\beta = -.155$, $p < .09$).

Positive interaction with specific police groups was associated with a statistically significant reduction in psychological symptoms. Police friends (those with whom the spouse and the deceased had previously been acquainted) significantly related to decreased symptoms in SCL-90-R subscales and global scores. The GSI global score ($\beta = -.287$), for example, indicated a statistical decrease in distress as support of police friends became more positive. This may have been associated with the personal nature of interactions that occurred with police friends.

On the organizational level, support of police departments ($\beta = -.254$) and police fraternal organizations ($\beta = -.227$) was associated with a statistically significant reduction in GSI scores and all SCL-90-R subscale scores. This was somewhat surprising, since Stillman (1987) and Sawyer (1988) both reported that surviving wives expressed feelings of being abandoned by police organizations after the death of the officer. It may that the timing and longevity of support play a role in how survivors respond to the organization.

Trauma Reaction Index global scores showed a statistically significant decrease as positive interaction with police departments increased ($\beta = -.336$), followed by police friends ($\beta = -.157$) and police fraternal groups ($\beta = -.115$). Spouse interaction with the community was significantly associated with increased trauma global scores ($\beta = .212$). Trauma Reaction Index subscales were similarly affected. Police fraternal groups were significantly associated with decreased "trauma fixation" in survivors ($\beta = -.271$), followed by police friends ($\beta = -.188$) and the police department ($\beta = -.156$). Increased positive interaction with the police department was associated with decreased "behavior manifestations of trauma" scores ($\beta = -.335$), followed by police fraternal groups ($\beta = -.288$) and police friends ($\beta = -.246$). Positive interactions with the police department were associated with a significant decrease in "psychological disruption" ($\beta = -.336$).

Interaction with the community was associated with a significant increase in all dimensions of trauma. This was best reflected in the Trauma Reaction Index global score, where community responses to the death were associated with a significant increase in trauma ($\beta = .212$).

Interesting were survivor "caseness" scores, defined by Frederick as global scores above 40 on the Trauma Reaction Scale (1985). When this criterion was used, the prevalence of PTSD among police spouses was 58%. This percentage was higher than those found in prisoner of war populations (50%), rape victims (54%), and hostages (56%) (Frederick, 1985; Stillman, 1986a). Spouses who met

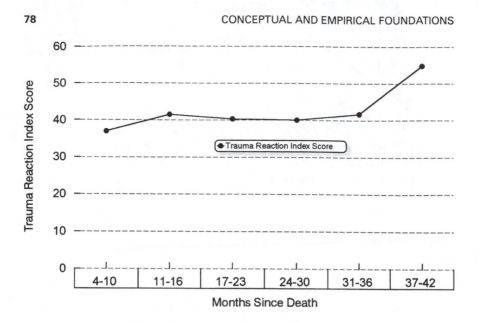

Figure 5.2   Trauma Reaction Index score and time since death.

this criterion had significantly higher scores than those who did not on subscales of depression, hostility, and anxiety (Stillman, 1986a).

   As time increased after the death of the officer, trauma caseness scores remained fairly constant. Figure 5.2 indicates that police spouse survivors maintained trauma caseness scores despite the passage of time. In fact, after 34 months, caseness scores increased. Thus, although increased positive interactions with the police group may have been associated with decreased trauma, such interactions may not have affected trauma enough to place survivors below caseness score criteria. It is also possible that positive group support was strong immediately after the death but later withdrawn. This may account for trauma levels increasing over time and for feelings of abandonment previously expressed by survivors (Stillman, 1986a). Future longitudinal studies are needed to confirm these hypotheses.

IMPLICATIONS FOR INTERVENTION AND TREATMENT

A surviving family never completely "gets over" the tragedy of a traumatic death; they continue on with their lives with the tragedy now a part of their personal history (Lindemann, 1944; Raphael, 1977; Burnett et al., 1994). The trauma of a death experience will somehow be integrated into their lives, and each time the death anniversary occurs, the family's sense of loss may surface. In instances of felonious death, every retrial, appeal, or parole forces the family to relive the injustice dealt to the fallen officer and loved ones (Van der Kolk, 1990; Stillman,

1987). In the case of the police family, intervention may best occur on two levels: (a) the group level, which this study suggests may be associated with reduced distress and trauma, and (b) the individual level, where specific characteristics of the death and individual grief responses must be dealt with.

Group-Level Intervention

As Van der Kolk (1990) stated, the essence of trauma is loss of safety and a continuation of psychological and physiological responses. The first step in intervention should therefore be to ensure that police survivors can retreat to a safe place of physical and psychological support. The present findings suggest that police groups may be such a safe place. Others (Figley, 1988b; Ochberg, 1995) have found that a supportive group or family is ideal for trauma recovery. Figley (1988b) described how such groups promote recovery by detecting trauma stress, confronting the trauma, urging recapitulation of the incident, and facilitating resolution. Egendorf, Kadushin, Laufer, Rothbart, and Sloan (1981) and Keane and Fairbank (1983) suggested that the presence of positive environmental support can be critical to the amelioration of war-related trauma in Vietnam veterans. Figley (1989, 1995) presented a generic model for treating families who have been traumatized. The goal of his therapy is to empower the family (or group, in the case of the police) to overcome and learn from their ordeal with duty-related death and, in so doing, be better prepared for future occurrences. Empowerment is a result of the development of social support among members of the group.

Unfortunately, not all police agencies are aware that they may be of benefit to survivors. Police agencies should strive to develop timely policies and practices that promote the development and maintenance of a supportive climate (Paton, 1996). Stillman (1987) found that 67% of law enforcement agencies lacked guidelines for continued emotional support for the survivors beyond the wake and funeral. Stillman commented that failure to provide continued support gave survivors the impression that they had been abandoned by the department. This may account for the present finding that trauma in survivors does not significantly decrease over time.

Since the findings of this study indicate that positive relations with police groups are associated with decreased symptomatology and trauma, it is important that such groups provide support for all problems associated with the death. Cook and Bickman (1989) found a high correlation between satisfaction with cohesive groups and support involving tangible factors (i.e., provision of concrete favors such as funeral arrangements, and transporting children to school). A national group called Concerns of Police Survivors (C.O.P.S.), organized in 1984, provides support to police survivors and assists law enforcement organizations with developing plans to help survivors. C.O.P.S. developed tangible (policy suggestions) and intangible (emotional support and counseling) organizational guidelines designed to mediate the impact of duty-related death. The sections to follow describe suggestions made by C.O.P.S. to help reduce the trauma of police survivors (Concerns of Police Survivors, 1997).

Death Notification   In many cases, the death of a law enforcement officer is sudden and unexpected. It is important for officers who notify survivors to be sensitive and caring. The name of the deceased officer should never be released to the media before immediate survivors are notified. Notification must always be made in person and never alone. The chaplain, psychologist, head of the agency (or representative), or another public safety survivor could appropriately accompany the informing officer. Gather everyone in the home and ask them to sit down. Inform them slowly and clearly of the information you have on the incident. Make sure you use the officer's name during the notification. If the officer has already died, relay that information and do not give the family a false sense of hope. Use words such as "died" and "dead" rather than "gone away" or "passed away."

The department should be prepared to handle immediate family needs. This is where coworkers' spouses or a spouse support group can be used. It is most reassuring to the family when the chief or another high-ranking designate responds to the home or hospital. In some cases, the absence was viewed by both the family and fellow coworkers not only as insensitive but as characteristic of poor leadership.

Supporting the Family During the Ordeal   Appointment of a liaison police officer to facilitate between the family and the department may help survivors feel that they are still part of the police family. Liaison officers provide a "connection" to the police agency and allow survivors to feel more comfortable in asking questions and making arrangements. This may be beneficial in reducing trauma. The liaison officer should meet with the family regarding funeral arrangements and be constantly available to the family throughout this traumatic time. Since most officers have not prearranged their wishes for the handling of their own funeral, the family will most likely need to decide all aspectsof the funeral. The department should only make the family aware of what it can offer in the way of assistance.

If there is a family support group organized in the police department, this group should have the responsibility of seeing that the needs of survivor families and their visitors are addressed. Departmental vehicles should be made available to the family if they desire transportation to and from the funeral home. The family should have access to other public safety survivors or other support groups (e.g., Concerns of Police Survivors, Survivors of Homicide Victims, Compassionate Friends, Parents of Murdered Children).

Although some police agencies may provide survivors access to the staff psychologist immediately following the death of the officer, the psychologist should provide only supportive services for the short term. Arrangements can be made for future sessions.

Follow-Up With the Police Family   Based on the present finding that trauma remains high in police survivors over time, it is important to help all survivors feel part of the police family for which the officer gave his or her life. Departments can easily keep in touch with the family through monthly phone calls during the first year after the death and less frequently afterward. Coworkers of the deceased officer should be encouraged to visit survivors on a regular basis. The department should always observe the officer's death anniversary date with a short note to the family. Keep in mind that, during the first year after the death, all holidays are traumatic events for the family. The department should maintain support as long as the family feels the need for support. The family will let you know when they are ready to move on with their lives without assistance from the department.

The police agency should be sensitive to the long-term needs of other family members as well as the spouse. When plaques and memorabilia are given to the surviving spouse, the same should be made available to the surviving parents. They have lost a child who can never be replaced. Remember to invite the surviving family to agency activities. Parents, adult-aged or younger children, siblings, and others are all experiencing grief (Gold, 1994). Realize that grief is a process and that everyone handles grief differently. It might be beneficial to have the psychologist see the entire family for a supportive service session shortly after the funeral. Do not set time limitations on when the family should recover from the death. The grief process has no timetable, and many survivors may experience a complicated grief process.

Individual Treatment Issues

While it is important to establish and maintain a supportive police group environment, it is also important to consider individual therapy for police survivors. The suddenness of duty-related death is an exacerbating factor in the impact of trauma. Sudden deaths are usually more difficult to grieve than deaths where there is some prior warning (Parkes, 1975). A sudden death will generally leave the police survivor with a sense of unreality about the loss. A first appropriate intervention might be to heighten the reality of the event. This may be accomplished by allowing the body to be openly viewed and explaining the circumstances of the death to survivors. I recall an incident where a chief of police was murdered and his body so badly mutilated that the coffin was closed. Police investigators were extremely wary about talking to the widow about the gruesome details of the incident. Upon learning of this, the police psychologist called a family meeting some 3 months after the death and requested that police detectives explain how the chief was killed. Both the widow and family members were afforded closure, and they expressed considerable relief.

Guilt feelings are also common among survivors of sudden deaths. I recall a police officer's surviving spouse repeatedly blaming herself for his death because she was unable to persuade him to put on his bullet-proof vest before he went on duty. Worden (1991) points out that the need to blame someone for the sudden death is very strong, and often survivors will either blame themselves or react harshly toward other family members or close friends. A sense of helplessness and rage is often associated with blame. An important intervention issue in these cases is to help the survivor focus on issues of the reality of responsibility for the death. The counselor should also be aware that the desire for retribution may be a psychological defense against both the reality and pain of the officer's death (Rynearson & McCreery, 1984).

Unfinished business is another special concern for survivors of sudden deaths. The death may leave them with many regrets for things they did not say to or do with the deceased officer. For example, one police spouse commented that she "didn't say good-bye" on the day her husband went to work and was killed. Another survivor said that "I never told him enough that I loved him." A counselor might attempt to focus on such unfinished business and find a way to bring closure.

The legal issues associated with duty-related deaths represent one of the most difficult obstacles for police survivors. Getting on with the task of mourning is sometimes impossible until legal aspects are resolved. Many police survivors feel that they have been traumatized over and over again by the courts and the criminal justice system. Delays in the trial of the accused murderer can delay the grief process.

Again, the support of the police agency and other officers may be crucial here to help reduce the negative impact of the justice system. Concerns of Police Survivors (1997) has made several suggestions to help survivors through the ordeal of the legal process. First, it is the police department's responsibility to keep the family informed of the legal proceedings. Public safety's surviving families are no different than any other victims. They must know how the incident occurred, down to the smallest detail. Many departments keep the family in the dark about the incident, stating that it could influence the outcome of the trial if the family is informed of the investigation. If this is the case, department officials should sit down with the family and explain their reasons for not sharing information. At the earliest opportunity following the trial, the investigators should sit down with the family and answer their questions about the ordeal. The facts will be far less shocking than what the family has already imagined happened during the incident. Should the department show a reluctance to share information on the incident, the survivors may view it as an attempt to hide something.

Second, it is important that the family attend the trial. Many survivors feel they are the only ones who can represent the deceased officer's interests. The department should assign a support person to accompany the survivors to the trial. If physical material evidence is going to be presented that will be upsetting to the family, this support person can suggest that the family leave the courtroom for that portion of the trial or prepare the family for what they will be seeing. The department should show support for the fallen officer during court proceedings by having as many coworkers as possible attend. This support should come from all segments of the department: management, the labor organization, coworkers, and even friends from other departments.

Surviving Children of Police Officers   Child survivors often are traumatized by the death of their parent. The extent of a child's trauma reaction is influenced by the reactions of supportive others (Williams, 1994; Gruler, 1994). The ability of the surviving parent to provide such support is often limited by the parent's own healing process (Williams, 1992). It is important to bring in others to help provide the child with understanding and support. Williams (1994) suggests that it is important not to hide the death from the child and to explain the death clearly in understandable terms. All questions should be answered honestly and openly. It is also important that children feel safe after the death and that some semblance of order is maintained. According to Willams (1994), the goal for counselors who work with children who have lost a parent in the line of duty is to help them manage psychological distress without incurring a major change in development. Therapy can help a child reestablish control, find alternative ways to deal with tension, and regain the process of ordinary existence in a world that seems difficult.

Other Considerations   Although the immediate family suffers greatly the loss of a loved one, coworkers should also be considered. They are part of the extended work family of policing. Departments must provide emotional support and debriefing sessions for friends of slain officers, from the partner and shift coworkers to station clerks and dispatchers. Departments should develop in-depth general orders that logistically deal with the department's handling of an officer's funeral. They should also develop a system focusing on timely reviews of beneficiary papers. Important considerations such as continued health insurance coverage for the family after the officer's death, educational benefits for surviving children, and arranging surviving spouse pension benefits should be included as part of policy.

CONCLUSION

The job of policing presents a clear and present danger for traumatic death. When such deaths do occur, police families are left in the wake of trauma. In this chapter, I have described a study on the effects of duty-related death on surviving spouses. Specifically, the study examined the quality and satisfaction of group social interactions following a traumatic death as they affect psychological distress and trauma. The results provide correlational evidence that an increase in the quality of interaction with police groups after the death of the officer decreases psychological distress and trauma in survivors. Positive interactions with police friends, the department, and police fraternal groups were statistically associated with a decrease in distress in police spouse survivors. This may indicate that cohesiveness and a sense of belonging to the police culture somehow influence experiences of distress and trauma.

Although the length of time that support was provided by police groups is not known, the present findings suggest that such support may be associated with decreases in psychological distress and trauma. It is hypothesized that initial tangible support by the police group is correlated with decreased distress and trauma and that prolonged support may further decrease such psychological symptomatology. Unfortunately, the present study was cross sectional in design and could not adequately explain variance in distress and social interaction over time.

This study also suggests that, regardless of increased survivor satisfaction with some groups outside of policing (media, justice system, etc.), distress and trauma scores still increased in police survivors. Surviving spouses may have been satisfied with the reaction of the justice system and community but may not have received essential personal support directly related to the officer's death. Apparently, police groups provided more meaningful types of support than outsiders to the survivor spouse and were associated with decreased distress.

The study was limited both in design and in that data were obtained from a previous study conducted by Stillman (1987). Although lack of an equivalent control group limited findings, comparisons of police spouses with nonpatient women and psychiatric outpatient normative groups lend credence to the officer's death as a powerful precipitating trauma. In terms of generalizability, this study infers that close-knit police groups that provide a sense of cultural belonging may be associated with decreased distress among the groups' members in times of crisis. It is uncertain whether or not this finding holds true for other work populations or groups that are less cohesive than the police.

In cooperation with Concerns of Police Survivors and the Bureau of Justice Assistance, my colleagues and I are presently conducting another study on police spouse survivors. In addition to tangible factors associated with spouse survival, our new research will measure factors on a personal and organizational level that may affect trauma. Examples are personal grief responses, coping strategies, relationships with others, psychological resources, and effects on physical health. As a comparison base, a control group of police spouses who have not experienced a duty-related death in their family will be introduced into the study. A survey will also be sent out to police departments throughout the United States to determine the extent of policies that are in place for duty-related deaths. Analysis will include the presence of survivor policies suggested by C.O.P.S. and professionals in psychology.

Effective intervention and treatment for surviving families of police deaths may be important for the amelioration of distress and trauma. In the present study, intervention was viewed as occurring on the group as well as individual level. If the hypotheses described hold true, then police organizations and group culture play an important associative role in decreasing trauma in survivors.

It is important, however, for police groups to understand specifically what they must do to assist survivors. Emotional as well as tangible support through the entire process of grieving is essential. The police group must therefore be available for the survivor during the ordeal and afterward. A police widow commented to me: "When my husband was alive, we were told that we would always be part of the police family. Now that he is gone, where is our police family when we need them the most?" Perhaps future longitudinal research will help to confirm that support over time is important in reducing trauma.

Treatment for police survivors on an individual level must address many of the same problems associated with anyone who has suffered a loss. Along with these are special problems involving the suddenness and violence of the officer's death, public notice of the death, and dealing with an often slow, unresponsive criminal justice system. Quite often, psychological closure is delayed for many years as legal issues concerning the death are argued in the courts and discussed in the media.

It is timely to consider the families and survivors of persons who choose law enforcement as a profession. The recent focus on the exposure of police officers to stress and trauma often overshadows the same residual exposure of their families. The ripple of police traumatic death flows outward, touching all in its wake and leaving a discernible path of grief. We should strive to understand and ameliorate the pain of those left behind.

REFERENCES

Amick-McMullin, A., Kilpatrick, D. G., Veronen, L. J., & Smith, S. (1989). Family survivors of homicide victims: Theoretical perspectives and an exploratory study. *Journal of Traumatic Stress, 2*, 21–35.

Bard, M., Arnone, H. C., & Nemiroff, D. (1985). Contextual influences on the post-traumatic stress adaptation of homicide survivor-victims. In C. R. Figley (Ed.), *Trauma and its wake: Vol. 2. Traumatic stress theory, research, and intervention* (pp. 90–112). New York: Brunner/Mazel.

Boman, B. (1979). Behavioral observations on the Grainville train disaster and the significance of stress for psychiatry. *Social Science and Medicine, 13A*, 463–471.

Bonafacio, P. (1991). *The psychological effects of police work.* New York: Plenum.

Burnett, P., Middleton, W., Raphael, B., Dunne, M., Moylan, A., & Martinek, N. (1994). Concepts of normal bereavement. *Journal of Traumatic Stress, 7*, 113–128.

Cohen, S., & McKay, G. (1984). Social support, stress, and the buffering hypothesis: A theoretical analysis. In A. Baum, J. Singer, & S. Taylor (Eds.), *Handbook of psychology and health* (Vol. 4). Hillsdale, NJ: Erlbaum.

Cohen, S., Mermelstein, R., Kamarck, T., & Hoberman, H. (1985). Measuring the functional components of social support. In I. Sarason & B. Sarason (Eds.), *Social support theory: Research and applications* (pp. 25–48). Amsterdam: Martinus Nijhoff.

Concerns of Police Survivors. (1997). *The trauma of law enforcement deaths.* Washington, DC: Bureau of Justice Assistance.

Cook, J. D., & Bickman, L. (1989). Social support and psychological symptomatology following a natural disaster. *Journal of Traumatic Stress, 3*, 541–556.

Danto, B. L. (1975). Bereavement and the widows of slain police officers. In R. Shoenberg (Ed.), *Bereavement: Its psychological aspects* (pp. 150–163). New York: Columbia University Press.

Derogatis, L. R. (1975). *The SCL-90-R manual.* Baltimore: Clinical Psychometric Research.

Derogatis, L. R. (1983). *Administration, scoring, and procedures manual-II for the SCL-90-R.* Baltimore: Clinical Psychometric Research.

Drabek, T. (1986). *Human system responses to disaster: An inventory of sociological findings.* New York: Springer.

Egendorf, A., Kadusihin, C., Laufer, R., Rothbart, G., & Sloan, L. (1981). *Legacies of Vietnam: Comparative adjustment of veterans and their peers*. Washington, DC: U.S. Government Printing Office.

Federal Bureau of Investigation. (1989). *Uniform crime reports: Law enforcement officers killed and assaulted*. Washington, DC: U.S. Department of Justice.

Figley, C. R. (1988a). Toward a field of traumatic stress. *Journal of Traumatic Stress, 1*, 316.

Figley, C. R. (1988b). Post-traumatic family therapy. In F. M. Ochberg (Ed.), *Post-traumatic therapy and victims of violence* (pp. 83–109). New York: Brunner/Mazel.

Figley, C. R. (1989). *Helping traumatized families*. San Francisco: Jossey-Bass.

Figley, C. R. (1995). Systemic PTSD: Family treatment experiences and implications. In G. S. Everly & J. M. Lating (Eds.), *Psychotraumatology: Key papers and core concepts in post-traumatic stress* (pp. 341–358). New York: Plenum.

Finister, S. R. (1994). The law enforcement organization: A unique family community. In J. T. Reese & E. Srivner (Eds.), *Law enforcement families* (pp. 275–279). Washington, DC: U.S. Government Printing Office.

Frederick, C. J. (1980). Effects of natural vs. human induced violence upon victims. *Evaluation & Change*, 71–75.

Frederick, C. J. (1985). Selected foci in the spectrum of post traumatic stress disorder. In J. Laube & S. Murphy (Eds.), *Perspectives on disaster recovery* (pp. 110–130). Norwalk, CT: Appleton-Century.

Gold, D. N. (1994). I had no room to breathe: Line-of-duty death of the adult child. In J. T. Reese & E. Srivner (Eds.), *Law enforcement families: Issues and answers* (pp. 185–190). Washington, DC: U.S. Government Printing Office.

Green, B. L. (1993). Identifying survivors at risk. In J. P. Wilson & B. Raphael (Eds.), *International handbook of traumatic stress syndromes* (pp. 135–144). New York: Plenum.

Green, B. L., Lindy, J. D., Grace, M. C., & Glaser, G. C. (1989). Multiple diagnosis in post-traumatic stress disorder: The role of war stressors. *Journal of Nervous and Mental Disorders, 177*, 329–335.

Green, B. L., Wilson, J. P., & Lindy, J. D. (1985). Conceptualizing PTSD: A psychosocial framework. In C. R. Figley (Ed.), *Trauma and its wake: The study and treatment of post-traumatic stress disorder* (pp. 53–69). New York: Brunner/Mazel.

Gruler, A. M. (1994). Assisting a child with the loss of a police parent. In J. T. Reese & E. Srivner (Eds.), *Law enforcement families* (pp. 191–194). Washington, DC: U.S. Government Printing Office.

Hartsough, D. M. (1988). Traumatic stress as an area of research. *Journal of Traumatic Stress, 1*, 145–153.

Hartsough, D. M. (1990). Stress, spouses, and law enforcement: A step beyond. In J. T. Reese, J. M. Horn, & C. Dunning (Eds.), *Critical incidents in policing* (pp. 193–201). Washington, DC: U.S. Government Printing Office.

Horowitz, M. J. (1986). *Stress response syndromes* (2nd ed.). Northvale, NJ: Aronson.

Horowitz, M. J., Wilner, N., Kaltreider, N., & Alverez, W. (1980). Signs and symptoms of posttraumatic stress disorder. *Archives of General Psychiatry, 37*, 85–92.

Kazak, A. E. (1991). The social context of coping with childhood chronic illness: Family systems and social support. In A. LaGreca, L. J. Siegel, J. L. Wallander, & C. E. Walker (Eds.), *Stress and coping in child health* (pp. 262–278). New York: Guilford Press.

Keane, T., & Fairbank, J. (1983). Survey analysis of combat-related disorders in Vietnam veterans. *American Journal of Psychiatry, 140*, 138–140.

Kirshner, E. (1982). Data on bereavement and rehabilitation of war widows. In C. D. Spielberger & I. G. Sarason (Eds.), *Stress and anxiety* (Vol. 8, pp. 219–224). New York: Hemisphere.

Kroes, W. H., Margolis, B. L., & Hurrell, J. J., Jr. (1974). Job stress in policemen. *Journal of Police Science & Administration, 2*, 145–155.

Lin, N., Woelfel, M. W., & Light, S. C. (1985). The buffering effect of social support subsequent to an important life event. *Journal of Health and Social Behavior, 26*, 247–263.

Lindemann, E. (1944). Symptomatology and management of acute grief. *American Journal of Psychiatry, 101*, 141–148.

Lindy, J. D., Grace, M. C., & Green, B. L. (1981). Survivors: Outreach to a reluctant population. *American Journal of Orthopsychiatry, 51*, 468–479.

Matsakis, A. (1988). But military wives never. In A. Matsakis (Ed.), *Vietnam wives: Women and children surviving life with veterans suffering from post traumatic stress disorder* (pp. 147–161). Baltimore: Woodbine House.

Mitchell, J. T. (1994). Critical incident stress interventions with families and significant others. In J. T. Reese & E. Srivner (Eds.), *Law enforcement families* (pp. 195–202). Washington, DC: U.S. Government Printing Office.

Niederhoffer, A., & Niederhoffer, E. (1978). *The police family: From station house to ranch house.* Lexington, MA: D.C. Heath.

Ochberg, F. M. (1995). Post-traumatic therapy. In G. S. Everly & J. M. Lating (Eds.), *Psychotraumatology: Key papers and core concepts in post-traumatic stress* (pp. 245–263). New York: Plenum.

Ottenberg, D. J. (1987). Initiation of social support systems: A grass roots perspective. In E. Gottheil, K. A. Druley, S. Pashko, & S. P. Weinstein (Eds.), *Stress and addiction* (pp. 209–224). New York: Brunner/Mazel.

Parkes, C. M. (1975). Determinants of outcome following bereavement. *Omega, 6*, 303–323.

Parkes, C. M. (1993). Psychiatric problems following bereavement by murder or manslaughter. *British Journal of Psychiatry, 162*, 49–54.

Paton, D. (1996). Traumatic stress in critical occupations: Current status and future issues. In D. Paton & J. M. Violanti (Eds.), *Traumatic stress in critical occupations: Recognition, consequences and treatment* (pp. 206–226). Springfield, IL: Charles C. Thomas.

Raphael, B. (1977). Preventative intervention with the recently bereaved. *Archives of General Psychiatry, 34*, 1450–1454.

Raymond, C. A. (1988). Study says memories of violent death linger in survivors, trigger psychological problems. *Journal of the American Medical Association, 259*, 3524–3529.

Reiser, M., & Geiger, S. P. (1984). Police officer as victim. *Professional Psychology: Research and Practice, 15*, 315–323.

Rynearson, E. K., & McCreery, J. M. (1984). Bereavement after homicide: A synergism of trauma and loss. *American Journal of Psychiatry, 150*, 258–261.

Sawyer, S. (1988). *Support services to surviving families of line-of-duty death.* Maryland: Concerns of Police Survivors.

Shaw, J. H. (1986a). Duty-related deaths: Family policy considerations. In J. T. Reese, J. M. Horn, & C. Dunning (Eds.), *Critical incidents in policing* (pp. 439–446). Washington, DC: U.S. Government Printing Office.

Shaw, J. H. (1986b). The death of an officer: Surviving the first year. In J. T. Reese, J. M. Horn, & C. Dunning (Eds.), *Critical incidents in policing* (pp. 447–453). Washington, DC: U.S. Government Printing Office.

Solomon, R. M., & Horn, J. M. (1986). Post shooting trauma reactions: A pilot study. In J. T. Reese & H. T. Goldstein (Eds.), *Psychological services for law enforcement* (pp. 383–394). Washington, DC: U.S. Government Printing Office.

Stillman, F. A. (1986a). The invisible victims: Myths and realities. In J. T. Reese & H. T. Goldstein (Eds.), *Psychological services for law enforcement* (pp. 143–146). Washington, DC: U.S. Government Printing Office.

Stillman, F. A. (1986b). *Psychological responses of surviving spouses of public safety officers killed accidentally or feloniously in the line of duty.* Unpublished doctoral dissertation, Johns Hopkins University.

Stillman, F. A. (1987). *Line-of-duty-deaths: Survivor and departmental responses.* Washington, DC: National Institute of Justice.

Stillman, F. A. (1990). *Concerns of police survivors* (database). Ann Arbor, MI: Interuniversity Consortium for Political and Social Research.

Tyler, M. P., & Gifford, R. K. (1991). Field training accidents: The military unit as a recovery context. *Journal of Traumatic Stress, 4*, 233–249.

Ursano, R. C., Holloway, D. R., Jones, A. R., Rodriguez, A. L., & Belenky, G. L. (1989). Psychiatric care in the military community: Family and military stressors. *Hospital and Community Psychiatry, 40*, 1284–1289.

Van der Kolk, B. A. (1990). The psychological processing of traumatic events: The personal experience of post traumatic stress disorder. In J. T. Reese, J. M. Horn, & C. Dunning (Eds.), *Critical incidents in policing* (pp. 495–502). Washington, DC: U.S. Government Printing Office.

Violanti, J. M. (1996). The impact of cohesive groups in the trauma recovery context: Police survivors and duty-related death. *Journal of Traumatic Stress, 9*, 379–386.

Violanti, J. M., & Aron, F. (1994). Ranking police stressors. *Psychological Reports, 75*, 824–826.

Williams, C. (1987). Peacetime combat: Treating and preventing delayed stress reactions in police officers. In T. Williams (Ed.), *Post-traumatic stress disorders: A handbook for clinicians* (pp. 267–292). Cincinnati, OH: Disabled American Veterans.

Williams, G. (1992). Children of the wall. *The American Legion, 132*, 30–31.

Williams, M. B. (1994). Impact of duty-related death on officers' children: Concepts of death, trauma reactions, and treatment. In J. T. Reese & E. Srivner (Eds.), *Law enforcement families* (pp. 251–260). Washington, DC: U.S. Government Printing Office.

Wojcik, E. H. S. (1987). *Description of pre-trauma social support considered as a factor in post-traumatic stress reaction.* Unpublished doctoral dissertation, Purdue University.

Worden, J. W. (1991). *Grief counseling and grief therapy: A handbook for the mental health practitioner* (pp. 98–104). New York: Springer.

Young, M. B., & Erickson, C. A. (1988). Cultural impediments to recovery: PTSD in contemporary America. *Journal of Traumatic Stress, 1*, 431–443.

Chapter 6

Emotional Dissociation, Self-Deception, and Adaptation to Loss

George A. Bonanno

How we conceptualize the factors that influence the course and severity of grief will, to a large extent, influence how we think about and interact with the bereaved. For those who share an intimate relationship with a bereaved individual or encounter the bereaved in a clinical capacity, this is a matter of no small importance. A wide range of factors have been considered in the bereavement literature as possible moderators and mediators of grief severity (see Chapter 3), including personality disposition (Horowitz, Bonanno, & Holen, 1993; Sanders, 1993; W. Stroebe & Stroebe, 1987), coping habits (Folkman et al., 1996), features of the loss event (e.g., type of death, degree of forewarning) (Parkes & Weiss, 1983), quality of the survivor's relationship to the deceased (Bowlby, 1980; Freud, 1917/1957; Horowitz et al., 1993; Raphael, 1983; Raphael, Middleton, Martinek, & Misso, 1993), and the survivor's history of previous losses (Raphael et al., 1993), stressful live events (Parkes, 1970), or emotional difficulties (Jacobs et al., 1990; Zisook & Schuster, 1991). Yet, despite the idiosyncratic nature of grief and the myriad possible variables that might predict its course, most professionals whose work brings them into the arena of bereavement attribute successful recovery to the degree that the bereaved individual completed the "work" of mourning (i.e., reviewed and expressed the emotional and cognitive meanings of the loss) (Bonanno, in press; W. Stroebe & Stroebe, 1987).

In this chapter, I review the basic tenets of this "grief work" approach to bereavement, with a particular emphasis on the assumption that avoiding, minimizing, or otherwise limiting awareness and expression of the emotional pain of a loss is maladaptive. Also, I review the empirical status of the grief work approach and several recent alternative conceptualizations of how people cope with loss, along with recent research conducted by my colleagues and myself demonstrating the adaptive value of emotional dissociation and self-deception during bereavement. Finally, I consider relevant cross-cultural data suggesting a some-what similar conclusion.

THE TRADITIONAL GRIEF WORK APPROACH TO BEREAVEMENT

Grief work has been described as a multidimensional process involving verbal, cognitive, and emotional components. The precise nature of these components and how they might interact have, however, not been well defined (W. Stroebe & Stroebe, 1993). Typically, theories of clinical intervention with the bereaved have stressed the importance of the *review* and *experience* of the emotional meanings of the loss (Horowitz et al., 1993; Osterweis et al., 1984), the *expression* of grieving affect (Raphael, 1983, p. 368), and the overt, *verbal disclosure* of the cognitive and emotional meanings to others (Bowlby, 1980; Parkes & Weiss, 1983; Schuster & Zisook, 1993). Discussions of the possible benefit of reviewing and expressing the emotional meanings of a loss have generally centered around negative emotion (Bowlby, 1980; Lazare, 1989; Osterweis et al., 1984), with a particular emphasis on the expression of anger (Bowlby, 1980; Belitsky & Jacobs, 1986; Cerney & Buskirk, 1991). The avoidance of negative material during bereavement is widely assumed to be maladaptive and to result from a defensive inhibition of the "nat-ural" release of affect related to the loss (Raphael et al., 1993). Thus, bereaved individuals who "show no evidence of having begun grieving" (p. 65) have been described as suffering from "some form of personality pathology" (p. 81) and as requiring "professional help" (p. 65) (Osterweis et al., 1984). By extension, fre-quent or intense expression of positive emotion during bereavement is generally viewed as escapist and as a form of maladaptive denial of the loss, and it has simi-larly been assumed to contribute to chronic (Bowlby, 1980; Horowitz et al., 1993) or delayed (Deutsch, 1937; Sanders, 1993) mourning.

DO EMPIRICAL DATA SUPPORT THE GRIEF WORK APPROACH?

Despite its widespread acceptance, recent reviews of the grief work approach to bereavement have noted the absence of empirical support for its basic tenets. Wortman and Silver (1989) detailed four major assumptions inherent in the be-reavement literature: Distress is necessary following a loss; failure to experience grief-related distress is pathological; it is crucial to "work through" the experience of loss; and resolution and full recovery are to be expected after a loss. They con-cluded that, although there was little in the way of systematic research available that had attempted to operationalize and evaluate these assumptions, the available evidence failed to support—and, in some cases, contradicted—the assumptions. Thus, in Wortman and colleagues' view, the prescriptive goal of working through grief-related emotions may owe its origins more to "clinical lore" than to system-atic inquiry (Wortman & Silver, 1989; Wortman, Silver, & Kessler, 1993). Ex-tending this view, one might easily conclude that clinical interventions based on

such lore could potentially exacerbate rather than am
example, that the majority of bereaved individuals '
culties coming to terms with the meaning of their l(
This finding is not easily reconciled with an appr(
and grief resolution as its normative end point.

M. Stroebe and colleagues (M. Stroebe, 1992–19.
Bout, & Schut, 1994) recently affirmed the conclusion that assu.
in the grief work approach have yet to receive empirical support, altu.
noted that the absence of clear empirical definitions for these assumptions h.
made their empirical evaluation difficult. My colleagues and I have also expressed
a similar conclusion and noted the incompatibility of the grief work approach with
theories and rituals of mourning from other, non-Western cultures (Bonanno, in
press; Bonanno & Siddique, in press).

Only a few empirical studies are available that have attempted to directly
evaluate the grief work assumption. These investigations have been largely incon-
clusive. Mawson, Marks, Ramm, and Stern (1981) attempted to assess the possible salutary effect of grief work by comparing a focused, "guided mourning"
treatment group with an alternative treatment that encouraged bereaved individuals to avoid thoughts and feelings about the loss and to practice distraction. The
sample used in the study was, however, very small ($N = 12$) and consisted ex-
clusively of "morbidly grieved" individuals whose bereavement was, on average,
already into its third year. Not surprisingly, Mawson et al. (1981) concluded that
the expected positive influence of the guided mourning treatment was only "mod-
est" and "not as potent as might have been hoped" (Mawson et al., 1981, p. 191).

M. Stroebe and Stroebe (1991) attempted to assess grief work using a small
set of self-report and interview questions pertaining to grief suppression and grief
confrontation, avoidance of reminders, distraction, emotional control, and nondisclosure. They administered these questions to a recently bereaved sample (4–7
months postloss) and followed them over an 18-month period. However, only a
few of the items were linked to adjustment and only for the male participants.
Thus, Stroebe and Stroebe concluded that "the view 'Everyone needs to do grief
work' is an oversimplification" (p. 481).

ALTERNATIVE PSYCHOLOGICAL APPROACHES TO BEREAVEMENT

Although the grief work approach has dominated the bereavement literature, the
paucity of data in its support has recently stimulated the development of alternative conceptualizations of how people might best cope with loss. W. Stroebe and
Stroebe (1987, 1993) suggested an approach to conjugal loss based on the interactionist cognitive stress perspective (Lazarus, 1985; Lazarus & Folkman, 1984).
Similarly, Dacher Keltner and I have proposed that the pain of a loss may be better
understood using a social-functional account of emotional expression (Bonanno
& Keltner, 1997).

ractionist Stress Perspective

viewed under the lens of an interactionist stress perspective, events are ssful" to the extent that they meet or exceed an individual's perceived coping ources (Lazarus & Folkman, 1984). Coping mechanisms that are appraised as having successfully reduced stress can be considered adaptive (Lazarus, 1985). The stress perspective also places a greater emphasis on the importance of situational factors and individual variation in subjective grief responses (M. Stroebe, 1992–1993; W. Stroebe & Stroebe, 1987). In this view, the absence of grief may be evaluated simply as a mild stress reaction rather than as a denial of symptoms. Furthermore, in contrast to the grief work approach, a stress perspective suggests that avoidant mechanisms may serve a potentially adaptive purpose, as may humor and benign distractions, in that they allow a temporary escape from and possible reduction in the pain of the loss.

The stress perspective suggests a more measured emphasis on emotional experience and expression than was considered in the grief work approach. In this context, for example, practitioners and others who have intimate contact with the bereaved would most likely encourage exploration of grief-related thoughts and emotions only to the extent that such a process would be consistent with the survivor's personality and natural inclinations (Bonanno & Castonguay, 1994; Bonanno & Siddique, in press). For example, explorations of the meanings of the loss might be planned for specified time periods, while, at other times, the survivor might practice "letting go" of the emotional pain of the loss by engaging in distractions (e.g., watching a funny movie) or focusing on positive memories and experiences. Such attentional shifts to more benign content would help lessen the stress of the loss (W. Stroebe & Stroebe, 1987), provide time to gradually integrate its more painful implications (Paulay, 1985), and foster the survivor's ability to meet the ongoing demands of work and to remain available for other important people in his or her life (Keltner & Bonanno, in press; Schuster & Zisook, 1993). The capacity to maintain connectedness and intimacy in relationships with others appears to be particularly important as a buffer against the isolation and disconnectedness often characteristic of severe grief reactions (Horowitz et al., in press).

A Social-Functional Account of Emotion

From the context of a social-functional perspective, emotional experience and expression play an important mediating role in self-regulation and in adaptation to the social environment and significant life events (Barrett & Campos, 1987; Bowlby, 1980; Darwin, 1872; Ekman, 1992). In this context, the experience of emotion helps to inform and to regulate intrapersonal processes (Izard, 1990), while the expression of emotion communicates internal states to others and helps mediate social interactions with others (Keltner, 1995).

In general, intense negative emotion has been shown to result in immediate psychological and physical health consequences (e.g., increased visits to a doctor for health problems) (Dua, 1993, 1994). The consistent experience and expression of negative emotion have been associated with increased stress and health problems (Watson, 1988; Watson & Clark, 1984; Watson & Pennebaker, 1989), with depression (Nolen-Hoeksema, 1987), with disrupted social and personal relationships (Lemerise & Dodge, 1993; Keltner, 1995; Keltner, Moffitt, & Stouthamer-Loeber, 1995; Levenson & Gottman, 1983), with pessimism and hopelessness (Keltner, Ellsworth, & Edwards, 1993), and with conflictual relations (Caspi, Elder, & Bem, 1987; Keltner, 1995; Lemerise & Dodge, 1993). During bereavement, early levels of distress tend to be one of the strongest predictors of subsequent grief severity (Bornstein, Clayton, Halikas, Maurice, & Robins, 1973; Vachon et al., 1982; Wortman & Silver, 1989; Zisook & Schuster, 1991). Thus, from a social-functional perspective, the intense or prolonged emphasis on negative affect during bereavement would probably increase psychological and physical distress and prolonged grief (Bonanno & Keltner, 1997).

In contrast to negative emotion, the tendency to experience and express positive emotion has been associated with increased personal well-being and goal-directed activity (Schwarz, 1990; Taylor & Brown, 1988) and with more satisfying personal and social relationships (Keltner, 1995). The expression of positive emotion may also enhance social connectedness and support (Malatesta, 1990). Consistent with this interpretation, positive emotional expressions have been found to be most prevalent among individuals with higher scores on the socially oriented personality characteristics of extraversion, agreeableness, and conscientiousness (Keltner et al., 1995). Thus, in the social-functional perspective, experiencing and expressing positive emotions during bereavement may enhance coping and facilitate social support from those in the bereaved's circle of important others (Bonanno & Keltner, 1997; Keltner & Bonanno, in press).

THE ADAPTIVE VALUE OF EMOTIONAL DISSOCIATION AND SELF-DECEPTION

In an attempt to explore the predictions of these various approaches to loss further, my colleagues and I recently conducted a systematic, longitudinal study of midlife conjugal bereavement. In particular, this research focused on assessing avoidant or emotionally dissociative mechanisms and the question of whether the use of such mechanisms will prove adaptive or maladaptive over the course of bereavement. Because the bereavement literature has suffered from an absence of precise operational definitions, we used well-validated behavioral measures of emotional experience, expression, and avoidance and developed an interview-based measure of grief symptoms. Furthermore, whenever possible, we also obtained evidence of convergent and discriminant validity to support these various constructs.

The study involved the longitudinal assessment of middle-aged individuals who had recently lost their spouses, beginning approximately 3 months after the loss and continuing over the next several years. To assess the natural experience, expression, and disclosure of grief-related thoughts and emotions, we asked participants, at the 6-month point in bereavement, to describe their prior relationship with the deceased with a trained clinical interviewer. Physiological and self-report data were obtained, and the interviews were videotaped for later analyses. Long-term outcome was assessed via self-reported somatic complaints and a structured clinical interview addressing grief-specific difficulties. The grief interview provided a relatively objective index of the degree to which the loss impeded general functioning and well-being and was validated against standardized measures of grief and depression, as well as clinical ratings of grief severity made blindly and independently by a team of psychotherapists (see Chapter 3) (Bonanno, Keltner, Holen, & Horowitz, 1995).

In an initial study from this project, emotional experience and emotional dissociation were examined in relation to long-term outcome (Bonanno et al., 1995). Emotional dissociation was measured via a well-validated method of comparing standardized levels of subjective emotional experience and autonomic arousal. Emotional dissociation was operationally defined as a *verbal-autonomic response dissociation* such that the level of negative emotion participants reported was relatively low in comparison with the level of autonomic arousal they exhibited during the interview. A verbal-autonomic dissociation of this type is generally considered to reflect participants' reduced awareness of their emotional arousal (Asendorpf & Scherer, 1983; Newton & Contrada, 1992; Shedler et al., 1993; Weinberger & Davidson, 1994; Weinberger et al., 1979). This assumption was further supported in the Bonanno et al. (1995) bereavement study by the fact that the verbal-autonomic dissociation score converged with clinician ratings of avoidance of emotional awareness. In addition, discriminant validity for the verbal-autonomic dissociation score as a relatively automatic mechanism was evidenced in its inverse correlation with a self-report measure of deliberate avoidance behaviors (e.g., deliberately trying not to talk about an event). Finally, the possibility that verbal-autonomic dissociation represents an enduring aspect of personality or cognitive style, as suggested earlier, was supported by its relatively high test-retest correlation ($r = .63$) when measured over an 8-month span of bereavement.

In contrast to the predictions of the grief work approach but compatible with the social-functional and stress perspectives, verbal-autonomic dissociation at the 6-month point in bereavement was associated with low levels of interviewer-rated grief through the 25 months measured in the study (Bonanno et al., 1995; Bonanno, Znoj, Siddique, & Horowitz, 1996). This finding was observed even when initial levels of grief were statistically controlled. Thus, regardless of participants' initial coping behaviors and grief course, the capacity or propensity to dissociate emotion when discussing the loss at 6 months predicted a better grief course over the ensuing 2 years. There was some evidence for a physical cost of avoidance early in bereavement in that verbal-autonomic dissociation at 6 months was coupled with concurrent elevations in reported somatic symptoms. Importantly, however, over the long-term course of the study, verbal-autonomic dissociation predicted relatively low levels of somatic symptoms and, thus, was *not* linked to either a cumulative or delayed physical cost.

A second study from this project (Bonanno & Keltner, 1997) examined the expression of emotion early in bereavement using a precise scoring method for coding facial muscle movements—the Facial Action Coding System (FACS; Ekman & Friesen, 1976, 1978)—that focuses only on the visible emotion-relevant facial muscle movements that have been derived from previous theory and research (Ekman, 1984). Consistent with descriptions of emotion in the bereavement literature (Schuster & Zisook, 1993), a range of both positive and negative emotions were evidenced in participants' facial expressions as they described their loss at the 6-month point in bereavement. Consistent with the emotional dissociation findings, facial expressions of negative emotion while describing the loss at 6 months predicted increased grief and decreased perceived health at later assessments.

This study also provided new evidence about the adaptive role of positive emotion during bereavement. Facial expressions of positive emotion, typically associated in the literature with maladaptive denial, were predictive of decreased grief over time. When viewed through the lens of the stress and social-functional perspectives, however, these data are consistent with the idea that minimizing or regulating negative emotions helps foster connection to—and support from— important people in the bereaved person's life. Clearly, the experience of listening to a depressed or distressed individual can be quite stressful (Harber & Pennebaker, 1992; Silver, Wortman, & Crofton, 1990) and may drive away potential avenues of support (Coyne, 1976; Gottlieb, 1991; Pennebaker, 1993). Minimizing negative emotion may help reduce the perceived burden or discomfort in the listener and foster the bereaved person's sense of ongoing affiliation with and potential support from that listener. The same may be true of positive emotional expression. Genuine positive emotions tend to be incompatible with or attenuate negative emotion (Levenson, 1988) and, thus, may also foster prosocial exchanges (Bonanno & Keltner, 1997).

Consistent with these speculations, Keltner and Bonanno (in press) found that bereaved individuals who showed genuine laughter and smiling (as evidenced in the obicularis oculi muscles around the eye) while they discussed their relationship to their deceased spouses also reported better relationships with other important people in their lives. Expressions of genuine laughter were more readily evidenced as well in those individuals who had also shown emotional dissociation, while individuals who did not evidence emotional dissociation tended to display only nongenuine or social laughter. Thus, it appears that all of the bereaved participants in the study attempted to honor the social context of moderating their disclosure of painful experiences with periodic expressions of positive emotion and laughter. Yet, only those participants who could genuinely dissociate the pain of the loss managed to convey genuine laughter expressions, while participants who were unable to temporarily dissociate or distance themselves from the painful feelings managed only social (non-Duchenne) laughter expressions.

In addition, to further explore the social impact of laughter and smiling during bereavement, Keltner and Bonanno (in press) showed videotapes of the same bereaved participants to untrained observers without sound (i.e., observers watched only the nonverbal behavior of the bereaved participants). The observers were told that they would view videotapes of individuals who had recently suffered the loss of their spouses and instructed to report their own honest feelings as they watched the tapes. In this context, observers perceived bereaved individuals who did not laugh as suffering more, and they reported a greater desire to comfort these individuals as well. However, the observers also reported more frustration and less positive emotion when they viewed the nonlaughers. Furthermore, nongenuine (social) laughter actually evoked less positive emotion in observers, and nongenuine (social) smiling evoked less compassion and less desire to comfort. In contrast, both genuine laughter and genuine smiling evoked greater positive emotion, and genuine laughter was also associated with reduced frustration in observers.

It is important to note that these emotion findings illustrate the mediating role of emotional regulation in long-term adaptation; even when the facial expression data were partialed for their overlap with initial levels of grief or somatic complaints, they still showed robust prediction of later outcome scores (Bonanno & Keltner, 1997). Interestingly, the grief work approach is fully consistent with the idea that the experience and expression of emotion mediated later outcome, yet it predicts the direction of that mediation as almost the exact opposite as that observed in the study.

The fact that these emotion findings were obtained from the same 6-month interview, however, raises the question of whether similar types of emotional experience and expression occurring at earlier points in bereavement may have had a similar influence on long-term outcome. To address this question further, we reexamined the outcome data in relation to two personality variables empirically associated with habitual patterns of emotional avoidance and self-deception: the repressor personality style (Weinberger et al., 1979) and self-deceptive enhancement (SDE; Paulhus, 1984, 1991). The association of these dimensions with the habitual avoidance of unpleasant information (see Chapter 3). Bonanno & Singer (1990) provides the opportunity to examine the grief course of individuals who would not be likely to engage in either cognitive or emotional processing of the loss at any point during bereavement.

In support of the presumed habitual, or traitlike, nature of these dimensions, both the repressor and SDE measures showed adequate test-retest reliability across 8 months of bereavement. Consistent with the 6-month emotion findings reported earlier, individuals categorized as repressors showed earlier reductions in interviewer-rated grief than all other participants and remained at low levels through 25 months (Bonanno, Siddique, Keltner, & Horowitz, 1996). The SDE findings showed an even more robust advantage. SDE was associated with less distress, better perceived health, and fewer interviewer-rated grief symptoms across time, and these results remained significant when partialed for initial symptom levels or for their possible overlap with more general negative affectivity, as measured by self-reported trait anxiety. Thus, individuals who, by personality disposition, tend to avoid emotional information and engage in self-deceptive biases or "self-enhancement" show a shorter, less distressed, and less symptomatic grief course.

Finally, in addition to these emotion and personality variables, we also recently analyzed the narrative transcripts from the 6-month bereavement interviews. In the initial analyses, we coded several variables indicative of the degree to which participants verbally disclosed thoughts and emotions related to the loss (Bonanno & Eddins, 1997). The grief work approach clearly endorses the importance of verbally disclosing the meanings of a loss to another person. The verbal disclosure of traumatic or painful material has also been consistently linked to improved health and well-being in the general psychological literature (Greenberg & Stone, 1992; Pennebaker, 1989, 1993). Interestingly, however, Kelly and McKilltop (1996) recently noted that the process of revealing personal secrets is more complex than is usually acknowledged and that there are many circumstances in which withholding personal information may be advantageous.

The results of our narrative analysis were consistent with the emotion findings and again contradicted the grief work view: More frequent disclosure of negatively valenced thoughts predicted increased grief at later assessments, while more frequent disclosure of negatively valenced emotion predicted increased distress and somatic symptoms at later assessments. Again, as in the previous findings, these results were significant after initial symptom levels had been statistically controlled.

LIMITATIONS OF THE EVIDENCE

Despite the strength of these various findings, their standing as evidence against the grief work approach must be considered with a measure of caution. There are several important limitations that must be acknowledged. First, all of the data reviewed earlier in support of emotional dissociation and self-deception, as well as the salutary effects of positive emotion, were derived from the same longitudinal study. If these results are to have any lasting meaning to the bereavement literature, their replication with different samples is imperative. Second, it must be acknowledged that the participants in this sample had all endured the same type of loss, conjugal loss, at the same point in the life span, midlife. It is entirely possible that emotional avoidance is particularly adaptive under these circumstances. For instance, midlife is typically a highly active and demanding period in most people's lives, often including the multiple responsibilities of career, caring for children, and aging parents (Bumpus & Aquilino, 1995). Furthermore, it is still possible that emotional avoidance is less advantageous at other points in life or in response to other losses. These questions await further empirical data.

Another potential limitation of the evidence reported in this chapter is that the observed links between the emotion and disclosure variables and grief course were limited to the first 3 years of bereavement. Previous bereavement studies have shown that symptom levels change very slowly beyond the first year of the loss (Wortman & Silver, 1989). Thus, even by a conservative criterion, 3 years may be considered an adequate duration to assess the various theoretical predictions. The 3-year duration of the study may have been inadequate, however, to fully investigate a related assumption of the grief work approach, that emotional avoidance may eventually manifest in the form of delayed grief or delayed somatic symptoms (Horowitz et al., 1993; Sanders, 1993; Osterweis et al., 1984; Worden, 1991). To address this limitation, we are currently in the beginning stages of additional data collection on the same sample at 5 to 7 years postloss.

CROSS-CULTURAL EVIDENCE

The strength of the findings in support of the adaptive influence of emotional dissociation and self-deception and the absence of support for the predictions of the grief work approach raise intriguing questions about possible historical and cultural developments in bereavement theory. There is compelling evidence, for instance, that the assumptions inherent in the grief work approach arose relatively recently, in response to the rapid social changes wrought by the industrial revolution (Bonanno, in press; M. Stroebe, Gergen, Gergen, & Stroebe, 1992).

Equally as compelling, however, are the cross-cultural data. Even a cursory review of the cross-cultural literature illustrates that the assumed importance of individual grief work is primarily limited to Western thought and culture. Obviously, some features of the human experience of death and bereavement will tend to manifest themselves in a similar manner across all cultures. Indeed, the capacity to experience grief over the death of another human being is, for many, the defining feature of "culture." Archaeological evidence of the ritualized burial of the dead, for example, is often cited as a marker for the emergence of human consciousness and the origins of society (Leakey, 1994). Yet, despite the limitations of generalization, when mourning rituals and beliefs about death are compared across Western and Eastern cultures, differences become readily apparent (Rosenblatt, 1993).

I have elsewhere (Bonanno, in press) described three such differences. First, rather than letting go of the attachment to the deceased and moving toward grief resolution, as prescribed by the Western grief work tradition, Eastern cultures tend to share belief in a continuity between the living and the dead as well as in the deceased's continued presence and influence from the world of the dead. This is perhaps most poignantly illustrated in the African view of death as "a journey to man's original home, not as an anihilation" (Opoku, 1989, p. 15).

> The terms "this life," "next life," "after life," "eternal life" are terms borrowed from European Christian philosophy which are foreign to the African system of thought. Life is one continuous stretch of existence and is not split up into "this life" and "the next life." The concept of time is cyclic, not lineal [sic]. What happens after death is not the terminal, definitive stages of man's life, it is only a phase in the continuing round of human existence. (Metuh, 1982, p. 153)

Extending beyond African cultures, the Hopi Indians of the southwestern United States consider the dead to exist in a separate realm that may influence the living but should under no circumstances be bridged with the world of the living (Mandelbaum, 1959). The Hopi are reported to "feel the pain of loss as deeply as do mourners in any society"; in contrast to the Western grief work approach, however, the Hopi actively dissuade the overt expression of grief (Mandelbaum, 1959, p. 210). Those mourners who feel the need to cry are admonished to do so alone and in a manner that will not be observed by others (Brandt, 1954). Furthermore, as soon as possible, the Hopi "try to forget the deceased and continue with life as usual" (Eggan, 1950, p. 58). They are reported to show little interest in recalling the memory of the deceased (Mandelbaum, 1959) and have been observed clearly and explicitly avoiding reminders of the deceased (Titiev, 1944).

A second difference is that Eastern cultures do not share the Western emphasis on the serious, realistic "work" of mourning; rather, they readily include humor and fantasy in their mourning rituals. For example, Octavio Paz (1961) observed that "the Mexican is familiar with death, jokes about it, caresses it, sleeps with it, celebrates it; it is one of his favorite toys and his most steadfast love" (p. 58). This familiarity and humor and their contrast to the typical Western view are aptly illustrated in the festive use of the *Calavera* or skeleton during the Mexican Day of the Dead celebration.

> The rich European imagery of death—Dürer's engravings, Holbein's woodcuts of the *danse macabre*—is clearly meant to affright us and at the same time to compel us to repent of our sins. The symbolic representation of death, the skeleton, seems to say: "Remember that soon you shall be like I am. Meditate on the vanity of your life in the world. Your destruction, your putrefaction, is very close to you. It is right here, it touches you!" The Mexican skeleton, in striking contrast, is no spook. It is a policeman, a city dandy, a hired ranch hand, or a bartender. "It is neither more horrible nor more frightening than men," wrote Paul Westheim. A *Calavera*, though a skeleton, poses no threat. (Gonzalez-Crussi, 1993, pp. 80–81).

Similar cultural differences have also been evidenced among expatriate Mexicans living in the United States (Corr, Nabe, & Corr, 1994). Mexican Americans have been reported to spend more time viewing, touching, and even kissing the body of the deceased than other Americans, and they spend greater periods of time at burials and grave sites (Kalish & Reynolds, 1981; Moore, 1980). Ironically, the contrast of this behavior with the Western grief work approach has resulted in frequent conflicts between Mexican Americans and professionals in the American funeral and cemetery industries (Kalish & Reynolds, 1981).

The use of humor and fantasy during bereavement is also a fascinating aspect of the funeral rites of the Saramaka of Suriname, in which a large group of relatives and neighbors

> in effect agree to transport themselves into a separate reality that they collectively create and maintain: *kóntu-kôndè* ("folktale-land," an earlier time as well as a distant

place).... Sitting by torchlight or the light of the moon, the participants at a tale-telling wake come face to face with age-old metaphysical problems and conundrums; by turns frightened by the antics of a villainous monster, doubled over with laughter at a lascivious song, or touched by a character's sentimental farewell, they experience an intellectually and emotionally rich evening of multimedia entertainment. (Price & Price, 1991, p. 1)

These tale-telling funeral evenings may last for up to several weeks during which "everyone present steps over the invisible barrier into folktale-land" (p. 3).

Finally, a third difference is that Eastern cultures tend to downplay the private, individual nature of bereavement suggested by the grief work approach and instead emphasize the community's loss and the surviving relative's place in the larger community. Most descriptions of the so-called preindustrial, primitive, or aboriginal "healing" rites emphasize their communal rather than individual basis (Ellenberger, 1970). In general, Eastern communal patterns are associated with "collectivism" (Triandis et al., 1988), in which the relations and values of the family and community, rather than the individual, "are the primary sources of demands and rewards, and the primary arbiters of what is desirable, what is permissible, and what is unthinkable" (Ross & Nisbett, 1991, p. 181). The opposite tends to be true of Western "individualist" cultures, which typically emphasize personal goals, preferences, and interests and, unlike collectivist cultures, tend to be "relatively free of the dictates of family, neighbors, or others to whom one might be linked in traditional role relations" (Ross & Nisbett, 1991, p. 181).

In the transcendent Saramakan fantasy rituals just described, for example, there is an almost complete absence of reference to the deceased or to the private experience of mourning (Price & Price, 1991). The handling of the body, the funeral ritual, and the care of the bereaved are seen as the responsibility of the entire community (Price & Price, 1991). During the actual burial ceremony, "rites of separation" (p. 56) are shared by the entire community so that the deceased may leave for the land of the dead in a symbolic, "final separation, from the village itself" (p. 57).

Similarly, the African view of death in general has been characterized by a proverb: "The ladder of death is not climbed by only one person" (Opoku, 1989, p. 20). A death among Africans is traditionally viewed as "not an individual affair" (Opoku, 1989, p. 20) but an event that "binds up relationships in society, revitalizing the living and underscoring their sense of community" (Dickson, 1984, p. 196). Death becomes an opportunity to "give concrete expression to community solidarity" (Opoku, 1989, p. 20). This same emphasis on communal rather than individual mourning has also been associated historically with African Americans (Kalish & Reynolds, 1981; Marsella, 1980), Mexicans and Mexican Americans (Kalish & Reynolds, 1981; Moore, 1980), Asians (Kastenbaum, 1995), and the Hopi Indians of the southwestern United States (Eggan, 1950).

CONCLUSION

The empirical and cross-cultural findings presented in this chapter robustly challenge the legitimacy of the traditional grief work approach to bereavment. Perhaps more important, these findings provide for the first time unambiguous evidence that emotional avoidance and self-deceptive processes, far from impeding the work of mourning, appear to serve an adaptive function during bereavement and to foster successful coping with the pain of loss. The importance of these findings is further highlighted by their consistency with views of death and mourning in many Eastern cultures. Nonetheless, caution must still be exercised in speculating from the limits of these data. Most of the positive findings reviewed in this chapter came from the same longitudinal study of midlife conjugal loss. Until further data can be evaluated, these conclusions must be considered promising but tentative. Yet, they also stand as part of an exciting ferment in contemporary research and theory about bereavement (see Chapter 3), a ferment that suggests that more solid answers about the legitimacy of traditional and newer conceptions of bereavement should soon become available.

REFERENCES

Asendorpf, J. B., & Scherer, K. R. (1983). The discrepant repressor: Differentiation between low anxiety, high anxiety, and represssion of anxiety by autonomic–facial–verbal patterns of behavior. *Journal of Personality and Social Psychology, 45*, 1334–1346.

Barrett, K. C., & Campos, J. J. (1987). Perspectives on emotional development II: A functionalist approach to emotions. In J. D. Osofsky (Ed.), *Handbook of infant development* (2nd ed., pp. 555–578). New York: Wiley Interscience.

Belitsky, R., & Jacobs, S. (1986). Bereavement, attachment theory, and mental disorders. *Psychiatric Annals, 16*, 276–280.

Bonanno, G. A. (in press). The concept of "working through" loss: A critical evaluation of the cultural, historical, and empirical evidence. In A. Maercker, M. Schuetzwohl, & Z. Solomon (Eds.), *Posttraumatic stress disorder: Vulnerability and resilience in the life-span*. Seattle, WA: Hogrefe & Huber.

Bonanno, G. A., & Castonguay, L. G. (1994). On balancing approaches to psychotherapy: Prescriptive patterns of attention, motivation, and personality. *Psychotherapy, 31*, 571–587.

Bonanno, G. A., & Eddins, C. (1997). *Talking about the loss of a spouse: Dimensions of verbal disclosure and the prediction of long-term bereavement outcome*. Manuscript submitted for publication.

Bonanno, G. A., & Keltner, D. (1997). Facial expressions of emotion and the course of conjugal bereavement. *Journal of Abnormal Psychology, 106*, 126–137.

Bonanno, G. A., Keltner, D., Holen, A., & Horowitz, M. J. (1995). When avoiding unpleasant emotion might not be such a bad thing: Verbal-autonomic response dissociation and midlife conjugal bereavement. *Journal of Personality and Social Psychology, 46*, 975–989.

Bonanno, G., & Siddique, H. I. (in press). Emotional dissociation, self-deception, and psychotherapy. In J. A. Singer & P. Salovey (Eds.), *At play in the fields of consciousness*. Hillsdale, NJ: Erlbaum.

Bonanno, G. A., Siddique, H., Keltner, D., & Horowitz, M. J. (1996). *How do repressors and self-deceivers grieve the loss of a spouse?* Manuscript submitted for publication.

Bonanno, G. A., & Singer, J. L. (1990). Repressor personality style: Theoretical and methodological implications for health and pathology. In J. L. Singer (Ed.) *Repression and dissociation* (pp. 435–470). Chicago: University of Chicago Press.

Bonanno, G. A., Znoj, H., Siddique, H., & Horowitz, M. J. (1996). *Verbal-autonomic response dissociation and the course of midlife conjugal bereavement: A follow-up at 25 months.* Manuscript submitted for publication.

Bornstein, P. E., Clayton, P. J., Halikas, J. A., Maurice, W. L., & Robins, E. (1973). The depression of widowhood after thirteen months. *British Journal of Psychiatry, 122,* 561–566.

Bowlby, J. (1980). *Loss: Sadness and depression.* New York: Basic Books.

Brandt, R. B. (1954). *Hopi ethics.* Chicago: University of Chicago Press.

Bumpus, L. L., & Aqvilino, W. S. (1995). A social map of midlife: Family and work over the middle life course. Unpublished manuscript, University of Wisconsin-Madison.

Caspi, A., Elder, G. H., Jr., & Bem, D. J. (1987). Moving against the world: Life-course patterns of explosive children. *Developmental Psychology, 23,* 308-313.

Cerney, M. W., & Buskirk, J. R. (1991). Anger: The hidden part of grief. *Bulletin of the Menninger Clinic, 55,* 228–237.

Corr, C. A., Nabe, C. M., & Corr, D. M. (1994). *Death and dying, life and living.* Pacific Grove, CA: Brooks/Cole.

Coyne, J. C. (1976). Toward an interactional description of depression. *Psychiatry, 39,* 28–39.

Darwin, C. (1872). *The expression of the emotions in man and animals.* New York: Philosophical Library.

Deutsch, H. (1937). Absence of grief. *Psychoanalytic Quarterly, 6,* 12–22.

Dickson, K. A. (1984). *Theology in Africa.* London: Darton, Longman, & Todd.

Dua, J. K. (1993). The role of negative affect and positive affect in stress, depression, self-esteem, assertiveness, Type A behaviors, psychological health, and physical health. *Genetic, Social, and General Psychological Monographs, 119,* 515–552.

Dua, J. K. (1994). Comparative predictive value of attributional style, negative affect, and positive affect in predicting self-reported physical health and psychological health. *Journal of Psychosomatic Research, 38,* 669–680.

Eggan, F. (1950). *Social organization of Western Pueblos.* Chicago: University of Chicago Press.

Ekman, P. (1992). An argument for basic emotions. *Cognition and Emotion, 6,* 169–200.

Ekman, P. (1984). Expression and the nature of emotion. In K. Sherer & P. Ekman (Eds.) *Approaches to emotion* (pp. 319–344). Hillsdale, NJ: Erlbaum.

Ekman, P., & Friesen, W. V. (1976). Measuring facial movement. *Journal of Environmental Psychology and Nonverbal Behavior, 1,* 56–75.

Ekman, P., & Friesen, W. V. (1978). *Facial Action Coding System: A technique for the measurement of facial movement.* Palo Alto, CA: Consulting Psychologists Press.

Ellenberger, H. F. (1970). *The discovery of the unconscious: History and evolution of dynamic psychiatry.* New York: Basic Books.

Folkman, S., Chesney, M., Collette, L., Boccellari, A., & Cooke, M. (1996). Postbereavement depressive mood and its prebereavement predictors in HIV+ and HIV− gay men. *Journal of Personality and Social Psychology, 70,* 336–348.

Freud, S. (1957). Mourning and melancholia. In J. Strachey (Ed.), *The standard edition of the complete psychological works of Sigmund Freud* (Vol. 14, pp. 152–170). London: Hogarth Press. (original work published 1917)

Gonzalez-Crussi, F. (1993). *The day of the dead and other mortal reflections.* New York: Harcourt Brace.

Gottlieb, B. H. (1991). The contingent nature of social support. In J. Eckenrode (Ed.), *Social context of stress.* New York: Plenum.

Greenberg, M. A., & Stone, A. (1992). Emotional disclosure about traumas and its relation to health: Effects of previous disclosure and trauma severity. *Journal of Personality and Social Psychology, 63,* 75–84.

Harber, K. D., & Pennebaker, J. W. (1992). Overcoming traumatic memories. In S. A. Christianson (Ed.), *The handbook of emotion and memory* (pp. 359–388). Hillsdale, NJ: Erlbaum.

Horowitz, M. J., Bonanno, G. A., & Holen, A. (1993). Pathological grief: Diagnosis and explanations. *Psychosomatic Medicine, 55,* 260–273.

Horowitz, M. J., Siegel, B., Holen, A., Bonanno, G. A., Milbrath, C., & Stinson, C. (in press). Diagnostic criteria for complicated grief disorder. *American Journal of Psychiatry.*

Jacobs, S., Hansen, F., Kasl, S., Ostfeld, A., Berkman, L., & Kim, K. (1990). Anxiety disorders during acute bereavement: Risk and risk factors. *Journal of Clinical Psychiatry, 51,* 269–274.

Kalish, R. A., & Reynolds, D. K. (1981). *Death and ethnicity: A psychocultural study.* Farmingdale, NY: Baywood.

Kastenbaum, R. J. (1995). *Death, society, and human experience* (5th ed.). Boston: Allyn & Bacon.

Kelly, A. E., & McKilltop, K. J. (1996). Consequences of revealing personal secrets. *Psychological Bulletin, 120,* 450–465.

Keltner, D. (1995). Facial expressions of emotion and personality. In C. Malatesta-Magai & S. H. McFadden (Eds.), *Handbook of emotion, aging, and the lifecourse.* New York: Academic Press.

Keltner, D., & Bonanno, G. A. (in press). A study of laughter and dissociation: Distinct correlates of laughter and smiling during bereavement. *Journal of Personality and Social Psychology.*

Keltner, D., Bonanno, G. A., Caspi, A., Krueger, R. F., & Stouthamer-Loeber, M. (1995). *Personality and facial expressions of emotion.* Manuscript submitted for publication.

Keltner, D., Ellsworth, P. C., & Edwards, K. (1993). Beyond simple pessimism: Effects of sadness and anger on social perception. *Journal of Personality and Social Psychology, 64,* 740–752.

Keltner, D., Moffitt, T., & Stouthamer-Loeber, M. (1995). Facial expressions of emotion and psychopathology in adolescent boys. *Journal of Abnormal Psychology, 104,* 644–652.

Lazare, A. (1989). Bereavement and unresolved grief. In A. Lazare (Ed.), *Outpatient psychiatry: Diagnosis and treatment* (2nd ed., pp. 381–397). Baltimore: Williams & Wilkins.

Lazarus, R. S. (1985). The costs and benefits of denial. In A. Monat & R. S. Lazarus (Eds.), *Stress and coping* (2nd ed., pp. 154–173). New York: Columbia University Press.

Lazarus, R. S., & Folkman, S. (1984). *Stress, appraisal, and coping.* New York: Springer.

Leakey, R. E. (1994). *The origins of humankind.* New York: Basic Books.

Lemerise, E. A., & Dodge, K. A. (1993). The development of anger and hostile interactions. In M. Lewis & J. M. Haviland (Eds.), *Handbook of emotions* (pp. 537–546). New York: Guilford Press.

Levenson, R. W. (1988). Emotion and the autonomic nervous system: A prospectus for research on autonomic specificity. In H. L. Wagner (Ed.), *Social psychophysiology and emotion: Theory and clinical applications.* New York: Wiley.

Levenson, R. W., & Gottman, J. M. (1983). Marital interaction: Physiological linkage and affective exchange. *Journal of Personality and Social Psychology, 45,* 587–597.

Malatesta, C. Z. (1990). The role of emotions in the development and organization of personality. In R. A. Thompson (Ed.), *Nebraska Symposium on Motivation: Vol. 36. Socioemotional development* (pp. 1–56). Lincoln: University of Nebraska Press.

Mandelbaum, D. G. (1959). Social uses of funeral rites. In H. Feifel (Ed.), *The meaning of death* (pp. 189–217). New York: McGraw-Hill.

Marsella, A. J. (1980). Depressive experience and disorder across cultures. In H. C. Triandis & J. G. Draguns (Eds.), *Handbook of cross-cultural psychology: Psychopathology* (Vol. 6, pp. 237–290). Boston: Allyn and Bacon.

Mawson, D., Marks, I. M., Ramm, L., & Stern, L. S. (1981). Guided mourning for morbid grief: A controlled study. *British Journal of Psychiatry, 158,* 185–193.

Metuh, I. E. (1982). *God and man in African religion: A case study of the Igbo of Nigeria.* London: Chapman.

Moore, J. (1980). The death culture of Mexico and Mexican Americans. In R. A. Kalish (Ed.), *Death and dying: Views from many cultures* (pp. 72–91). Farmingdale, NY: Baywood.

Newton, T. L., & Contrada, R. J. (1992). Repressive coping and verbal-autonomic response dissociation: The influence of social context. *Journal of Personality and Social Psychology, 62,* 159–167.

Nolen-Hoeksema, S. (1987). Sex differences in unipolar depression: Evidence and theory. *Psychological Bulletin, 101*, 259–282.

Opoku, K. A. (1989). African perspectives on death and dying. In A. Berger, P. Badham, A. H. Kutscher, J. Berger, M. Perry, & J. Beloff (Eds.), *Perspectives on death and dying* (pp. 14–23). Philadelphia: Charles Press.

Osterweis, M., Solomon, F., & Green, F. (Eds.). (1984). *Bereavement: Reactions, consequences, and care.* Washington, DC: National Academy Press.

Parkes, C. M. (1970). The first year of bereavement. *Psychiatry, 33*, 442–467.

Parkes, C. M., & Weiss, R. S. (1983). *Recovery from bereavement.* New York: Basic Books.

Paulay, D. (1985). Slow death: One survivor's experience. In R. H. Moos (Ed.), *Coping with life crisis* (pp. 227–234). New York: Plenum.

Paulhus, D. L. (1984). Two-component models of socially desirable responding. *Journal of Personality and Social Psychology, 46*, 598–609.

Paulhus, D. L. (1991). *Assessing self-deception and impression management in self-reports: The Balanced Inventory of Desirable Responding, Version 6.* Unpublished manual, University of British Columbia.

Paz, O. (1961). *The labyrinth of solitude—Life and thought in Mexico.* New York: Grove.

Pennebaker, J. W. (1989). Traumatic experience and psychosomatic disease. In L. Berkowitz (Ed.), *Advances in experimental social psychology* (Vol. 22, pp. 211–214). New York: Academic Press.

Pennebaker, J. W. (1993). Social mechanisms of constraint. In D. M. Wegner & J. W. Pennebaker (Eds.), *Handbook of mental control* (pp. 200–219). Englewood Cliffs, NJ: Prentice Hall.

Price, R., & Price, S. (1991). *Two evenings in Saramaka.* Chicago: University of Chicago Press.

Raphael, B. (1983). *The anatomy of bereavement.* New York: Basic Books.

Raphael, B., Middleton, W., Martinek, N., & Misso, V. (1993). Counseling and therapy of the bereaved. In M. S. Stroebe, W. Stroebe, & R. O. Hansson (Eds.), *Handbook of bereavement: Theory, research, and intervention* (pp. 427–456). Cambridge, England: Cambridge University Press.

Rosenblatt, P. (1983). *Bitter, bitter tears: Nineteenth century diarists and twentieth century grief theories.* Minneapolis: University of Minnesota Press.

Ross, L., & Nisbett, R. E. (1991). *The person and the situation.* New York: McGraw-Hill.

Sanders, C. M. (1993). Risk factors in bereavement outcome. In M. S. Stroebe, W. Stroebe, & R. O. Hansson (Eds.), *Handbook of bereavement: Theory, research, and intervention* (pp. 255–270). Cambridge, England: Cambridge University Press.

Schwarz, N. (1990). Feelings as information: Information and motivational functions of affective states. In E. T. Higgins & R. M. Sorrentino (Eds.), *Handbook of motivation and cognition: Foundations of social behavior* (Vol. 2, pp. 527–561). New York: Guilford Press.

Schuster, S. R., & Zisook, S. (1993). The course of normal grief. In M. S. Stroebe, W. Stroebe, & R. O. Hansson (Eds.), *Handbook of bereavement: Theory, research, and intervention* (pp. 23–43). Cambridge, England: Cambridge University Press.

Silver, R. K., Wortman, C. B., & Crofton, C. V. (1990). The role of coping in social support provision: The self-presentation dilemma of victims in crisis. In B. R. Sarason & G. Pierce (Eds.), *Social support: An international review* (p. 52). New York: Wiley.

Stroebe, M. (1992–1993). Coping with bereavement: A review of the grief work hypothesis. *Omega, 26*, 19–42.

Stroebe, M., Gergen, M. M., Gergen, K. J., & Stroebe, W. (1992). Broken hearts or broken bonds: Love and death in the historical perspective. *American Psychologist, 47*, 1205–1212.

Stroebe, M., & Stroebe, W. (1991). Does "grief work" work? *Journal of Consulting and Clinical Psychology, 59*, 479–482.

Stroebe, M., van den Bout, J., & Shut, H. (1994). Myths and misconceptions about bereavement: The opening of a debate. *Omega, 29*, 187–203.

Stroebe, W., & Stroebe, M. (1987). *Bereavement and health: The psychological and physical consequences of partner loss.* Cambridge, England: Cambridge University Press.

Stroebe, W., & Stroebe, M. (1993). Determinants of adjustment to bereavement in younger widows and widowers. In M. S. Stroebe, W. Stroebe, & R. O. Hansson (Eds.), *Handbook of bereavement: Theory, research, and intervention* (pp. 208–226). Cambridge, England: Cambridge University Press.

Taylor, S. E., & Brown, J. D. (1988). Illusion and well-being: A social psychological perspective on mental health. *Psychological Bulletin, 103*, 193–210.

Titiev, M. (1944). Old Oraibi. *Papers of the Peabody Museum, Harvard University, 22*.

Triandis, H. C., Bontempo, R., Villareal, M. J., Asai, M., & Lucca, N. (1988). Individualism and collectivism: Cross-cultural perspectives on self-ingroup relationships. *Journal of Personality and Social Psychology, 54*, 323–338.

Vachon, M. L. S., Rogers, J., Lyall, W. A. L., Lancee, W. J., Sheldon, A. R., & Freeman, S. J. J. (1982). Predictors and correlates of adaptation to conjugal bereavement. *American Journal of Psychiatry, 139*. 998–1002.

Watson, D. (1988). Intraindividual and interindividual analyses of positive and negative affect: Their relation to health complaints, perceived stress, and daily activities. *Journal of Personality and Social Psychology, 54*, 1020–1030.

Watson, D., & Clark, L. A. (1984). Negative affectivity: The disposition to experience averse emotional states. *Psychological Bulletin, 96*, 465–490.

Watson, D., & Pennebaker, J. W. (1989). Health complaints, stress, and distress: Exploring the central role of negative affectivity. *Psychological Review, 96*, 234–254.

Weinberger, D. A., Schwartz, G. E., & Davidson, J. R. (1979). Low-anxious and repressive coping styles: Psychometric patterns of behavioral and physiological responses to stress. *Journal of Abnormal Psychology, 88*, 369-380.

Worden, J. W. (1991). *Grief counseling and grief therapy: A handbook for the mental health practitioner*. New York: Springer.

Wortman, C. B., & Silver, R. C. (1989). The myths of coping with loss. *Journal of Personality and Social Psychology, 57*, 349–357.

Wortman, C. B., Silver, R. C., & Kessler, R. C. (1993). The meaning of loss and adjustment to bereavement. In M. S. Stroebe, W. Stroebe, & R. O. Hansson (Eds.), *Handbook of bereavement: Theory, research, and intervention* (pp. 349–366). Cambridge, England: Cambridge University Press.

Zisook, S., & Schuster, S. R. (1991). Depression through the first year after the death of a spouse. *American Journal of Psychiatry, 148*, 1346–1352.

Part Two

Applications

Chapter 7

Bereavement After Homicide: Its Assessment and Treatment

E. K. Rynearson and Russell Geoffrey

It seems paradoxical that a clinical text on the uniqueness of traumatic dying has been so slow in appearing. While traumatic dying has been universally acknowledged with alarm and abhorrence, this anomalism of death has not been recognized in our literature. Perhaps the repugnancy of traumatic dying has resulted in a "blind spot" for the researcher. The responsibility for the avoidance and retribution of unnatural dying takes precedence. Emotional responses and needs are overshadowed by the social imperative of understanding how the death occurred, apprehending and punishing whomever was responsible, and protecting the rest of us from such a trauma.

A systematic, prospective, controlled study of the effects of traumatic dying and its treatment has not been completed, leaving us with a very rudimentary understanding. A review of the convergent histories of trauma and bereavement research can prepare us in developing a preliminary model of homicidal dying, a model that would guide our understanding of phenomenology, mechanism, and intervention.

HISTORICAL REVIEW: THE COCONUT GROVE FIRE REVISITED

Conceptual models of bereavement and trauma have their origins in distinctly different contexts: bereavement from the death of one emotionally valued and trauma from the horror of disaster and war. Bereavement and trauma research have reflected this distinction from the outset. The bereavement model focused on the personal relationship with the deceased and the task of unconscious acceptance of the loss. Conversely, the trauma model concentrated on the impersonal effects of an overwhelming event and the conscious task of reestablishing autonomy from that event.

Pathologic grief reactions were first delineated by Freud (1957) in his highly speculative and ingenious observations associating prolonged melancholia with unresolved ambivalence and decathexis. Deutsch (1937) later extended this model to include delayed responses, and Abraham (1924) and Klein (1948) further widened the model to explain identificatory symptoms and depressive psychosis. Any mention of "trauma" by these authors referred to overwhelming feelings (anger and/or sexual) engendered by cruel, repressive, or neglectful relationships and treatment focused on the retrospective task of examining unconscious defensive mechanisms.

"Shell shock" became a generic diagnosis for traumatized soldiers after World War I, and it was Kardiner (1941) who first formalized the posttraumatic descriptive model in the title of his 1941 book *The Traumatic Neuroses of War*. In that volume, he described a syndrome that virtually coincides with the criteria of the *Diagnostic and Statistical Manual of Mental Disorders* (4th edition: American Psychiatric Association, 1994) for posttraumatic stress disorder. He viewed this response as primarily reactive and physiologic ("physioneurosis") instead of relational and unconscious. His therapeutic objectives focused on support, symptom removal, and early return to "duty" (i.e., autonomy).

In November 1942, the Coconut Grove disaster inaugurated the first study of traumatic death. It occurred at a time and place that might have provided a blending of these parallel models of trauma and bereavement. There have been few disasters that compressed so much horror and death into so small a space and duration. It is a wonder that anyone survived at all. Within 15 to 20 minutes, the searing heat and suffocating gases swept over the crowd of nearly 1,000 nightclub patrons who stampeded from one blocked exit to another. It took several days for the final death toll of 491 to be established because the survivors were scattered to the two major Boston hospitals. For every four sent to Boston City, only one went to Massachusetts General (Benzaquim, 1959). Boston City Hospital admitted 129 living patients (nearly 300 were dead on arrival), and Massachusetts General admitted 39 (75 were dead on arrival). The excessive exposure to death and the entrapment and suffocation of the witnessed dying must have presented an overwhelming trauma to those who survived. Certainly not all of the survivors had suffered the death of a relative or close friend with the fire, so the more impersonal and traumatic effects of the disaster itself represented the more common factor. Separate psychiatric studies of the survivors were begun, by Lindeman at Massachusetts General and by Adler at Boston City Hospital. According to Dr. Adler, there were some tentative conversations about the possibility of sharing preliminary observations and research design, but issues of territoriality and politics prevented a joint study.

Within months (June 1943), Cobb and Lindeman published a report on their initial observations of 17 of the 39 patients admitted to Massachusetts General. They cited those who met criteria for psychiatric diagnosis (organic brain syndrome [1 patient], psychosis [2 patients], and neurosis [2 patients]), but their novel insight described their management of 7 patients who presented with "severe grief" after learning that a relative had also died in the fire. A year later (September 1944), Lindeman published a more detailed paper on acute grief and its management based on his work with 101 patients (the patients from the Coconut Grove disaster were a distinct minority of the total sample). He noted in his introduction that the management of acute grief reactions was of special importance because of "the enormous increase in grief reactions due to war casualties" (p. 142). Perhaps it was this attitude of crisis that impelled him to recommend short-term abreactive psychotherapy treating severe grief, focusing on hostility in grief as the unconscious determinant.

Adler's report was later in appearing (December 1943). She reported on 54 of the 129 patients admitted after the disaster and obtained 9-month follow-up data on 46 of those initially screened. Her study included more data and rigor than Lindeman's but is rarely quoted. She found that 20 of the 46 patients whom she initially screened did not present with any psychiatric complications. Psychiatric complications (which she called "posttraumatic mental complications") included anxiety, phobias, recurring nightmares, and survivor guilt. She dismissed bereavement as a significant variable, since the 23 subjects who had lost a close friend or relative were equally distributed between those with and without complications. As Alfred Adler's daughter, she was more than familiar with psychoanalytic theorists' concepts of unconscious determinism, but she did not believe they were of significance in this context of disaster. Instead, she felt that neurogenic "unconsciousness" was a protective factor, noting that 12 of 15 survivors who were comatose for longer than 1 hour did not develop any psychiatric complications. Nine months after the disaster, she found that 13 of the 46 patients maintained their traumatic symptoms and viewed these sustained reactions as physiologic. She anticipated they would spontaneously remit and would not require psychotherapy.

Each of the authors approached traumatic death in a highly creative but divergent way. Criticism of the research design might be softened by recognizing that psychiatric research at that time was impelled more by intuition and anecdote than by reliable measurement.

More recently, these extreme models have been modified so that they are no longer as mutually exclusive. Jacobs (1993) has theorized that "traumatic" distress and "separation" distress commonly coexist during bereavement after traumatic dying. Traumatic responses (fear, horror, vulnerability, and disintegration of cognitive assumptions) are primarily related to motivation for autonomy and self-protection. Separation responses (longing, loneliness, searching, and sorrow) are primarily related to motivation for attachment. Traumatic death responses would presumably contain both traumatic and separation distress. While both emotional processes share in the dynamic of intrusion and avoidance of strong affect and secondary anxiety, depression, or somatic symptoms, the task of future clinical research will be to test the specific etiology, description, and treatment of these types of distress. Development of reliable measurements of trauma and separation distress would be a priority before the systematic study of the various forms of unnatural death bereavement could proceed.

Recent reviews of bereavement after disasters (Raphael, 1986), suicide (Ness & Pfeffer, 1990), and homicide (Rynearson & McCreery, 1993) demonstrate the lack of rigorous research designs and reproducible measurements of observations. The collected literature lacks coherence, consistency, and cross validation. However, a common clinical finding with these studies is the presence of posttraumatic responses. Several authors are noteworthy in their novel insights about trauma at the time of unnatural dying. Frankl (1972) and Lifton (1967) first noted intrusive death imagery as a pathogenic response in survivors of mass killing in concentration camps or nuclear attack. Van der Kolk and Van der Hart (1989) noted the pioneering work of Janet, who first described the maladaptive responses of avoidance, repression, and dissociation following traumatic dying. Ochberg (1988) was the first to formalize the victim response of helplessness and defilement in survivors of traumatic dying. Horowitz (1976) first theorized a model of traumatic adjustment with bereavement. The recent traumatic death studies of Pynoos and Nader (Pynoos et al., 1987) have documented the high frequency of traumatic responses in children with standardized and reliable testing of PTSD responses.

Homicidal dying has received the least attention of all forms of traumatic death. There are a handful of descriptive studies (Rinear, 1988; Rynearson, 1984; Parkes, 1993) suggesting that this form of unnatural death may be particularly traumatic, each author noting the prominence of chronic PTSD symptoms in unrecovered subjects. There are even fewer studies of homicidal bereavement that include standardized measures of intense trauma and grief coexisting in unrecovered subjects (Amick-McMullen et al., 1988; Nader et al., 1990; Rynearson, 1994a; Vargas et al., 1989; North et al., 1994), and no comparable study has been completed with unrecovered subjects following natural death.

THE SPECIFIC EFFECTS OF HOMICIDE

Homicidal dying presents at least three peculiarities that differentiate it from natural dying: (a) The dying is violent, a forceful, suddenly traumatic act; (b) the dying is a violation, a transgressive act; and (c) the dying is a volition, an intentional act. Rynearson (1987a) has presented a preliminary model of traumatic dying in which it is suggested that these three "Vs" (violence, violation, and volition) are associated with syndromal effects, including responses of posttraumatic stress disorder (intrusion/avoidance), victimization (rage, defilement), and compulsive inquiry (socially mandated investigation and punishment of the murderer). A therapeutic corollary of this model suggests that a family member closely identified with the deceased will, to some degree, identify with the violent, violational, and volitional effects of the dying itself, an additional adjustive burden to the grief associated with the loss of the relationship. Therapeutic strategies will need to include management of PTSD, victimization, and compulsive inquiry. If not, there is preliminary evidence that these sequelae of homicidal dying will be associated with prolonged recovery, suggesting that their management takes precedence. It will be difficult for family members to begin grief work associated with loss un-

til they have begun to accommodate the highly traumatized responses associated
with the dying.

VULNERABILITY AND RESILIENCY

Clinical studies previously cited suggest that the majority of subjects will endorse
some degree of time-limited distress to trauma or bereavement, and nonrecovery
is associated with intensification of the same signs and symptoms that normally
subside. However, there is impressive evidence that predisposing risk factors are
associated with prolonged recovery so that unresolved subjects differ in kind as
well as degree (Stroebe et al., 1988).

Whether these same associations pertain when the specific act creates simultaneous trauma and bereavement would appear to be consistent, but at this point
is untested.

In an effort to focus on clinical principles that clarify both risks (vulnerability) and resiliency (recovery and therapy), we have limited ourselves to clinical
observations and measures that are relevant to the clinical tasks of assessment and
treatment.

Vulnerability (Risk Factors)

Although there are numerous literature references citing risk factors for prolonged
responses to trauma and bereavement, there are relatively few controlled studies
(see Parkes 1990, and Bremner et al., 1993, for recent reviews). Table 7.1 contains
a comparative listing of risk factors noted before, during, and after the event.

Several recent well-controlled studies have demonstrated the co-occurrence
of trauma and bereavement responses with depressive disorders (30%), anxiety
disorders (20%–30%), substance abuse (15%–20%), and somatization disorder
(5%) (Green et al., 1992; Smith et al., 1990; Jacobs & Kim, 1990). The explanation for this co-occurrence is presumably multifactorial: (a) A number of the

Table 7.1   Risk Factors

	Trauma	Grief
Relationship	Family member	Ambivalence
		Child (1–5 years)
		Spouse
Pre-Event	History of childhood abuse	Young age (< 15)
		Poverty
		Multiple prior losses
Event	Degree of exposure	Sudden death
	Perceived responsibility	Unnatural death
Post-Event	Perceived lack of support	Perceived lack of support

symptom criteria overlap, and (b) psychiatric disorders may be associated with increased risk of occurrence of the event or with development of the disorder given exposure. Clinicians should be alert to the significant incidence of coexistent psychiatric disorders following trauma or loss, since recognition will indicate specific pharmacotherapy and/or behavioral treatment.

Resiliency

It is beyond our purpose to present a detailed overview of this topic. Resiliency has always been of interest to metapsychologists who have linked resiliency to secure mother-infant bonding (i.e., with a "good enough" mother, the developing individual will be able to tolerate and verbalize strong affects). Indeed, the basis for the metapsychologists' definition of resiliency pivots around the ability to verbalize, which necessarily conforms to the primarily verbal context of psychotherapy. There is an insistence in this literature of the infant's absolute dependency upon the mother for rescue from the potential chaotic preverbal fantasies that are harbingers of psychopathology.

Recent infant neurobehavioral studies have documented that the preverbal, inborn behaviors of reactivity and self-soothing are accurate predictors of later resiliency, influenced but not instilled by "good enough" mothering (Seifer et al., 1992; Wyman et al., 1992).

The majority of any population adjusting to loss or trauma will follow a spontaneous time-limited recovery. There has been no systematic research to define, measure, and explain the elements of resiliency that facilitate this process of recovery. Instead, clinical researchers monitor risk factors of dysfunctional clinical syndromes that are associated with an impairment in rather than a positive definition of resiliency itself.

We propose a limited definition of resiliency in loss and trauma to explain its function in recovery so that the clinician can assess for and reinforce its role in therapy.

Trauma and loss share in the dynamic of intense, sustained, aversive affect. The major function of resiliency is to maintain the intensity of aversive affect at a tolerable level (Krystal, 1970; Sahin, 1985). The intense affective responses of trauma and separation distress are particularly overwhelming because of their preverbal, preoperational, neuropsychologic basis. These responses resonate our earliest aversive experiences, before we could objectify and reify with words. We propose three preverbal elements of resiliency that are presumably basic for accommodation.

1   Pacification: This refers to the capacity for self-soothing. The real and/or fantasized apperception of loss and trauma, with its associated affects, can be sustained through *modulation* or *diversion*. Perhaps modulation of and diversion from aversive affect occur on a clinical continuum; with the relative absence, there is an associated responsive disintegratory paralysis, and, with hypertrophy, a numb and avoidant hyperactivity.

2   Partition: This refers to the capacity to separate one's experiential self from one's simultaneous experiential apperception of others. People's aversive reactions to loss and trauma belong to them, and this discrimination allows a focus on their own responses rather than being dependent upon (anxious attachment) or dependable for (compulsive caregiving) the aversive responses of others.

3   Perspective: This refers to the capacity to maintain a simultaneous consideration of one's experiential self in time: who one was, who one is, and who one will be. The aversive affect of loss and trauma stretched by the dimension of time creates an *interpenetration* of one's aversive responses of the present reverberating with those from the past and anticipating some hope of change in the future. Without this interpenetration, the responses may remain static, relegated to one's forgotten past, intrusively flooding one's shattered present, or distorting one's future with fear or a counterphobic omnipotence. The resilient perspective allows an ironic detachment, a wider and deeper acknowledgment of loss and trauma and the residual ambiguity rather than a transcendent surrender of self.

These concepts of resiliency (capacity for pacification, partition, and perspective) are distilled from our clinical work with family members struggling to accommodate to a homicidal death. We are not prepared to defend their essentiality to recovery in other clinical contexts. However, with this group of patients, the diminished capacity for one or a combination of these resilient capacities appears to have considerable face validity in predicting nonrecovery, and efforts to reinforce these capacities appear to be important during the initial phase of therapy.

A CLINICAL SURVEY OF RESILIENCY AND VULNERABILITY IN HOMICIDAL BEREAVEMENT

We initiated the Support Project for Unnatural Dying in 1990 to study and offer preventive intervention to family members bereaved by homicide. In our first study, we examined a group ($N = 18$) of adult subjects who were referred to us for treatment because of their dysfunctional responses after the homicidal death of a family member. Measures of bereavement and trauma showed higher levels of intensity than reported in studies of control subjects and other cohorts of bereaved individuals. We also noted the high correlation of antecedent psychiatric treatment ($n = 12$), the death of a child ($n = 12$), and recurrent and disorganizing flashbacks and dreams of homicidal dying (Rynearson & McCreery, 1993).

As an extension of that initial survey, we have gathered a matched comparison group of family members who were contacted through the medical examiner's office but refused treatment. While they were willing to cooperate for assessment, they felt no need for additional support or psychotherapy. We presume that those subjects who would not seek treatment would present with less evidence of vulnerability by structured assessment and self-report measures. Since there are no reliable measures for resiliency, there is no standardized method of testing our presumption that treatment refusal and resiliency show a positive correlation. However, we interviewed each of the treatment refusal group members in an effort to gain some clinical impressions of resilient dynamics.

A detailed presentation of this comparative research study has been published elsewhere (Rynearson, 1995). In this chapter, we include the findings that are most clinically relevant for assessment and psychotherapy.

Comparison of Vulnerabilities

Table 7.2 is a tabulation of the variables that approached ($p < .1$) or showed significant ($p < .05$) variation between those seeking ($n = 32$) and refusing ($n = 20$) treatment. Demographic comparison shows the two groups are matched; those refusing treatment listed church membership more frequently ($p = .08$). Variables of antecedent psychiatric history and childhood abuse were prevalent in those seeking treatment, as was their apperception of deficient external support. There were multiple variables detailing the specifics of the dying, the criminal judicial process, and viewing and disposition of the deceased, all of which were comparatively insignificant.

Table 7.3 details the remarkably strong ($p = .001$) variation of standardized measures of grief (Texas Revised Inventory of Grief), trauma (Revised Impact of Events Score), and dissociation (Dissociative Experience Scale). Those seeking treatment reported high levels of distress differentiating them from the treatment refusal group as well as bereaved groups from other clinical studies.

Table 7.4 compares the presence and frequency of imagery of the homicidal dying. Imagery experiences were divided into reenactment (McFarlane, 1992; Schwarz & Kowalskis, 1991) of the homicide (where the events are nonreflectively witnessed), rescue, reunion, and revenge (where the events are actively reversed and/or retributed by a fantasized autonomous self). We hypothesized that

Table 7.2   Seeking vs Refusing Treatment

	Rx seeking (N=32)	Rx refusal (N=20)	p value
Demographics			
Intervention	6 months	7 months	N.S.
Loss of child	17	10	"
Age	42	49	"
Gender	26F/6M	13F/7M	"
Education	13	13.5	"
Religion	17 yes	16 yes	.08
Psych Hx			
Physical abuse	9	1	.09
Sexual abuse	8	1	.04
Psych Rx	16	4	.06
Perceived Support			
Social	28 neg	10 neg	.008
Church	25 neg	9 neg	.03
Family	12 neg	2 neg	.06

Table 7.3 Self-Report Measures (Mean Scores)

	Rx seeking (N=32)	Rx refusal (N=20)	p value
TRIG			
Part 1	29.7	20.9	<.001
Part 2	56.0	44.6	<.001
RIES			
Intrusion	29.4	18.3	<.001
Avoidance	24.2	9.8	<.001
DES	19.7	8	<.001

Table 7.4 Presence and Frequency of Imagery

	Reenactment		Rescue		Revenge		Reunion	
	Rx+	Rx−	Rx+	Rx−	Rx+	Rx−	Rx+	Rx−
None	2	11	18	16	16	14	20	12
Monthly	1	2	2	1	3	3	1	3
Weekly	13	4	9	1	7	2	7	2
Daily	16	3	2	2	5	1	4	3
p Value	.0004		.1954		.3392		.4683	

subjects seeking treatment would present with more intense and frequent intrusive imagery of reenactment than the comparison group. Only 2 of the 52 subjects had actually witnessed the homicide.

Of the four types of imagery, reenactment showed the only significant association, with those subjects seeking treatment ($p = .001$) reporting intense and frequent intrusive recurrences.

These data would tend to confirm the hypothesis that those subjects who seek treatment within the first year of homicidal bereavement present with higher levels of distress and antecedent psychiatric vulnerability than those who refuse treatment. A criticism of this confirmation might suggest that those who refuse treatment are following a "delayed" trajectory, and serial monitoring would show higher levels of distress by Year 2 or 3. While we plan on repeating measures, there is abundant prospective study of bereaved and traumatized subjects to discount anticipation of "delayed" distress. Those subjects who show significant distress at Years 2 and 3 have been similarly distressed during the initial months of bereavement.

Comparison of Resiliency

We propose several clinical impressions of enhanced resiliency in those subjects refusing treatment. These impressions are necessarily vague and arbitrary because they are condensed from unstructured interviews with each of the 20 subjects. They should be viewed as preliminary concepts that might be considered more systematically and reliably in future research. We believe that they are noteworthy and highlight resiliency dynamics, and we attempt to initiate and/or reinforce them in therapy.

- *Accommodation to reenactment imagery*: While many treatment refusal subjects noted reenactment imagery during the early phases of recovery, it did not persist. Some subjects were able to actively suppress the image, but most reported a calming, contrapuntal image of the deceased that they were able to summon to counterbalance the horrific fantasy. Sometimes the image was composed of pleasant past memories, but more often it contained fantasies of release and spiritual restoration. It would appear that the capacity to tolerate and restructure reenactment imagery is an essential first step in accommodation.
- *Maintenance of altruism*: All of the treatment refusal subjects reported the continuance of nurturing contact between themselves and others following the homicide. Many of the resilient subjects had been comfortable in assuming the role of primary caregiver within the family before the homicide and maintained a concern for the emotional needs of remaining family members that superseded their own. This altruism allowed the early active installation of hope into the process of recovery for others as well as oneself. We have also been surprised by the importance of pets (particularly for subjects with no remaining children) who became the objects of intense caring.
- *Maintenance of coherence*: The capacity to find some meaning in this tragedy allowed a less discordant perspective. Most of the subjects cited a strong pre-existent concept of death that was anticipated without dread. Many of the subjects associated this concept with their strong religious or spiritual belief systems. For the deceased, death was synonymous with release (for some, with reunion) and resynthesis in some "universal" context that promised perpetuity. If this belief system was based in an organized church (as demonstrated by the majority of the treatment refusal group), then it was supported by liturgy, ritual, and resonance from other members. The belief system was sometimes nonreligious and based on an elemental natural connection between death and new life; this was supported more by contact with nature than by human society. Two of the subjects were adherents of reincarnation, and, for them, the homicide was an inevitable scene in a never-ending drama of disappearance and reemergence of self. These belief systems appear to have buffered the incoherence of death and unnatural dying, both the loss and the trauma.

If we attempt to connect these clinical impressions with our limited definition of resilient capacities, there would appear to be considerable overlap. Pacification and its preverbal capacity to modulate and divert appears to correspond with accommodation to reenactment imagery; partition and its capacity to discriminate appears to correspond with maintenance of altruism; perspective and its capacity to establish ironic detachment appears to correspond with maintenance of coherence. We do not suggest that these are univariate connections; they are so vague that it would be wiser to assume a multivariate relationship.

ASSESSMENT

We have already cited the theoretical and empirical data that outline an understanding of vulnerability and resiliency during homicidal bereavement, and it would seem to be a simple process to apply this understanding to a clinical case. Unfortunately, whenever one resorts to a written, relatively reasoned explanation, one assumes an attitude of intellectual detachment.

Since one of our strongest findings with those who seek treatment is intense experiential imagery, we appreciate that our reasonings are far removed from the immediate needs of our patients. Recognizing that intrusive reenactment imagery will probably be the most prominent debilitating sign in those seeking assessment suggests we ask directly about it at the outset. The interviewer assumes a reassuring and participatory alliance in the way questions are offered:

> What a terrible time for you. We need to focus on what is most upsetting. I know that you did not witness the murder, but we know that many family members are left with a vivid fantasy of what happened and that they can't stop thinking or dreaming about it. Has this been a problem for you?

Those who are overwhelmed by this traumatic imagery are reassured to know that they are not "going crazy" and that recovery will involve calming and distancing themselves from such horrific imagery.

During early assessment, we emphasize the need for and reinforcement of resiliency and do not actively inquire about sources of vulnerability until our patient has begun to master the trauma of the homicide. Since a high percentage of those seeking treatment are familiar with therapy, it is reassuring to emphasize that homicidal bereavement has presented a psychological challenge that cannot be avoided. No matter how many vulnerabilities or resiliencies or how comprehensive previous therapy, homicide is going to have a lasting impact on their lives, and there is no therapy that is going to offer complete relief.

> There is no question that your reaction is going to be less painful with time, but it takes months and months for these changes. Please don't burden yourself with the expectation that you should recover quickly.

Another principal focus of assessment is the patient's matrix of perceived support. Early inclusion of family members and friends allows a clinician to begin educating these individuals about the importance of reinforcing resiliency and the long-term nature of recovery. This is not the time for family therapy that attempts to delineate sources of discord or dynamics of the homicide.

Inquiry about the patient's private symbology of dying and death is another early task of assessment. Nihilism and despair are common early responses, and helping the patient recover or develop sustaining beliefs or actions can assist in buffering the disintegratory effects of homicidal dying.

PRELIMINARY THOUGHTS ABOUT
PSYCHOTHERAPY

To our knowledge, there has been no controlled prospective treatment study of bereavement after homicide. We emphasize the preliminary nature of our own observations, which might serve as useful guides rather than tested principles.

An important initial caveat for the therapist and patient is the finding, common to systematic studies of grief therapy, that 20%–30% of subjects will remain nonresponsive (Rynearson, 1987b). This suggests that the promise of short-term recovery is, at best, naive and, at worst, an unrealistic goal that might reinforce diminished self-esteem and demoralization. Presumably, there is a positive association between premorbid psychopathology and nonrecovery, and the clinician will be alert to the possibility that the tragedy of homicide is only the latest in a long procession of major life disruptions. Given this situation of premorbid vulnerability, the therapist might become involved in therapy issues distantly connected to the focus of homicidal bereavement. It would seem prudent, then, to clarify at the outset the differential between the proximal goal of recovery from homicidal bereavement and the more distal and vague reverberations of a childhood of neglect and trauma.

If the patient presents in a flooded state of reenactment imagery, then restructuring this traumatic fantasy will be the initial goal of therapy. It would be premature to begin individual or group therapy until patients have recovered enough resiliency to pacify and partition themselves, which is the basis of psychological accommodation to trauma (Pitman et al., 1987; Sheikh, 1983). Without these capacities, the patient will feel such disintegratory anxiety with exposure to cues of homicidal dying that he or she will necessarily avoid treatment.

STRATEGIES FOR PACIFICATION AND PARTITION

Exercises that encourage relaxation (modulation) and guided imagery (diversion) are nonverbal capacities that we actively initiate. Our commitment to ally ourselves in this process of accommodation so that we can survive the trauma together offers nonverbal reassurance and hope. We introduce positive imagery vis-à-vis the deceased through scenes that contain active mastery and autonomy, scenes that are often discovered by reviewing family picture albums together. Some pictures can serve as catalysts in creating comforting, counterbalancing images when the patient is flooded by horrific reenactment.

It should be noted that our approach to accommodation (Rynearson, 1996) is different than the operant conditioning model based on extinction. While recent modified techniques of extinction of traumatic imagery and avoidance have been reported as effective (Grigsby, 1987; Vaughan & Tarrier, 1992; Kellner et al., 1992), we are similarly encouraged by our goal of active ongoing mastery. We are more comfortable with the creative and symbolic task of restructuring the trauma than the more extirpative goal of implosion and extinction. We believe (but cannot validate) that our treatment stance encourages and strengthens psychological autonomy.

Medications to diminish panic and anxiety and anticonvulsants to counteract disruptive flashbacks are sometimes indicated as important adjuncts in patients' initial recovery of pacification.

As the capacities for modulation and diversion are reestablished, we can begin to confront the traumatic imagery more directly. The assignment to draw the death scene provides a nonverbal expression of reenactment that can be directly viewed and shared with the therapist. The process of responding to the horror is followed by questioning in which the patient places him- or herself in the drawing. It is rare that patients portray themselves at all, and this is presumably a sign of their traumatic overidentification with the dying itself. Efforts to place themselves within the reenactment drawing allow a beginning partition instead of mute participation. It is not unusual for patients to imagine themselves beside the deceased—sometimes defending, sometimes holding, sometimes rescuing. This exercise allows a more active and supportive presence and a counterbalancing identification as enclosed and safe.

While this initial phase of resiliency reinforcement may be accomplished after two or three visits and several weeks of daily repetition, it is an important first step in recovery. It is very difficult for the patient who is nonresilient to focus on the verbal and conceptual demands of therapy. The state of hyperarousal and traumatic introjection might explain the high dropout rate in support groups in which patients feel the need to avoid the trauma of others when they cannot tolerate their own.

The longer term goals of treatment may now be addressed, and these goals may include (a) self-esteem enhancement, (b) acceptance of survivor guilt, and (c) delineation of antecedent vulnerabilities and resiliencies in the relationship with the deceased.

At this point, it becomes clear which patients have had severe long-term characterologic problems, irrespective of their homicidal bereavement. As always, finding a resource of care for this chronically dysfunctional population is challenging. We have been hesitant in committing ourselves to these patients after the initial assessment and efforts to reestablish resiliency. Their therapeutic needs exceed our limited treatment focus, and their involvement with other patients in groups is often psychologically disruptive and enervating for all concerned.

GROUP PSYCHOTHERAPY

The resilient phenomena of accommodation, altruism, and coherence are anticipated and encouraged during recovery. Their emergence and combination are so idiosyncratic that it would be misleading to recommend a specific strategy. However, the context for their development involves active interaction with others. We have been impressed with the opportunities offered by group therapy in which the patient is engaged with others who are also having difficulty in recovery. As a group, the subjects share an empathic effort to accommodate to the trauma of unnatural dying, now mutually resonated. Their efforts to support one another contain the rudiments of altruism and coherence, which are more purposeful than self-disclosure.

Group therapy has become an integral part of our treatment program (Rynearson & Sinnema, in press). We meet on a weekly basis for 90-minute sessions, and patients agree to attend 12 consecutive sessions. The therapists maintain the group's focus on the dysfunctional affect of unnatural dying and actively guide the group in developing resilient responses. Most patients want to remain in the support group for 6–9 months. Those who remain longer need more time for accommodation or, more commonly, are focused on longer term problems that predated the homicide. Every 3 months, the group experiences turnover, and the remaining group members serve as a cohesive nidus for the acculturation and care of new members. Concurrent individual therapy sessions are available.

CASE HISTORIES

Case presentations provide a "telling" way to convey the ebb and flow of treatment. We can become more directly immersed in the story of the dying and the narrative of recovery as created by the writer. Since the cases present themselves in the form of a highly subjective interplay between patient and therapist, it must be acknowledged that this is a highly biased accounting of the how and why of improvement (Schafer, 1992).

The cases presented here share one common challenge beyond the murder itself: In each case, the murder was an intrafamily event. In our series of 52 cases, 9 were intrafamily homicides and were proportionately distributed between treatment seeking (5 of 32) and treatment refusal (4 of 20) groups.

Instead of highlighting and emphasizing the dynamics of recovery, we have decided to include patients who were difficult to engage, showed only limited recovery, or claimed no need for therapy at all. In our experience, it is the more challenging and resistant patients who teach us more about not only the intricacies of recovery but our therapeutic limitations as well.

Case 1: Treatment Avoidance

A 44-year-old woman was referred by a bereavement support group after attending two sessions "because I can't stand to hear other people's tragedy when I can't handle my own." She had had no previous history of psychiatric disorder or treatment.

Two years before, her mother had been murdered by the patient's brother, who was schizophrenic. The patient was overwhelmed with reenactment fantasies and nightmares, often accompanied by panic attacks. Unable to concentrate, she had stopped working as a secretary and had become reclusively agoraphobic and dependent upon her husband.

She asked to leave our initial 1-hour appointment after 30 minutes because of the terror she anticipated in talking about her mother's murder. We tried to reassure her that she retained primary control over the way and the time she would discuss the subject. It was recommended that we try to enhance her trust and her support system, and together we might initially diminish her panic attacks.

During the second session, she felt compelled to explain her role as primary caregiver during her childhood. When she was 5, her father abandoned the family, and her mother decompensated and began to drink. For the next 45 minutes, the patient wept and raged about her mother's death, about the physical and sexual abuse she and other family members had suffered from her alcoholic stepfather, and about her incapacity to protect her mother and her four younger half-sibs during her childhood and adolescence. At the end of that session, she felt unrelieved, as if this childhood terror of unremitting abuse and her incapacity to control the situation were an inevitable preface to her mother's murder. Efforts to comfort or divert her during this monologue had no apparent effect. She agreed to a short-term trial of an anti-anxiety agent (clonazepam).

During the third session, she expressed her gratitude for the medication, which had controlled the panic attacks. However, the reenactment flashbacks and nightmares persisted.

We inquired about cohering belief systems and learned that her religious faith and faith in the future had been dissolved by the murder.

She began to talk about her incapacity to trust her husband and her desperate emotional commitment to her male lover, with whom she had been involved for 5 years. At the end of the session, she handed us a copy of her brother's written confession, detailing the specifics of the murder. She asked that we read the account before our next scheduled session. It was an appalling document, not only because of its brutality (he had decapitated the mother) but because of its absurdity (his certitude that he was saving the family from the mother instead of being traumatized or remorseful about his act).

She failed to attend her next appointment, and when contacted by phone she said she was enraged at us. She felt that we were critical and uncaring. She had decided that she needed to recover with the support of her male lover, who would mutely reassure and comfort her by his embrace.

Since that brief contact 2 years ago, she continues to call every 4 to 6 months to ask for a refill of the minor tranquilizer when her panic attacks recur. There has apparently been no substantive change in her skewed support system, and her traumatic response has only diminished to the point that she can now leave home.

Although we continue to offer treatment, she still feels too threatened but acknowledges that she will return at some point.

Comment   The brutal death of her mother apparently realized a long suppressed fear (or fearful wish for the brother) that occurred in a family context of chronic violence. The patient has remained unable to pacify or partition herself from this trauma without the nonverbal proximity of a clandestine lover. Presumably, the massive transferential distortion of the early dependency upon the therapist was so threatening that she had to escape. At the same time she offered, but could not directly share, the traumatic description of her mother's murder. Despite her need for avoidance, she maintains a tenuous but ongoing contact, requesting medication and our assurance that we are still available to help.

Case 2: Short-Term Recovery

A 35-year-old male attorney was referred by the medical examiner's office 3 months after the murder of his sister by her husband. There was no previous history of psychiatric disorder or treatment.

The patient was unable to sleep because of the nearly constant reenactment images of his sister's dying. She had been chained to a bed, sodomized, and strangled while her 2-year-old son watched from a crib. Her husband was amnesic from the murderous behavior that was associated with multiple intoxicants—alcohol, cocaine, and PCP.

The patient was confused by his incapacity to control his thoughts and perplexed at the rage, concern, and disillusionment he felt toward his brother-in-law, who had been a very close friend before the murder.

After our initial efforts to reinforce his capacity for pacification, he felt considerable relief. As the older brother, he had been very caring of the murdered sister and was able to summon a series of these images. As we reviewed his drawing of the death scene, we noted that he was not portrayed in his fantasy. When he was directed to project himself into the reenactment, he first placed himself beside his sister to rescue her, then his brother-in-law to restrain and arrange for his hospitalization, and, finally, with his 2-year-old nephew, whom he wanted to hold. The nephew now became an altruistic preoccupation. The patient was determined that the child receive psychiatric assessment and a series of visits to ensure his support after the trauma of the murder.

The patient did not feel treatment was indicated after four sessions.

He contacted us 2 years later to refer one of his friends to the Support Project for Unnatural Dying and stated that he was doing well. However, he continued to worry about his nephew, for whom he had become a virtual parental surrogate.

Comment   This homicidal death occurred as an aberrant and intoxicated act in a family with a history of stability. There was an abundant historical substrate of nurturance and resiliency from which the patient could gain comfort. He was able to accommodate to the traumatic dying with alacrity and saw a purpose in this recovery for others as well.

Case 3: Limited Recovery

A 35-year-old woman was referred by her psychiatrist, who had been unsuccessful in treating her depression the previous year despite weekly outpatient visits and therapeutic levels of antidepressant medication (fluoxetine). In addition, she had been inconsistently attending AA meetings and a bereavement support group since the homicidal death of her mother 3 and a half years before.

Her mother was killed by her father. He had become psychotically depressed and paranoid after the neurosurgical removal of a brain tumor 2 years before the murder. Her mother and the patient's three younger sisters had sought multiple consultations with the father's physicians because of his pathologic jealousy and persistent threats. Desperate entreaties to the police and efforts to commit the father failed to prevent the shooting. The mother died instantly from a head wound, and the father survived a self-inflicted gunshot wound to the chest. Her sisters were able to mourn openly and recover, but the patient began to drink while compulsively caring for her close friend who was dying of cancer and visiting her father several times each week at the state hospital where he had been committed. The combination of alcohol and compulsive caregiving diverted her from acknowledgment of her mother's death. The alcohol also distanced her from the repetitive reenactment flashbacks and dreams of her mother's dying. Within months of the murder, she also joined a conservative and fundamentalistic church that offered social support along with an absolute promise of eternal salvation for her mother and a simplistic explanation of her father's murderous behavior as an act of the devil.

Our initial objective was to assist her in mastering the traumatic imagery. We insisted on sobriety and attendance at AA meetings as a condition of ongoing assessment and treatment. She felt relief in sharing the traumatic reenactment imagery, which had heretofore remained a dreaded secret. She had misinterpreted these flashbacks as hallucinations and feared that she was "going crazy like my dad." It was explained that the flashbacks and dreams were a common experience that needed her accommodation rather than avoidance. In addition to techniques of progressive relaxation and guided imagery, we examined her paintings through verbalization of the dying scene to promote a sense of safety and separateness from the dying image. We recommended that she curtail her visits to her father. She was incapable of integrating her desperate feelings of nurturance and rage toward her father, whom she loved as a caring parent but feared and hated as a murderer. Clonazepam was added to the fluoxetine to control the anxiety and panic that accompanied the flashbacks.

Within a short time, she was able to express the long-suppressed longing and sadness for her mother's loss, which was a milestone in her recovery. At subsequent group and individual therapy, we learned of her lifelong dependency upon her mother and her masochistic relationship with men (two unhappy marriages). Her vulnerability to separation and her inability to accept her own anger in relationships had persisted since her childhood. Despite her improvement after 6 months of treatment, we were apprehensive about her impulsive decision to marry a 53-year-old disabled construction worker who lived in a remote area of Alaska.

Four months later, she returned for several outpatient visits while separating from her new husband, who had physically abused her in a fight she had provoked after several weeks of mutual heavy drinking. He enrolled in an inpatient alcohol rehabilitation program, while she refused to do so. She denied any persistence of traumatic imagery or depression; however, the images of reenactment would fleetingly recur. Eventually she decided to return to Alaska and her marriage.

Comment   This case report illustrates the limitations of recovery in the ongoing psychotherapy of a patient whose chronic mixed character disorder and alcohol dependence complicated her adjustment to her mother's homicidal dying. While focused individual therapy, group therapy, and pharmacotherapy have offered short-term improvement in her traumatic grief, the prognosis remains guarded, and we remain available for continued support.

Case 4: Treatment Refusal

A 64-year-old woman came to our attention because of her lack of reported difficulties after her husband murdered her son. Her scores on all of the standardized measures were the lowest recorded by any of our subjects.

While her husband had always been an angry, autocratic man, his volatility and lack of impulse control dramatically increased after the neurosurgical removal of a massive meningioma 3 years before. During a physical fight with a 33-year-old son who lived with the family, the husband became overtly paranoid and murdered the son with a shotgun 11 months before we contacted the family.

Her husband was imprisoned and declared temporarily deranged because of his organic brain syndrome, and he was placed in an anger management program. After 6 months of incarceration, he returned home and was in residence at the time of our interview.

Most important to the woman was her faith in God and the firm belief that there were lessons in all of this for her entire family. She was sure this was not a punishment; rather, there was a more positive reason behind the tragedy that remained to be discovered.

She reported that she had been able to maintain a sense of altruism toward her husband. Indeed, during her description of the murder, she firmly identified with the husband rather than her murdered son and could understand how her husband's paranoia had forced him to protect himself. She was enraged at him for what he had done but forgave him for what he could not control.

She noted reenactment imagery during the initial weeks of her recovery, which she was able to transform by visualizing her son's death as a release from his pain and terror into heaven, where he awaited the remainder of the family in peace. She was persuaded that God had created this crisis as a challenge for her to establish enough harmony within the family that they would welcome one another when reunited in heaven.

She felt that, at some point in the future, the entire family might benefit from therapy to resolve the hurt and anger she recognized in everyone.

Comment In a seemingly intolerable conundrum of violence and family disintegration, this woman was able to remain nurturant and hopeful. She stated that the reason was her belief that God would reveal a purpose and healing to the murder. While her overidentification and need to nurture her murderous husband may be viewed as a reaction formation, she was quite candid about the rage that she and the other family members experienced and was open to the need for therapy at some point.

Since our purpose during the interview was to understand her recovery, we did not challenge or question her efforts to cope so much as celebrate how well she was doing.

PREVENTION

The public health paradigm of primary, secondary, and tertiary prevention of disease is useful in ordering some tentative recommendations.

Primary prevention focuses on elimination of the causes of disease. While eliminating the causes of violence is becoming an urgent public demand, there can be no generic or proscriptive remedy. An obvious, long-resisted "elimination" will be the control of handguns and automated weapons, which cause the vast majority of homicidal deaths. Unfortunately, the social, cultural, and economic causes of violence are so inherent in our country that their solution will take many generations. So long as unlimited possession of weapons and unrestrained marketing of violence by the media remain more of a constitutional right than a public health risk, violence and traumatic dying will escalate. It would appear that intensifying the harshness of criminal judicial control of violence is as misdirected and shortsighted as it has been in curbing the use and distribution of drugs.

Secondary prevention focuses on early intervention in high-risk populations. One major well-controlled study of early intervention in reducing prolonged distress after traumatic dying was conducted by Raphael (1977). The intervention (short-term individual supportive psychotherapy) occurred within the first 3 months of bereavement after the sudden death of a spouse. Depressive and anxiety disorders in the early course of bereavement are also harbingers of prolonged recovery (6 times the risk for nonrecovery). When to intervene with appropriate pharmacotherapy is still uncertain, since these disorders will spontaneously clear within the first 4–6 months of bereavement in 70%–80% of subjects. Several pilot studies (Jacobs et al., 1987; Pasternak et al., 1991) have demonstrated marked improvement in coexistent depressive and anxiety disorders with judicious use of medications in combination with ongoing psychotherapy. Preliminary findings from the present study would suggest that intense and frequent reenactment in imagery is another risk factor indicating a combination of pharmacotherapy and focused psychotherapy.

Tertiary prevention focuses on early rehabilitation and education to minimize chronic disability and relapse during recovery from a disease. Several studies have documented the effectiveness of support groups with bereavement (Vachon et al., 1980; Marmar et al., 1988), although none of these studies have included homicidal bereavement. A mutual support group composed of family members in homicidal bereavement might be introduced during the early phase of recovery. If family members are involved in an active investigation and/or trial of the homicide, they are well served by a support group that provides didactic and clarifying information to help in guiding them through the criminal judicial system. At the conclusion of the investigation and trial, a longer term support group allows the exploration of trauma and separation distress and their management.

CONCLUSION

Bereavement after homicidal dying creates a discordant response of trauma (loss of autonomy) and bereavement (loss of an altruistic relationship). The persistence of intense reenactment imagery of the dying appears to be an indirect sign of traumatic and unresolved bereavement connoting a traumatic overidentification with the nonautonomy of the murder victim. There is preliminary evidence that premorbid psychiatric vulnerabilities are associated with this response of traumatic overidentification. However, clinical experience would suggest that subjects seeking treatment are so overwhelmed and reactive (as documented by significant elevations on measures of reenactment imagery, trauma, dissociation, and bereavement) that the initial treatment strategy should focus on supportive reestablishment of resilient capacities (pacification, partition, and perspective) rather than preexistent vulnerabilities (ambivalence, guilt, repression and/or denial) (Rynearson, 1994b).

We have outlined some guidelines during assessment and initial treatment to help in clarifying and modifying traumatic homicidal bereavement responses. These interventions include nonverbal techniques applied to individual and group therapy whose comparative effectiveness must await future study and validation.

Adjusting to homicidal dying is a lifetime enterprise, so the therapist and patient will be better served by acknowledging the limitations of a dialectic change than by hoping for a restorative recovery.

REFERENCES

Abraham, K. (1924). A short study of the development of the libido; viewed in the light of mental disorders. In *Selected papers on psychoanalysis*. London: Hogarth Press.

Adler, A. (1943). Neuropsychiatric complications in victims of Boston's Coconut Grove disaster. *Journal of the American Medical Association, 123*, 1098–1101.

American Psychiatric Association. (1994). *Diagnostic and statistical manual of mental disorders* (4th ed.). Washington, DC: Author.

Amick-McMullen, A., Kilpatrick, D. G., Veronen, L. J., & Smith, S. (1988). Family survivors of homicide victims: Theoretical perspectives and an exploratory study. *Journal of Traumatic Stress, 2*, 21–35.

Benzaquin, P. (1959). *Fire in Boston's Coconut Grove*. Boston: Branden Press.

Bremner, J. D., Southwick, S. M., Johnson, D. R., Yehuda, R., & Charney, D. S. (1993). Childhood physical abuse and combat-related post traumatic stress disorder in Vietnam veterans. *American Journal of Psychiatry, 150*, 235–239.

Cobb, S., & Lindeman, E. (1943). Neuropsychiatric observations. *Annals of Surgery, 117*, 814–824.

Deutsch, H. (1937). The absence of grief. *Psychoanalytic Quarterly, 6*, 12–22.

Frankl, V. (1972). The feeling of meaninglessness: A challenge to psychotherapy. *American Journal of Psychoanalysis, 32*, 85–89.

Freud, S. (1957). Mourning and melancholia. In *Standard edition of the complete psychological works of Sigmund Freud* (Vol. 14). London: Hogarth Press.

Green, B. L., Lindy, J. D., Grace, M. C., & Leonard, A. C. (1992). Chronic post traumatic stress disorder and diagnostic comorbidity in a disaster sample. *Journal of Nervous and Mental Disease, 180*, 760–766.

Grigsby, J. P. (1987). The use of imagery in the treatment of post traumatic stress disorder. *Journal of Nervous and Mental Disease, 175*, 55–59.

Horowitz, M. J. (1976). *Stress response syndromes*. New York: Jason Aronson.

Jacobs, S. (1993). *Pathologic grief maladaptation to loss*. London: American Psychiatric Press.

Jacobs, S., & Kim, K. (1990). Psychiatric complications of bereavement. *Psychiatry Annals, 20*, 314–317.

Jacobs, S. C., Nelson, J. C., & Zisook, S. (1987). Treating depressions of bereavement with antidepressants: A pilot study. *Psychiatric Clinics of North America, 10*, 501–510.

Kardiner, A. (1941). *The traumatic neuroses of war*. New York: Paul B. Hoeber.

Kellner, R., Niedhardt, J., Krakow, B., & Pathak, D. (1992). Changes in chronic nightmares after one session of desensitization or rehearsal instructions. *American Journal of Psychiatry, 149*, 659–662.

Klein, M. (1948). Mourning and its relation to manic depressive states. In *Contributions to psychoanalysis*. London: Hogarth Press.

Krystal, H. (1970, December). *The genetic development of affects and affect regression*. Paper presented at the meeting of the Michigan Psychoanalytic Society, Detroit, MI.

Lifton, R. J. (1967). *Death in life: Survivors of Hiroshima*. New York: Simon & Schuster.

Lindeman, E. (1944). Symptomatology and management of acute grief. *American Journal of Psychiatry, 101*, 141–148.

Marmar, C. R., Horowitz, M. J., Weiss, D. S., Wilner, N. R., & Kaltreider, N. B. (1988). A controlled trial of brief psychotherapy and mutual help group treatment of conjugal bereavement. *American Journal of Psychiatry, 145*, 203–209.

McFarlane, A. C. (1992). Avoidance and intrusion in post traumatic stress disorder. *Journal of Nervous and Mental Disease, 180*, 439–445.

Nader, K., Pynoos, R. S., Fairbanks, L., & Frederick, C. (1990). Childhood PTSD reactions one year after a sniper attack. *American Journal of Psychiatry, 147*, 1526–1530.

Ness, D., & Pfeffer, C. (1990). Sequelae of bereavement resulting from suicide. *American Journal of Psychiatry, 147*, 279–285.

North, C., Smith, E., & Spitznagel, E. (1994). Post traumatic stress disorder in survivors of a mass shooting. *American Journal of Psychiatry, 151*, 82–88.

Ochberg, F. M. (1988). *Post traumatic therapy and victims of violence*. New York: Brunner/Mazel.

Parkes, C. M. (1990). Risk factors in bereavement: Implications for the prevention and treatment of pathologic grief. *Psychiatry Annals, 20*, 308–313.

Parkes, C. M. (1993). Psychiatric problems following bereavement by murder or manslaughter. *British Journal of Psychiatry, 162*, 49–54.

Pasternak, R. E., Reynolds, C. F., Schlernitzauer, M., Hoch, C. C., Buysse, D. J., Houck, P. R., & Perel, J. M. (1991). Acute open-trial nortriptyline therapy of bereavement-related depression in late life. *Journal of Clinical Psychiatry, 52*, 307–310.

Pitman, R. K., Orr, S. P., Forgue, D. F., de Jong, J. B., & Claiborn, J. M. (1987). Psychophysiologic assessment of post traumatic stress disorder imagery in Vietnam combat veterans. *Archives of General Psychiatry, 44*, 970–975.

Pynoos, R. S., Frederick, C., Nader, K., Arroyo, W., Steinberg, A., Eth, S., Nunez, F., & Fairbanks, L. (1987). Life threat and post traumatic stress in school-age children. *Archives of General Psychiatry, 44,* 1057–1063.

Raphael, B. (1977). Preventive intervention with the recently bereaved. *Archives of General Psychiatry, 34,* 1450–1454.

Raphael, B. (1986). *When disaster strikes.* New York: Basic Books.

Rinear, E. E. (1988). Psychosocial aspects of parental response patterns to the death of a child by homicide. *Journal of Traumatic Stress, 1,* 305–322.

Rynearson, E. K. (1984). Bereavement after homicide: A descriptive study. *American Journal of Psychiatry, 141,* 1452–1454.

Rynearson, E. K. (1987a). Psychological adjustment to unnatural dying. In *Biopsychosocial aspects of bereavement* (pp. 77–93). Washington, DC: American Psychiatric Press.

Rynearson, E. K. (1987b). Psychotherapy of pathologic grief: Revisions and limitations (grief and bereavement). *Psychiatry Clinics of North America, 10,* 487–499.

Rynearson, E. K. (1994a). Support project for bereavement after homicide. *Virginia Mason Clinic Bulletin, 48,* 33–41.

Rynearson, E. K. (1994b) Psychotherapy of bereavement after homocide. *Journal of Psychotherapy Practice and Research, 3,* 341–347.

Rynearson, E. K. (1995). Bereavement after homicide: A comparison of treatment seekers and refusers. *British Journal of Psychiatry, 166,* 507–510.

Rynearson, E. K. (1996). Psychotherapy of bereavement after homicide: Be offensive. *In Session: Psychotherapy in Practice, 2,* 47–57.

Rynearson, E. K., & McCreery, J. (1993). Bereavement after homicide: A synergism of trauma and loss. *American Journal of Psychiatry, 150,* 258–262.

Rynearson, E. K., & Sinnema, C. S. (in press). Supportive group therapy for bereavement after homicide. In: D. Blake & B. H. Young (Eds.), *Group treatment for post-traumatic stress disorders.*

Sahin, J. I. (1985). Affect tolerance: A model of affect-response using catastrophe theory. *Journal of Social and Biological Structures, 8,* 175–202.

Schafer, R. (1992). *Retelling a life. Narration and dialogue in psychoanalysis.* New York: Basic Books.

Schwarz, E. D., & Kowalski, J. M. (1991). Malignant memories: PTSD in children and adults after school shooting. *Journal of the American Academy of Child and Adolescent Psychiatry, 30,* 936–944.

Seifer, R. S., Sameroff, A. J., Baldwin, C. P., & Baldwin, A. (1992). Child and family factors that ameliorate risk between 4 and 13 years of age. *Journal of the American Academy of Child and Adolescent Psychiatry, 31,* 893–903.

Sheikh, A. A. (1983). *Imagery. Current theory, research, and application.* New York: Wiley.

Smith, E. M., North, C. S., McCool, R. E., & Shea, J. M. (1990). Acute postdisaster psychiatric disorders: Identification of persons at risk. *American Journal of Psychiatry, 147,* 202–206.

Stroebe, W., Stroebe, M. S., & Domittner, G. (1988). Individual and situational differences in recovery from bereavement: A risk group identified. *Journal of Social Issues, 44,* 143–158.

Vachon, M., Lyall, W., Rogers, J., Freedman-Letofski, K., & Freeman, S. (1980). A controlled study of self-help intervention for widows. *American Journal of Psychiatry, 137,* 1380–1384.

Van der Kolk, B. A., & Van der Hart, O. (1989). Pierre Janet and the breakdown of adaptation in psychological trauma. *American Journal of Psychiatry, 146,* 1530–1540.

Vargas, L. A., Loya, F., & Hodde-Vargas, J. (1989). Exploring the multidimensional aspects of grief reactions. *American Journal of Psychiatry, 146,* 1484–1488.

Vaughan, K., & Tarrier, N. (1992). The use of image habituation training with post traumatic stress disorders. *British Journal of Psychiatry, 161,* 658–663.

Wyman, P. A., Cowen, E. L., Work, W. S., Raoof, A., Gribble, P. A., Parker, G. R., & Wannon, M. (1992). Interviews with children who experienced major life stress: Family and child attributes that predict resilient outcomes. *Journal of the American Academy of Child and Adolescent Psychiatry, 31,* 904–910.

Chapter 8

The Treatment of PTSD Through Grief Work and Forgiveness

Lee Hyer and Jeffrey M. Brandsma

The processes of grieving in trauma treatment are understated, yet critical. Loss is a very common experience in life and a large component of all trauma. But most times, people do not show the deficits or scars that are internal. These scars represent the loss of or damage to the internal organization that enables people to experience life as human beings: their self-theory (Epstein, 1978). Often, loss is initially thought of in terms of the effects resulting from the death of a valued, internalized other. Yet, there are many other kinds of losses. But always self-theory damage (soul loss) is registered and needs to be addressed in trauma care (Moore, 1994).

It is our position that, with trauma, one suffers a self-loss, a wound to one's identity, and damage to other parts of one's self-theory. As noted, there may be real external losses as well. But it is the self that is wounded and the self that requires "therapy." The self is the intention-driven actor that complies with its natural tendencies to heal. Rorty (1976) maintains that the person always acts a center, a self, and translates dissonant or oppressive data for consistency.

In this chapter, we argue that traditional approaches to bereavement are too restrictive; a multifactorial approach is now necessary that will include issues of trauma and vulnerability of the self (Hagman, 1995). First, we define self-theory and set it in the context of trauma. Second, the "necessary" commingling of grief with other diagnostic states (posttraumatic stress disorder [PTSD] and depression) is explicated. We believe that these states are inherent components of the trauma experience. Grief necessarily accompanies trauma. As implied, a critical component in the treatment of trauma involves the issues of loss in the trauma re-experience. Third, we outline eight tenets for the understanding and treatment of PTSD with its grief components. This is highlighted by the hypothesis that people are best understood in the context of the stored memories that form their identity (as mentioned, a crucial aspect of self-theory). Treating trauma is insufficient; treating the person and his or her self-theory is required. Fourth, we present a model of the processes and steps involved in grief treatment. In written form, this model may seem simplistic and "canned," but it does possess sufficient abstraction, generality, and flexibility so that respect for the person of the victim can be maintained while providing a road map for treatment. We believe that information now points to treatment of trauma memory that directly involves grief. Finally, we argue that the person is potentially transformed in this experience when there is an optimum level of frustration allowing for at least some disintegration, restabilization, and growth. In this growth-healing, we posit that forgiveness processes are central for change. Forgiveness too is a complex process based on one's relationship with God, others, oneself, and one's culture. Once this process is initiated, however, people can become more than they were; they repair and redefine their self-theory and grow.

SELF

The self, in an important way, is a consistent, organized set of memories, largely autobiographical memories, that capture in narrative form the important aspects of a person and the rules (propositions and hypotheses) that hold these aspects together. These dictate how information is to be processed. It has a set of core memories that reference the person, ones that both organize how information flows and what is the conceptual base camp of the person. The self usually also has a summary self-concept. This is a more generalized and abstracted icon of total self theory. It follows that the self has a set of inferences and hypotheses at various levels of abstraction and importance. The set of cognitions that apply to the self are the conscious or preconscious building blocks (presumptions) of a central aspect of a person's theory of self. These are organized into what has been called core cognitions or schemas (Hyer, 1994).

Trauma devastates the self theory: It has a critical role in deforming the context that then usurps all setpoints; it affects the typical internal structures of the self most tellingly. It devastates the explicit memories that are self-defining, as these cannot accommodate to the degree of stress (van der Kolk & Fisler, 1995). What is critical here is that the self (core memories and rules) shapes the trauma response, the specific cognitions and affects. And always the problem is one of loss, self-loss. When symptoms occur, the self has not been able to assimilate or accommodate to the trauma. The art of remembrance of the trauma, then, is suffused with the ineffable process of self-pain, grief. For true healing, the path must go through this affect state. Grief has a special role, one that affects core memories and alters the rules of their integrity. This involves the therapies of trauma, ones that require a coherent autobiography of self. But in addition to providing meaning to the old and the new, therapy also requires a necessary dialogue within the body and soul, a dialogue with the loss.

The decade of the 1990s has seen a vibrant discussion on self-injury in trauma. Hyer (1994) noted the relationship between the necessary abuse criterion (of PTSD) and schemas of the self. Several authors (e.g., Herman, 1992; Tedeschi & Calhoun, 1995) also noted the inherent pain in the trauma process. The most poignant psychic pain is experienced when the person's self-theory has been found to be inadequate, unable to assimilate the overwhelming meaning shifts or disintegration(s) that occur in trauma. As implied earlier, each individual has a self-theory, an amalgam of implicit or explicit assumptions, postulates, corollaries, hypotheses, laws, and concepts implied or enacted in his or her cognitions, behaviors, and affect that organize in schemas to process experiences and initiate action. Some important schemas are body image, sources of esteem, the nature of the world, important other people (introjects), the assumption of predictability, self-efficacy boundaries, the summary self-concept, and a host of just world and safety concepts, among others. Trauma disrupts these: Key schemas of the self are disorganized, and new information becomes impossible to assimilate. One's self-system thus breaks down in midst of great psychic pain.

This might seem an obvious conclusion to many clinicians: A person in trauma must deal on a basic organizational level with the assumptions, postulates, and guiding hypotheses of her or his current self-theory (i.e., "who I am in the world"). The self-theory is the organization of the postulate systems for the syntax of the person and the nature of the world as well as the necessary interactions with it. It is tuned to balance the pleasure/pain dynamic, to maintain self-esteem, and to organize the data of experience (cf. Epstein, 1978). And, from our perspective, since this is the basic meaning and coherence generator in the person, the warning of pain in this area—the actual grief component of the trauma response—is most insistent and intense.

From an information-processing perspective, we (Bagge & Brandsma, 1994) have argued that when trauma occurs, information is not assimilated into one's historical memory; it is stuck in one's immediate memory. van der Kolk and Fisler (1995) recently noted that people with PTSD initially hold traumatic experiences as sensations or feeling states that are not immediately transcribed into the self, the personal narrative. It is this failure to encode information in symbolic form that constitutes the core of PTSD pathology. We believe that this is especially a problem with loss (a grief process), where time does not heal the victim's blocked grief. The appreciation of one's vulnerability, a new philosophy of self, or a new meaning is not achieved. If psychotherapy of PTSD means anything, it implies the integration of the fragments of the self, its cohesion in explicit memory.

In treatment, a minidevelopmental process of grief occurs, and the loss part of the traumatic experience is accessed. The trauma must eventually be integrated into the narrative of the person's life. Guided imagery can be used to revise and then revisit the trauma memory. This dialogue of grief allows for completion of unfinished business, the expression of affect and affection, forgiveness, and finally the good-bye. The last step of mourning involves opening up to a new future, the new remembered future, by allowing for a safe past (cf. Melges, 1982). As

Erikson (cited in Sherman, 1991) noted, there is no other task in the philosophy of life (especially in stress) than to remember the self. We elaborate subsequently.

PTSD AND GRIEF

Definition

Loss is a necessary element in the etiology of PTSD. As noted, we believe that the grief response is virtually universal in PTSD, sometimes fueled by clinical depression and sometimes not. We realize that in some sense we are creating a "straw man" argument; to some extent, the survivor's self-concept must be disrupted. Basic components of the self—trust, individuation, object relations, reality experience, fullness of experience, coping mechanisms, integrative capacity, and self-analytic functions (Lingiardi, Madeddu, Fossati, & Maffei, 1994)— are, by definition, affected by trauma. We underline this loss again (self-theory loss), but also the loss or disruption of one's autobiographical memory, issues core to self-definition and continuity. We address both now, as well as the role of depression.

The concept of grief has been applied to PTSD in one form or another since the inception of the construct (Cook & Dworkin, 1992; Villereal, 1991; Widdison & Salisbury, 1990; Worden, 1991). In fact, grief and its complications are universal in trauma (Garb, Bleich, & Lerer, 1987): The issue is "how much?" At the one extreme, grief may simply be a part of the disorder and "responsible" for subclinical pain and sadness, often experienced years after the trauma event. At the other, grief may be the primary explanatory variable in the acquisition of PTSD. In this latter sense, it is a universal reaction in trauma victims, especially those who were victims of personal loss. As a component of PTSD, Shay (1994) and Lifton (1992), for example, posit that rage is a key by-product (of grief); hence these authors outline the need for personal and communal grief rituals. It is no surprise that several models of PTSD have implicated grief (Hyer, 1994).

Many terms have been used to address the complications of grief in the bereavement process, especially as it relates to PTSD: delayed, abnormal, pathological, and complicated. States of grief and PTSD are descriptively and conceptually close, sharing many common features (cf. Bagge & Brandsma, 1994). "Traumatic grief" is the phrase used to straddle the two diagnostic domains of pathological grief and PTSD (van der Hart, Brown, & Turco, 1990). It represents the complicated side of loss in PTSD, a state reflective of the "biphasic symptom-swings from symptoms of arousal, intrusive traumatic imagery, and anxiety, to defensive numbing and avoidance" (van der Hart, 1990, p. 264). Just as meaning in the process of dying is enhanced by a self-struggle, so too trauma survivors must genuinely make inner contact with the pain of loss (grief) if growth is to occur (Hyer, 1994).

Whether grief should have a separate diagnosis in the *Diagnostic and Statistical Manual of Mental Disorders* (*DSM*) has also been debated (Marwit, 1991). If grief is a universal reaction to a loss, stressors are often outside the range of past editions of the *DSM* for a PTSD diagnosis (Horowitz, Bonanno, & Holen, 1993). Even though the *DSM-IV* has been more liberal with the stressor in the diagnosis of PTSD, a psychological space for grief is unclear. In fact, many other complications are present. Few empirical studies on grief reactions with PTSD victims exist (e.g., Villereal, 1991). When the grief reaction is more simple, individuals face problems soon into the reaction; those with more complicated reactions avoid and are delayed (Cook & Dworkin, 1992). This avoidance may be a part of PTSD since individuals who show traumatic or complicated grief also show many signs of PTSD. Regardless, available literature suggests that grief reactions are abnormal when they are delayed or intense (Worden, 1991).

The fact that grief lies behind many of the functional problems related to PTSD and is present in nonclinical trauma populations is more important than finding its "correct place" in the nosology. If the clinician considers the act of maintaining meaning in the face of disintegration of the person's basic schemas as part of the process of PTSD, then grief becomes a part of treatment. Ideally, the clinician can focus on the excessive intensity of any grief response (Worden, 1991).

Depression

The relationship between depression and grief is another way to view grief as a problem state. Research seems to show that these are interdependent but different terms. Depressive symptoms can occur in a grief reaction and result in clinical depression. Often, the clinical depression remits, leaving the grief reaction. Also, depression can be complicated by a grief reaction. Kim and Jacobs (1991) examined the relationship between complicated grief, depression, and anxiety disorders in 25 bereaved individuals. Significant relationships were found between complicated grief and the anxiety disorders. Relationships were not as pronounced in the more depressed group. The authors conclude that these disorders share some common features but are not "isomorphic." More recently, Prigerson et al. (1991) assessed widowed people and found that grief is indeed different from depression and anxiety. Symptoms such as preoccupation with the dead, denial, yearning, and searching correlate with grief but not depression.

Major differences exist in the significant symptoms of lowered self-esteem versus the poorer sense of self found in depression. Grieving people suffer from the pangs of loss of another person and are preoccupied with this. Also, in grief, there is often an open display of affect. The symptoms are up front and present, unlike depression. Also, grief tends to involved more than one episode with distinct features, sadness, pangs of loneliness, and transient depression features. Interestingly, grief shares features of other diagnoses as well, especially anxiety disorders (other than PTSD), substance abuse, and psychosomatic problems (Cook & Dworkin, 1992).

Data suggest that rogue emotions, especially depression and other PTSD affect, are not assimilated and act as free radicals roaming the thalamic region of the brain unabated until a place can be found in explicit memory (van der Kolk & Fisler, 1995). PTSD is most of all an anxiety disorder, and the inability to encode the memory is due to the experience of high anxiety (Foa & Kozak, 1986). Also, most chronic PTSD sufferers are depressed. Seven symptoms of PTSD, as defined by the *DSM* (Category C or D), are directly related to depression (Joseph, Williams, & Yule, 1995). Among others, McCranie and Hyer (in press) have shown that combat veterans with PTSD have high scores on the self-criticism factor of the Depressive Experiences Scale, indicating a form of introjective depression (guilt based) independent of clinical depression. This self-criticism appears to be pervasive among PTSD sufferers, an existential dispiritedness that transcends and is different from clinical depression. From another perspective, Foa, Molnar, and Cashman (1995) have shown that clinical depression asserts a differential influence on the treatment of trauma response.

Perhaps what clinicians are seeing, then, is that the person's self-theory is being altered, and the prepotent emotion is a function of the meaning of the trauma event. In this way, the grief and depression of PTSD are modal and affect information processing. Depression does this in general, leading to a hypersensitive focus on self and to an overall negative or general recollection of memories. Depression predisposes the person to respond in a determined way to emotional states (state dependence), to bias cognitions, to develop avoidant coping strategies, and to eventually become numb. Depression can also form in comorbid affective states (Boudewyns, Woods, Hyer, & Albrecht, 1990). If it does not, residual depression states are visible, often affecting traumatic grief. This altered information processing, we believe, constitutes an important deficiency and provides for maintenance of the traumatic grief response.

Which emotion becomes prepotent (anxiety or depression, or others) is variable and dependent on the person's self-theory as well as the event. Whichever one is present, however, depression accompanies it, and the self is involved. We believe, then, that "PTSD depression" is present and is most related to grief. Most emotions disrupt the internal stability of the person, but the depressive features require "grief healing." This grief is based on damage to the self-theory of the person. In regard to the influence of depression in the treatment of trauma, Siegel (1995) notes:

> The working-through process is the overall therapeutic growth in which an initial trauma is recalled, abreacted, processed, and incorporated to the ongoing mental models and narrative of the patient's life. The working-through process invariably involves grieving as the advent of new knowledge destroys an often idealized sense of a significant other or of the self. Depression also commonly accompanies this grief. (p. 118)

GROWTH IN GRIEF

We believe that among the core issues of PTSD treatment are the transformational processes found in grieving. Grief is the motivational pain that is both specific

("I lost this") and human ("I survived and must find meaning here"). Several principles underline the importance of this relationship and its potential for healing. Some of these principles apply to the victim, and some apply to the therapy process. These tenets set the stage for and provide the basis for the grief process in trauma treatment.

Tenet 1

People often do not merely cope with trauma, they can be transformed in their struggle with it: As a result of assimilating trauma, individuals extend developmentally where they would not have been had the trauma not occurred. Positive reactions to trauma have been noted in the research literature (Hamera & Shontz 1987; Lehman et al., 1993; Lopata, 1973; Malinak et al., 1979). Affleck, Tennen, and Gershman (1985) noted that, after trauma integration, most people improve their perspective on life. Tedeschi and Calhoun (1995), more than others, noted that an important sense of self-reliance is learned through the struggle: Surviving trauma leads not only to an enhanced sense of one's vulnerability but to sensitivity and emotional strength as well. In another study, this group (Calhoun & Tedeschi, 1989–1990) found that 83% of a bereavement group realized that they could depend on their family and could better express emotions: Their interpersonal experiences were enhanced. Another result is that people who suffer from trauma are more likely later to be supportive of others (Tedeschi, 1989).

It is our belief that a kind of phylogenetic principle applies here: A transmutation of information occurs, moving from a dysfunctional to a functional form, from diffuse to specific, and from negative to positive. This can occur because the vulnerability of the grief reaction in trauma is unlocked over time. A self-healing of the person unfolds as the state-specific material of the obvious or subtle grief components is integrated into the core narrative of the person. Eventually, the person is actually better for this experience.

Tenet 2

Growth occurs only when schemas are challenged and changed by (traumatic) events. Tedeschi and Calhoun (1995) note that change is possible only because schemas are disrupted. If one manages the event well and does so with ease, little change in schemas occurs. But if one is rocked to the core, schemas are disrupted. Now the conditions appropriate for self-change are available and necessary.

We believe that one's theory of self provides a "platform" or perspective from which to view and initiate the information flow. Whatever the central metaphors of their living, people attempt to match the necessities of their personal needs with life's events in their own way. This is most notable when one ages. Here the recognition and reconstruction of the self in the course of life review is an inherently satisfying component. Life takes on a reauthoring process as the person attempts to separate self from specific problems. According to Epstein (1978), the dialectic important here is that one's self-theory is preserved, and the flow of information unfolds naturally.

Each person reconstructs memories, especially self-defining memories, to preserve identity (Singer & Salovey, 1993). As we have noted, usually a core of self-memories that are representative of the person become involved. It is these memories that provide the meaning and the consistency to self. One central part involves the drive toward sense making by the individual. Meaning implies that one has internal patterns to guide one's actions and behavior and to regulate emotions (Baumeister, 1991; Janoff-Bulman, 1989).

In the grief process of trauma, the person attempts to find meaning but is unable to complete the process as a result of self-loss. It is the job of the therapist to expose this process and to allow the affect to be assimilated. This can be accomplished only when core aspects of self (theory) are challenged. Frankl (cited in Sherman, 1991) noted that people find meaning in the suffering and struggle of their existence within the transitoriness and frailty of life. This occurs through self-pain, the survival-guilt pain of grief. Adversity introduces one to oneself.

Tenet 3

Memory is created in a present context and oriented by affect. This is a distinctly therapeutic tenet that is critical for an understanding of the change process. The emphasis here is on "now" experiencing and the process of meaning changing. Two personal experiences guarantee ongoing experiencing: affect and sensations. Singer and Salovey (1993) believe that affect is the phenomenon that provides the ordering for and association to multiple memories. Meaningful reprocessing of memories occurs in the present. When past and present commingle, the on-line expressions necessary for restructuring occur. The vehicle of change is most often affect (Safran & Greenberg, 1991).

In therapy, sensations also are accessed to cement the experiential component. Bacon noted that sensations do not lie, giving a "true snapshot" of the situation (cited in Guidano, 1991). For Shapiro (1995), sensations are the true governor of the change process. Brigham (1994) too notes that the real entrance to change is the body itself, when thinking stops.

This is not to eschew the past; to do so is costly (Hyer, 1994). It is only to endorse the fact that treatment gains are optimal when the past is alive in the present. Both past memories and present affect attract the therapist's interest when they are in conjunction (Fleming & Robinson, 1990). Survivors of traumatic grief benefit from talk and exposure to the past event in the "doing" of the present. Exposure may be accomplished in a gradual (Ganz et al., 1992), even nonsystematic way. According to Gendlin (1991), the change process never involves a (re)experiencing of anything. Rather, it entails the present experiencing of the past event; present tense processing is the curative component in the change process, not the past reintegration. Reorganization is a by-product.

Tenet 4

The narrative of one's life must be made coherent and understandable, encompassing the trauma experience. Over time, salient positive and negative events form one's memories. As noted earlier, core memories are organized and form one's autobiographocal self. Memories are summarizations of experiences; they are at the vestigial core of development. In effect, we are our selected memories. A "need" to organize the biographical self to maintain continuity of meaning is paramount for optimal functioning in our species.

From the perspective that we have been developing, information about the self is organized in stories (memories) dictated by the theory of the self. It is an attempt to capture who we are at a level of abstraction that allows for historical continuity. This organization is critical, because how one organizes information and scripts the story determines the adaptation process.

Importantly, trauma events must be taken in by their narrative. Strong negative events especially have difficulty becoming integrated into the self and require rescripting if change and assimilation are to occur. When one's self-theory becomes disorganized, the balancing processor of information is dyfunctional. Information does not move freely, and core experiences become damaged or frozen.

Rescripting is the treatment. We are arguing here that these negative events must be incorporated into the ongoing self in order to be completed and processed. Since they cannot be exorcised, they must be exercised. The person comes to know that she or he is greater than the pathology: The self is the director of and responsible for the change.

It is noteworthy that several personality patterns (the methods of operation of self-theory) reflect the potential for growth in the experience of stress. Most often, it is these features of the person that are given attribution for the change process. These include locus of control (Rotter, 1966), self-efficacy (Bandura, 1977), self-confidence (Schaefer & Moos, 1992), optimism (Scheier & Carver, 1985), hardiness (Kobasa, 1979), resilience (Beardslee & Podorefsky, 1986), sense of coherence (Antonovsky, 1987), creativity (Strickland, 1989), and intrapsychic strengths (Stuttman & Baruch, 1992). Similarly, people with rigid personality styles or personality disorders (Millon & Davis, 1995) have problems in the negotiation of trauma because of their limited, rigid, defensive organizations. Traits have an impact on the expression of grief (Lepore, Silver, & Wortman, 1995). "Person" components influence the stress response.

Tenet 5

There is a need for a degree of consistency and continuity in the theory of self. That is to say, there is a need to bind time, to have a connection of coherence with what happened then, what is happening now, and what will happen in the future. No superior new self is warranted; the person must be as she or he was, but with the incorporation of the new data. The aim is not a new rendering of the whole self-theory; it is to make the person aware again of postulate breakdowns, to bring back the past as it was, but alive and immediate and needing of attention for present and future. Price (1994) noted that the person moves on to the next "viable you," not a superior self.

The simple point here is that change occurs with genuine inner contact. This leads to evolutionary change, a sense of acceptance and renewal, not revolutionary re-creation. This is the consistency side of the change balance. The self is remarkably consistent, even in its own distortions. In reminiscence, the "earlier person" is made vivid to the self. As this occurs, the self becomes more coherent, consistent, and intelligent. The "binding of our days together," of past and present, is the magic of living that forms our identity. It starts in childhood, has new intensity in adolescence, and builds across the life span but is one's personal identity always (McAdams, 1993). The natural iterative process of fine-tuning past and present is ever unfolding.

Tenet 6

The person has to confront older schemas and grieve parts of self and certain experiences to grow. Organisms that ignore their own natural feedback do not adapt well. This involves giving up, for example, old assumptions of invulnerability and power and, sometimes, the harsh judgments of others. Also often required is the commitment to live life better and to be generative toward others. In the search of the examined life, the person becomes more what he or she intended to be (Jung, 1971). This is an unfreezing of the past, but not just nostalgia; it is a true generative process. If sufficiently close to the self-theory, the balance of pleasure/pain and esteem for oneself is incorporated. It is narrative truth, with acceptance for the only self that could have been at the time.

A self-narrative that denies truth to make events more pleasant or to "get by" runs counter to the possibility of change. One can "foreclose" in the Eriksonian sense, but this is a faulty compromise that allows for minimal satisfaction only. People must "come to terms" with their problems and feelings and accept life's events. This is why treating trauma is insufficient: Treating the person and his or her self-theory is required.

Tenet 7

Transformation occurs when the client's own interpretation of the good coming from negative events is respected. Again, this applies to the therapy protocol. Reflection and unconditional positive regard are only rarely overused. Then a gentle learning procedure, a dosed exposure that encourages change by facilitating choice and mastery over state-specific information, is always effacious.

Two issues are important here (Tedeschi & Calhoun, 1995): (a) being respectful of the individual's processes of coping and (b) letting the client do the work. In allowing clients to feel validated while listening to the narrative they create, respecting their pace and their self-protective ways, the therapist creates the holding environment for the healing work of therapy. Clients learn that fear does not kill and that anger does not have to be all-consuming. They unlearn maladaptive responses "naturally." Once old schemas and the inherent tensions are reexperi-enced, they become relieved, and new meanings emerge. Revised schemas gener-ate new behaviors and reactions.

In terms of the client doing the work, the trauma victim is requested to "just talk" from self. As the dialectic process with the inner self continues, presumably an old problem can create new meaning. Clients become witnesses to the rigid and chaotic musings of their inner dialogue. The therapist first helps by explicating the target memory and next commenting on the processing style.

Everyone has her or his own way to struggle with trauma. Some act out more than others; some immerse themselves in the emotions and struggles, others in more rational processes. Clearly, if the crisis is continuing or intense, the struggle will be more difficult and require a long period. A balance must be struck between passive acceptance of the problem, with denial/distortion of the event, and the problem solving that is required for change—between what must be and what can be.

The essence of the grief process in trauma is a transformation of fear/depres-sion into a new contact with self that allows for change. As the memory is changed, the person's self-theory is altered, and self-concept and self-efficacy are touched for the better (Shapiro, 1995).

Tenet 8

The treatment of trauma may never be complete; most often, the reason is grief related (i.e., the refusal to mourn and forgive). The life span of the grief reac-tion in the PTSD survivor appears to be set during the first few months, and the story becomes "bad start, bad finish" (Brandsma & Hyer, in press). Probably as a "result" of the early (mal)adjustment to trauma, the pathological types of compli-cated grief take form (Parkes & Weiss, 1983).

But something more important is implied. Marcel (cited in Sherman, 1991) noted that life is a mystery to be lived, not a problem to be solved. The grief in the trauma process is the "natural suffering" of life. It is a key aspect of life. It should not be removed fully—in fact, it cannot be. This is the reason that the narrative of one's life must be "understood" as one "becomes" and encompasses the wisdom of the processes that undergrid life.

Of course, people must come to terms with their problems and how they cope with daily events. This is only to say that life goes on and that practical issues must be attended to. Most therapists know that the amount of change that can occur in therapy is limited: "Real" change occurs in the life lived. It is probably folly to think of a person as an authentic self. Rather, people become realized selves in the sense that they are dealing with the realities of life and human nature itself. In response to self-damage, the person, it is hoped, comes to know that the only life that could have been lived was, in fact, lived. With trauma, this occurs in the feel and acceptance of the pain and the grief and the hard tasks of forgiveness. We elaborate in the following section.

TREATMENT MODEL

We expand here on the grief therapy model we have previously outlined (Brandsma & Hyer, in press). As we noted earlier, many grief therapies exist (e.g., Worden, 1982), sometimes outlined by the focus of the therapy, such as psycho-dynamic (e.g., Horowitz et al., 1984) or cognitive-behavioral (e.g., Fleming & Robinson, 1990); sometimes by components of the grief process (e.g., Melges, 1982); sometimes by stages (Parkes, 1985); and sometimes by tasks (e.g., Worden, 1982). When PTSD is chronic and unrelenting, however, these methods have only loose application clinically. After all, grieving in PTSD is "traumatic," resulting in an alteration of basic physiological responses (Hyer, 1994), as well as enduring dysfunction in basic character structure (self-theory) (Herman, 1992). In working with the chronic PTSD client, the healing of the human being may extend, we believe, beyond that required by the curing of the patient's symptoms.

Stages in Grief Work

Six identifiable stages in traumatic grief work were identified (Bagge & Brandsma, 1994). These stages overlap with the tenets just noted. We believe that this sequence encourages the therapist and client to respond to the grief aspects of trauma. The therapist can direct the therapy, and the client can sense the location/influence of the loss. Of course, in any "real" sense the process of the grief reaction is not stepwise and clear. It is muddled and nonlinear. Often, it falls short of acceptance.

Verbalization of the Loss   There is a stated recognition that a sense of loss was or is being experienced. Here the therapist's task is twofold: to get the "grief story" out and to create a healing atmosphere. Merleau-Ponty (1964) noted that "man expresses self to discover what he means to himself." The client articulates the trauma, and the therapist validates.

One form of validation is the universal sense that something deep in the soul was involved. In the pursuit of a narrative understanding, the therapist attunes to the client and makes the past vivid (validation). There is an increased saliency regarding the interiority of the person ("What happened inside?"), as well as a need to talk through important core self-issues. In addition, the therapist must create a healing atmosphere; he or she must listen and understand.

There is a critical element here. The grief side of loss requires expression. In the two classic motives for human striving, agency (striving for self-enhancement) and communion (need for contact with others), loss is inevitable. Direct queries into loss are helpful: What does this mean? Take away from you? Comparing you now to before the event, what do you notice? In some cases, even repressed subselves reflective of the loss may be exhumed so that a balance can be seen (e.g., the quiet self as contrasted to the active one).

At the risk of simplification regarding the trauma response, a chronic grief reaction is individually driven but tends to follow the two "classic" paths of PTSD: numbing and intrusion. That is, the person experiencing the grief tends to get stuck in a pain barrier, in the intensity of the experience (trying unsuccessfully to avoid it), or to severely suppress or inhibit the response, often becoming numb to feelings and given to acting out (Fleming & Robinson, 1990). These may be the "final common pathways" of the grief/trauma response; when the therapist accepts and truly validates the experience, however, information is forced to confess itself again, and an epiphany can unfold, often a reorganization of the core schema.

Psychoeducation of the Grief Process   The tasks of grief therapy are "taught." There are, of course, many informative pieces of data about grief, as well as many myths (Worden, 1982). The issues that are important (among others) involve experiencing the loss and identifying its components, its sequence, and predictable responses, among others. These are as important in the treatment of grief as they are in the treatment of any problem. Information titrates expectations and builds an appropriate compliance pattern in the service of realistic goals. Clients who are only vaguely aware of their problem have a more difficult course.

The therapist who truly believes that stories (memories) are habituations and that there are "epiphanies in the ordinary" can use this model and treat with confidence. The therapist who knows that memory exists only in present consciousness can be free to validate the pain and parse out its components. The therapist can make issues vivid that allow for an understanding of the grief process.

Tedeschi and Calhoun (1995) note too that the therapist can facilitate the psychoeducation process in several ways, including positive framings on the struggle, generic benefits accrued by the person in that context, a reengagement of hope, new perspectives on possible growth, and a selective reinforcement of competence, manageability, locus of control, and efficacy (i.e., those personality variables noted earlier). The therapist can also assist in integrating the problem into the larger life narrative.

Talking Through, Then Working Through, a Loss   This involves exposing the positive and negative aspects of loss, always guided by affect. The therapist's task is to foster any movement of information, to allow the story to unfold and to keep it moving. The therapist should keep statements simple, with affective involvement high, and thus allow the natural healing (integration) of the therapy. If the client remains stuck, the therapist's task is to keep data moving. The intent is to keep the client processing in present time to allow the natural healing processes of assimilation and accommodation.

As in most dynamic therapies, the therapist has one key rule: to keep information moving. This involves, it is hoped, a mix of expressive and instrumental tasks for the client. The therapist moves back and forth, being reflexive ("What does that say about you as a person?") and nonreflexive ("Stay with that"). Other tasks are to bring the focus into the present; to access other modalities, especially sensations, to allow for "genuine inner contact"; to appreciate the primacy of affect; to tag (label) emotions; to keep the client experiencing in the present ("Feel it now"); to support the toleration of unacceptable feelings ("It's okay"); to tighten poorly integrated concepts ("Tell me more about that"); and to loosen deviant cognitions ("When were you not that way?"). Eventually the therapist more actively facilitates change ("What prevents you from...?"). This leads to the next stage.

Guided Imagery   Resolution unfolds in imagination with an awareness of several blocks to the affective flow. The therapist's task again is to keep the information flowing and to tag problem areas.

Melges (1982) argues for the use of imagery in this process. He employed present-time guided imagery, which optimizes the imagery skills usually already present in these individuals. Melges advocates that imagery be used at two times in grief work, believing that in pathological bereavement feelings of loss and grief are components of the psychopathology of PTSD. The initial step is to identify the losses that the individual has experienced and the blocks that have become obstacles to resolution. A list of obstacles found frequently in grief work has been provided by Bagge and Brandsma (1994). For example, an individual who shows evidence of persistent yearning for the deceased may keep the clothing of the deceased in closets long after the loss. A key step is to help the individual remove the obstacles by revising scenes through the use of present tense imagery. This helps to reactivate the grieving process in a controlled manner.

In Table 8.1, it can be seen that guided imagery is the key to the entire grief process. Revision of the scene through talk or creation of new imagery is then planned with the client to allow opportunity for completion of unfinished business. It begins with a decision to regrieve the losses. Patients are asked to relive the scene(s) of the loss in their imagination as it happened at that time. The more traumatic and foreign the experience, the greater the difficulty with this stage. This reliving often helps to identify blocks to the grieving process (e.g., things not done or things done and regretted).

"Saying Good-bye"   This somewhat ritualized component can be a powerful closure to a traumatic memory. This is the logical extension of the previous stage. The person's blocks are negotiated to enable the saying of the needed "good-bye." In conjunction with the previous stage, one woman was unable to express a good-bye to her deceased son because of the presence at the funeral of her husband's former wife. In the revision, the scene could be reconstructed without the offending individual, thus facilitating the expression of unfinished business. This then is effected in a controlled environment by revisiting the scene and allowing opportunities for "dialogues with the dead." Affective exchanges (both love and anger), confrontation of conflicts, expressions of guilt, and finally (but

Table 8.1   Grief-Resolution Therapy

Techniques for removing obstacles	Process
1. Decision to regrieve	1. Decrease of defensive avoidance
2. Guided imagery Relive, revise, revisit scenes of the loss Last positive exchange News of the loss The viewing Funeral ceremony Burial	2. Controlled detachment
3. Future oriented Identity Reconstruction	3. Building new images and plans

empathically not of least importance) the giving and receiving of forgiveness are important elements. When carefully done, this allows for a controlled detachment from the deceased. These sessions are often intensely emotional, which supports Bowlby's (1980) contention that weeping and anger appear to be necessary components in helping the patient recognize and accept that the loss is final, the bond is broken.

Future Orientation   Imagery is used to help the individual construct a future in terms that recognize the finality of the loss and the need to continue in life. The therapist's task is to focus toward the future and to empower, give choice, and, if needed, reframe. Again, imagery is used. The therapist allows for a series of feasible steps in which the client creates a new future and then anchors it.

Withdrawing cathexes from the past allows the renewal of a present-future focus. Using guided imagery, the individual can look to the future (as well as to the past). This can be done shortly after completion of the guided imagery phase of grief-resolution therapy. The patient is asked to imagine that she or he is visiting a place once cherished by her- or himself and the deceased together, a place of safety and warmth (Melges, 1982, p. 207). Then the individual can look toward the future and, perhaps, look back on the present. This ability to distance (observing ego) is a good test of the efficacy of the grief work; it shows the new flexibility of the healed self-theory.

FORGIVENESS: THE SPECIAL INGREDIENT OF GRIEF THERAPY

Grief is a process that humans go through to mourn (process) their many possible losses. We believe that losses in traumatic grief are, for the most part, shame based. Shame and guilt are bookends that are often confused. Guilt refers to specific acts that one is sorry for, whereas "the experience of shame is directly about the self, which is the focus of evaluation" (Tangney, 1995). For example, if one were to list the losses related to guilt and shame with regard to combat, the guilt side of the equation would include such events as taking life, not saving friends, and illegal and immoral acts. The shame side of the equation is much longer and more insidious and pervasive. There is the loss of the ability to work and to behave appropriately and consistently, of the capacity to love, of the sense of a niche in humanity and community, of control, integration of self, potency, innocence, and vitality, all with their negative impact on the summary self-image (self-theory). These shame-based losses have an important impact on the theory of self because they are directed at the self, not at specific behaviors. Shame-based losses abuse the central valuations of the person, and they strike at the core of the person's belief system, the self-theory. In effect, the self-narrative is damaged, and the only way back is through self-healing.

Interestingly, more recent therapies for shame and guilt have involved cognitive (Kubany, 1994) or spiritual (Enright et al., 1992) interventions. For change to occur, forgiveness must play a crucial part. Forgiveness is central to all aspects of mental health. Forgiveness mainly deals with the insults and losses to one's theory of self. Mourning and forgiveness are intimately linked. They both represent processes that progress toward a more realistic acceptance of the self and world as it currently is.

In the last decade, forgiveness as a therapeutic concept has blossomed. Conceptual clarification has made great strides, and this has led to operational definitions and interventions useful both scientifically and clinically. There are now more than 70 books and even more articles published on this subject. A brief historical and philosophical analysis of this term has been presented by Enright et al. (1992) and provides an excellent conceptual foundation for interpersonal forgiveness. For our purposes, forgiveness is defined as overcoming negative thoughts, feelings, and behaviors not by some form of denying the offense or the right to be hurt or angry but by viewing the offender at least with acceptance so that the forgiver can be healed. At a simple level, it is the realization that one does not condone the transgressed act or absolve responsibility, but it releases resentment. It is a change in perception, a recognition that the situation is emotionally over. Forgiveness, then, is not forgetting. At a deeper level, it is an act of self-interest and self-love. When one forgives, one must own the pain that was experienced in the situation. Once it is owned, the pain of the past looks to the future.

Once again, we refer to our tenets: To begin the process of forgiveness, the client must be stabilized enough to feel that she or he is safe and in a relationship with a therapist that will be as supportive as necessary. The client must know that the therapist understands his or her predicament. As therapy proceeds, however, forgiveness depends on several higher level cognitive processes. Many of these are listed in Table 8.2.

Table 8.2   Ego Skills Necessary for Forgiveness

1. Ability to empathize and give up one's egocentric position; this involves a discovery of likeness or similarity and respect for the personhood of the other individual
2. Appreciation for the self and growth of the self-theory apart from the other person in a relationship
3. A differentiated theory of motives
4. Ability to discriminate boundaries between parties
5. Understanding of vulnerabilities in all parties
6. Ability to tolerate and clarify emotional contradictions (i.e., ambivalence, confusion, logical contradiction)
7. Acceptance of limitations in self and others

The growth of these ego skills requires a relationship, insight, and time for effective working through. Particularly mentioned is the operation of empathy and altruism as processes that underlie forgiveness. These are often hard to attain with trauma victims until a conceptual shift is experienced, from competition to cooperation and, eventually, compassion. This is a true reformulation of one's valuations.

One word of caution is necessary. Most psychotherapy outcomes covary inversely with chronicity in PTSD. Many clients with chronic PTSD will not benefit equally even with the practice of our musings. Over time, many simply do not have the "object relations abilities" to struggle with these issues; that is, they do not possess sufficient cognitive complexity, a flexible capacity for emotional investment and detachment, understanding of social causality, or affect tone in relationships (Ford, 1995). For these clients, simply fostering stable psychosocial adjustment may be preferable.

From the therapist side of the equation, McCullough and Worthington (1994) propose five elements that must be provided by the therapist: (a) unconditional positive regard to explore feelings, (b) refocusing attention away from negative emotions by reframing or viewing from a larger context or different perspective, (c) enabling empathy for the offender, (d) discussing reconciliation if possible, and (e) focusing attention on forgiveness of the self. These elements underlie the key therapeutic interventions with regard to forgiveness.

Most therapists trained in secular institutions do not think in terms of forgiveness or understand its various possibilities in technique. Thus, clinical questions abound, the primary one being how explicitly a therapist should encourage forgiveness and, if so, in what forms and at what points in time. There are now available psychoeducational, time-limited programs for teaching people the processes of forgiveness that address these issues by plowing through them. But there are many pitfalls and pseudo-forms of forgiveness interacting with personality diagnosis and level of moral development that limit effectiveness (Brandsma, in press; Hebl & Enright, 1993).

We propose that an engagement with the issues of forgiveness in some explicit form is very useful in the resolution of traumatic grief and PTSD. It is often the missing piece in the therapeutic puzzle that prevents movement toward a new gestalt or schema. While the processes of therapy surrounding forgiveness have been clarified greatly in recent years, especially where it involves other people, it is forgiveness of self that remains a more difficult conceptual conundrum. This is the ultimate act of humanity, perhaps what makes a person a person. It is often a silent personal war within a war; it is the essence of the human struggle. It involves a high degree of ego splitting and skill. It is the compassion for self, a friendly view of self. And it is the part of the PTSD response that applies to grief.

CONCLUSION

By way of recapitulation, a better understanding of the treatment of PTSD results by looking at grieving processes. PTSD and grief cohabitate, often in the form of the depressive components of PTSD. In fact, these are independent "symptoms." We argue that issues of loss necessarily influence the formation of PTSD. We have provided eight tenets that reflect the PTSD grief process and its treatment. Central to this understanding is that the person of the trauma victim is affected and, as such, is influenced by and influences the loss response, the grief reaction in PTSD. In addition, we have outlined a treatment model useful in the therapist's response to grief in the context of PTSD. We have ended with forgiveness, usually an ongoing task in one's life, as a necessary component in the care of grief in PTSD.

At a basic level, the inability to accommodate to trauma is due to the severity of the event and the internal resources of the person at the time of the trauma. After all, the traumatic memory is only a descriptive phrase for events that are experienced under high levels of arousal. In the past decade, we have come to know that treating trauma memories alone is insufficient. The trauma must be integrated into the person(ality). The existence of loss in this reaction is no less important than any PTSD symptom. To turn a phrase, the "care of the PTSD soul" demands this hearing (in treatment). To do less compromises the treatment of PTSD and certainly is not the treatment of traumatic grief.

REFERENCES

Affleck, G., Tennen, H., & Gershman, K. (1985). Cognitive adaptations to high-risk infants: The search for mastery, meaning, and protection from future harm. *American Journal of Mental Deficiency, 89*, 653–656.

Antonovsky, A. (1987). *Unraveling the mystery of health: How people manage stress and stay well.* San Francisco: Jossey-Bass.

Bagge, R., & Brandsma, J. (1994). Traumatic grief counseling. In L. Hyer (Ed.), *Trauma victim: Theoretical issues and practical suggestions.* Muncie, IN: Accelerated Press.

Bandura, A. (1977). Self-efficacy: Toward a unifying theory of behavioral change. *Psychological Review, 84*, 191–215.

Baumeister, R. F. (1991). *Meanings of life.* New York: Guilford Press.

Beardslee, W. R., & Podorefsky, D. (1986). Resilient adolescents whose parents have serious affective and other psychiatric disorders: Importance of self-understanding and relationships. *American Journal of Psychiatry, 145*, 63–69.

Boudewyns, P., Woods, M., Hyer, L., & Albrecht, W. (1990). Chronic combat-related PTSD and concurrent substance abuse: Implications for treatment of this frequent "dual diagnosis." *Journal of Traumatic Stress, 4*, 549–560.

Bowlby, J. (1980). *Attachment and loss: Vol. 3, Loss.* New York: Basic Books.

Brandsma, J. M. (in press). Forgiveness. In D. G. Benner & P. C. Hill (Eds.), *Baker's encyclopedia of psychology* (2nd ed.). Grand Rapids, IA: Baker Book House.

Brandsma, J., & Hyer, L. (in press). Resolution of traumatic grief. *NCS Newsletter.*

Brigham, D. (1994). *Imagery for getting well: Clinical applications for behavioral medicine.* New York: Norton.

Calhoun, L. G., & Tedeschi, R. G. (1989–1990). Positive aspects of critical life problems: Recollections of grief. *Omega, 20*, 265–272.

Casarjian, R. (1992). *Forgiveness.* New York: Bantam.

Cook, A., & Dworkin, D. (1992). *Helping the bereaved: Therapeutic interventions for children, adolescents and adults.* New York: Basic Books.

Enright, R. E., Eastin, D. L., Golden, S., Sarinopoulos, S., & Freedman, S. (1992). Interpersonal forgiveness within the helping professions: An attempt to resolve differences of opinion. *Counseling and Values, 36*, 84–103.

Epstein, S. (1978). The self-concept revised or a theory of a theory. *American Psychologist, 404–409.*

Fleming, S., & Robinson, P. (1990). The application of cognitive therapy to the bereaved. In T. Vallis (Ed.), *The challenge of cognitive therapy: Application to nontraditional populations* (pp. 135–157). New York: Plenum.

Foa, E. B., & Kozak, M. J. (1986). Emotional processing of fear: Exposure to corrective information. *Psychological Bulletin, 99*, 20–35.

Foa, E. B., Molnar, C., & Cashman, L. (1995). Change in rape narratives during exposure therapy for posttraumatic stress disorder. *Journal of Traumatic Stress, 8*, 675–690.

Ford, J. (1995, November). *Object relations and PTSD treatment outcomes.* Paper presented at the ISTSS conference, Boston, MA.

Ganz, F., Gallagher-Thomson, D., & Rodman, J. (1992). Inhibited grief. In A. Freeman & F. Datillio (Eds.), *Comprehensive textbook of cognitive therapy* (pp. 201–209). New York: Plenum.

Garb, R., Bleich, A., & Lerer, B. (1987). Bereavement in combat. *Psychiatric Clinics of North America, 10*.

Gendlin, E. (1991). On emotion in therapy. In J. D. Safran & L. S. Greenberg (Eds.), *Emotion, psychotherapy, and change* (pp. 255–279). New York: Guilford Press.

Guidano, V. F. (1991). Affective change events in a cognitive system approach. In J. D. Safran & L. S. Greenberg (Eds.), *Emotion, psychotherapy, and change* (pp. 50–79). New York: Guilford Press.

Hagman, G. (1995). Bereavement and neurosis. *Journal of the Academy of Psychoanalysis, 23*, 635–653.

Hamera, E. K., & Shontz, F. C. (1987). Perceived positive and negative effects of life-threatening illness. *Journal of Psychosomatic Medicine, 22*, 419–424.

Hebl, J. H., & Enright, R. D. (1993). Forgiveness as a psychotherapeutic goal with elderly females. *Psychotherapy, 30*, 658–667. Herman, 1992 in B & H.

Horowitz, M., Marmar, C., Krupnick, J., Wilner, N., Kaltreider, N., & Wallerstein, R. (1984). *Personality styles and brief psychotherapy.* New York: Basic Books.

Horowitz, M., Stinson, C., & Fridhandler, B. (1993). Pathological grief: An intensive case study. *Psychiatry Interpersonal and Biological Processes, 56*, 356–374.

Horowitz, R., Bonanno, G., & Holen, A. (1993). Pathological grief: Diagnosis and explanation. *Psychosomatic Medicine, 55*, 260–273.

Houck, P., George, C., & Kupfer, D. (1995). Complicated grief and bereavement-related depression as distinct disorders: Preliminary empirical validation in elderly bereaved spouses. *American Journal of Psychiatry, 152*, 22–30.

Hyer, L. (Ed.). (1994). *Trauma victim: Theoretical considerations and practical suggestions.* Munice, IN: Accelerated Press.

Janoff-Bulman, R. (1989). Assumptive worlds and the stress of traumatic events: Application of the schema construct. *Social Cognition, 7*, 113–136.

Joseph, S., Williams, R., & Yule, W. (1995). Psychosocial perspectives on post-traumatic stress disorder. *Clinical Psychology Review, 15*, 515–544.

Jung, C. G. (1971). The stages of life. In *The portable Jung.* New York: Viking Press.

Kim, K., & Jacobs, S. (1991). Pathological grief and its relationship to other psychiatric disorders. *Effective Disorders, 21*, 257–263.

Kobasa, S. C (1979). Stressful life events, personality, and health: An inquiry into hardiness. *Journal of Personality and Social Psychology, 37*, 1–11.

Kubany, E. (1994). A cognitive model of guilt typology in combat-related PTSD. *Journal of Traumatic Stress, 7*, 3–19.

Lehman, D. R., Davis, C. G., Delongis, A., Wortman, C., Bluck, S., Mandel, D. R., & Ellard, J. H. (1993). Positive and negative life changes following bereavement and their relations to adjustment. *Journal of Social and Clinical Psychology, 12*, 90–112.

Lepore, S., Silver, R., & Wortman, C. (1996). Social constraints, intrusive thoughts, and depressive symptoms among bereaved mothers. *Journal of Personality and Social Psychology, 70*, 271–282.

Lifton, R. (1992). *Home from the Vietnam war: Learning from Vietnam veterans.* Boston: Beacon Press.

Lingiardi, V., Madeddu, F., Fossati, A., & Maffei, C. (1994). Reliability and validity of the Personality Functioning Scale (PFS). *Journal of Personality Disorders, 8*, 111–120.

Lopata, H. Z. (1973). Self-identity in marriage and widowhood. *Sociological Quarterly, 14*, 407–418.

Malinak, D. P., Hoyt, M. F., & Patterson, V. (1979). Adults' reactions to the death of a parent. *American Journal of Psychiatry, 136*, 1152–1156.

Marwit, S. (1991). DSM-III grief reactions and a call for revisions. *Professional Psychology and Research, 22*, 75–79.

McAdams, D. P. (1993). *The stories we live by: Personal myths and the making of the self.* New York: Morrow.

McCranie, E. W., & Hyer, L. A. (in press). Self-critical depressive experience in posttraumatic stress disorder. *Psychological Reports.*

McCullough, M. E., & Worthington, E. L. (1994). Encouraging clients to forgive people who have hurt them: Review, critique, and research perspective. *Journal of Psychology and Theology, 22*, 3–20.

Melges, F. T. (1982). *Time and the inner future: A temporal approach to psychiatric disorders.* New York: Wiley.

Merleau-Ponty, M. (1964). *The primacy of perception.* Evanston, IL: Northwestern University Press.

Millon, T., & Davis, R. (1995). *Disorders and personality: DSM-IV and beyond.* New York: Wiley.

Moore, T. (1994). *Soul mates: Honoring the mysteries of love and relationship.* New York: Harper Perennial.

Parkes, C. M. (1985). *Recovery from bereavement.* New York: Basic Books.

Parkes, C. M., & Weiss, R. S. (1983). *Recovery from bereavement.* New York: Basic Books.

Price, R. (1994). *A whole new life.* New York: Atheneum.

Prigerson, H., Frank, E., Kasl, S., Reynolds, C., Anderson, B., Zubenko, G., & Sherman, E. (1991). *Reminiscence and the self in old age.* New York: Springer.

Rorty, A. Q. (1976). A literary postscript: Characters, persons, selves, individuals. In *The identity of persons.* Berkeley: University of California Press.

Rotter, J. B. (1966). Generalized expectancies for internal versus external control of reinforcement. *Psychological Monographs, 80*, 1–28.

Safran & Greenberg, L. S. (1991). *Emotion, psychotherapy, and change.* New York: Guilford Press.

Schaefer, J. A., & Moos, R. H. (1992). Life crises and personal growth. In B. N. Carpenter (Ed.), *Personal coping: Theory, research, and application* (pp. 149–170). Westport, CT: Praeger.

Scheier, M. F., & Carver, C. S. (1985). Optimism, coping, and health: Assessment and implications of generalized outcome expectancies. *Health Psychology, 4,* 219–247.

Shapiro, F. (1995). *Eye movement desensitization and reprocessing: Basic principles, protocols and procedure.* New York: Guilford Press.

Shay, J. (1994). *Achilles in Vietnam: Combat trauma and the undoing of character.* New York: Atheneum.

Siegel, D. J. (1995). Memory, trauma, and psychotherapy. *Journal of Psychotherapy: Practice and Research, 4,* 93–122.

Singer, J. A., & Salovey, P. (1993). *The remembered self: Emotion and memory in personality.* New York: Free Press.

Strickland, B. R. (1989). Internal-external control expectancies: From contingency to creativity. *American Psychologist, 44,* 1–12.

Stutman, S., & Baruch, R. (1992). A model for the process of fostering resilience. In H. Tomes (Chair), *The process of fostering resilience: Roles for psychologists and media.* Symposium conducted at the annual meeting of the American Psychological Association, Washington, DC.

Tangney, J. P. (1995). Recent advances in the empirical study of shame and guilt. *American Behavioral Scientist, 38,* 1132–1145.

Tedeschi, R. G., & Calhoun, L. G. (1995). *Trauma and transformation growing in the aftermath of suffering.* Thousand Oaks, CA: Sage.

van der Hart, O., Brown, P., & Turco, R. N. (1990). Hypnotherapy for traumatic grief: Janetian and modern approaches integrated. *American Journal of Clinical Hypnosis, 32,* 263–271.

van der Kolk, B. A., & Fisler, R. (1995). Dissociation and the fragmentary nature of traumatic memories: Overview and exploratory study. *Journal of Traumatic Stress, 8,* 505–525.

Villereal, G. (1991). *An application of the Veterans Diagnostic Scale as a rapid assessment instrument.* Unpublished doctoral dissertation, University of Pittsburgh.

Widdison, H., & Salisbury, H. (1990). The delayed stress syndrome: A pathological grief reaction? *Omega, 20,* 293–305.

Worden, J. W. (1991). *Grief counseling and grief therapy: A handbook for the mental health practitioner.* New York: Springer.

Chapter 9

Relieving the Naumatic Aspects of Death with Naumatic Incident Resolution and EMDR

Teresa Descilo

SIGNIFICANCE OF THE STRESSOR TO THE CHILD/ADULT SYSTEM

In Uganda, when someone loses a loved one, each person who knows the surviving family member spends time with her or him, letting the person recount her or his experience and what she or he is feeling (J. Nambi, personal communication, 1995). The visitor then recounts his or her experience with death. In their cultural wisdom, Ugandans understand that everyone is affected by a death, that normalizing and social supports prevent posttraumatic stress, and that telling one's story over and over again brings relief. I would wager that their cultural practice prevents posttraumatic symptoms from developing from the loss of a loved one, no matter what the circumstances were surrounding the death.

James (1994), in her book regarding children and attachment trauma, offers the following definition: "Trauma occurs when an actual or perceived threat of danger overwhelms a person's usual coping ability." This definition can be expanded: Trauma occurs when an actual or perceived threat of danger *or loss* overwhelms a person's usual coping ability. While James was defining trauma for children, the definition seems to describe what we all experience. This definition serves to explain how death could produce posttraumatic stress.

In our Western culture, where we tend to view death as an option, we are ill prepared to deal with the reality of a death, no matter what the circumstances. Because of our general lack of acknowledgment and discussion about death within our families, when it occurs, our usual coping mechanisms tend to be overwhelmed.

For those of us who do not have the cultural practice of recounting our loss to many willing listeners, seeking a professional who will help us relieve and integrate our loss becomes the solution. To this end, two approaches, which are person centered and have proven efficacy in relieving trauma (Figley, 1996), are offered here as part of our "cultural practice."

INTERVENTIONS FOR BEREAVEMENT

It is evident from the literature that bereavement will create symptoms that would be classified as traumatic stress symptoms. These include any of the *Diagnostic and Statistical Manual of Mental Disorders* (4th edition; *DSM-IV*) descriptors of posttraumatic stress disorder. For anyone who has experienced the death of a loved one, distress at reminders of the loved one, sleeplessness, having no energy for normal activities, feeling detached from others, and lack of concentration are all familiar feelings. While these are also descriptive of normal grief reactions, any symptoms that become long-term or debilitating require intervention. Long-term or debilitating mourning is also referred to as morbid grief or complicated bereavement. Potocky (1993) described morbid grief as "characterized by high distress and high symptom levels that are present four months after a death and may persist for a year or longer."

Those who are prone to developing morbid grief have one or more of the following characteristics:

> (1) a low level of social support during the crisis; (2) a moderate level of social support coupled with particularly traumatic circumstances of the death; (3) a highly ambivalent relationship with the spouse; and (4) the presence of a concurrent life crisis at the time of the death. In addition, coping with sudden loss should be seen as a special high-risk group. (Potocky, 1993)

Most of the interventions described in the literature reviewed were group interventions. Potocky's (1993) analysis of nine experimental studies of bereavement interventions were all therapeutic group interventions. Her article revealed "that grief intervention is effective in preventing or reducing symptoms of morbid grief among spouses who are at high risk or in high distress."

Rando (1995) defines complicated mourning as a state in which normal grief steps, which require recognizing the loss, processing it, and essentially moving on with life, are compromised, distorted, or not completed, resulting in debilitating psychological, behavioral, social, or physical symptoms.

In the book *Living With Grief After Sudden Loss*, most of the interventions offered could be used in conjunction with traumatic incident resolution (TIR) and eye movement desensitization and reprocessing (EMDR). For example, Rando (1996) summarized a number of steps that a caregiver attempts to achieve with someone following a traumatic death. The first step is as follows: "Bring into consciousness the traumatic experience; repeatedly reviewing, reconstructing, re-experiencing, and abreacting the experience until it is robbed of its potency" (p. 157). This is essentially a description of TIR, the family treatment approaches described by Figley could also incorporate either EMDR or TIR at various stages for family members who require them. Cable (1996) adapts the critical incident stress debriefing model to traumatic loss. A family or individual would benefit from completing the seven steps described in her article. Once these steps are completed, TIR or EMDR would be appropriate to obtain a deeper level of resolution.

THEORETICAL PERSPECTIVE: TRAUMATIC INCIDENT RESOLUTION

Moore (1993) describes TIR as "a guided cognitive imagery procedure [that is] a high-precision refinement of earlier cognitive desensitization procedures." According to Coughlin (1995):

> TIR is a unique procedure in comparison to traditional cognitive and behavioral therapies. Unlike traditional therapies, TIR bypasses clinician-centered directive and didactic ideas to the client in favor of working directly with the client's knowledge, perspective, and internal awareness. The clinician facilitates the processing of the client-identified issues (traumatic incidents and/or emotional or somatic symptoms) and does not interpret the material.

Gerbode's (1989) theory as to why TIR brings relief from traumatic events is explained by a definition of time as a series of subjective events set into motion by an individual forming an intention to do something. If the individual completes the intended event, that cycle of time is finished. However, if an event is not completed, it continues on into the present, holding a greater or lesser degree of the person's attention, whether or not the person is consciously aware that his or her attention is so occupied. In the case of trauma, the common experience of most of humankind is to repress the content of the event in whole or in part. The result of this repression is that the traumatic event is never given the opportunity to complete itself. To further compound the effects of the traumatic event, it is common for an individual to form a decision at the time of the event, similar to what is referred to as an "irrational belief" in cognitive-behavioral therapy. This decision carries forward in time as an incomplete cycle that an individual may or may not be aware of. On both counts, a traumatic event continues into the present, involving all or many of the symptoms of the original event.

Valentine (1995) offers a different view of TIR theory. She reports that TIR has its roots in cognitive theory:

> Since trauma is experienced forcefully and impairs the defense mechanisms (Everstine & Everstine, 1993), old constructs are shattered (Janoff-Bulman, 1992), and one begins operating from hastily made constructs formed during or immediately after the traumatic incident. Insight "is a luxury that the mind cannot afford when locked in a struggle for survival" (Everstine & Everstine, 1993, p. 18). Cognitive distortions follow. TIR presents clients with the opportunity to correct those distortions. Clients retell their story, relive the event in a safe, controlled environment, reexamine the conclusions that were drawn from the experience(s), and come to a different understanding of the event (Valentine, 1994).

In her dissertation, Coughlin (1995) describes how TIR "builds on the psychoanalytic, behavioral, and cognitive theories and techniques that precede it in the field of psychotherapy."

EYE MOVEMENT DESENSITIZATION AND REPROCESSING

EMDR is a controversial yet undeniably effective method for relieving trauma and stressful life issues. Part of the controversy regarding the approach lies in the fact that no one knows exactly why it works. Shapiro (1995) offers the following explanations:

> When someone experiences a severe psychological trauma, it appears that an imbalance may occur in the nervous system, caused perhaps by changes in neurotransmitters, adrenaline, and so forth. Due to the imbalance, the system is unable to function and the information acquired at the time of the event, including images, sounds, affect, and the physical sensations, is maintained neurologically in its disturbing state. Therefore, the original material, which is held in this distressing, excitatory state-specific form, continues to be triggered by a variety of internal and external stimuli and is expressed in the form of nightmares, flashbacks, and intrusive thoughts—the so-called positive symptoms of PTSD.

> The hypothesis is that the eye movements (or alternative stimuli) used in EMDR trigger a physiological mechanism that activates the information-processing system. Various mechanisms by which this activation and facilitation of processing occurs have been proposed, including the following:

> 1 Activation and facilitation of information processing due to the client's dual focus of attention as he simultaneously attends to the present stimuli and the past trauma
> 2 A differential effect of neuronal bursts caused by the various stimuli, which may serve as the equivalent of a low-voltage current and directly affect synaptic potential (Barrionuevo, Schottler, & Lynch, 1980; Larson & Lynch, 1989)
> 3 Deconditioning caused by a relaxation response (Shapiro, 1989a, 1989b; Wilson et al., 1995) (p. 30).

Another explanation for EMDR's effectiveness can be found in Weil's (1995) book, *Spontaneous Healing*. Weil, in stressing the importance of walking, wrote the following:

> When you walk, the movement of your limbs is cross-patterned: the right leg and the left arm move forward at the same time, then the left leg and the right arm. This type of movement generates electrical activity in the brain that has a harmonizing influence on the whole central nervous system—a special benefit of walking that you do not necessarily get from other kinds of exercise. Dr. Fulford, the old osteopath who first taught me the basic principles of healing, believed that cross-patterned movement was necessary for normal development and optimal functioning of the nervous system. When babies first start to crawl, this movement stimulates further brain development. I often heard Dr. Fulford instruct adult patients to crawl as a way of speeding recovery from injuries. "Go back to that simple movement, and you will help the nervous system move beyond any blocks," he would say (1995, pp. 188–190).

ription of the Intervention Approaches

ascribed best by comparing it with watching a movie. The clinician
nt to repeatedly review a traumatic or distressing event, asking him
d to the beginning of an incident, view the incident until the end,
what he or she saw, heard, felt, and thought while reviewing it.
`watching a movie a second, third, or fourth time, when a client
..peatedly views an event, different aspects emerge. It seems that repetition of
a technique is used to achieve a deeper level of resolution. This is possible because repetition of a concept or trauma reactivates the material connected to it.
This reactivation creates what is described under the concept of state-dependent
learning, wherein a person must be in a similar state to the time he or she learned
or experienced something in order to be able to recall it (Goodwin, Well, Brewer,
Hoine, & Stern, 1969). Repeating an emotionally uncomfortable concept or traumatic event serves to trigger the event or the material connected to the concept,
which is stored in state-dependent form. Through repeating material that is in a
client's conscious awareness, the preconscious material will begin to surface, and
as the repetition is continued, the client will become aware of what was previously
unconscious material.

EMDR has been described by Shapiro (1995) as an eight phase process, as
follows:

1 Client history and treatment planning.

2 Preparation, which includes establishing a therapeutic alliance, ensuring
that the client can successfully do a relaxation tape or exercise, and explaining
EMDR to the client, the procedures involved, and what is expected of the client.

3 Assessment, entailing determining the issue to address in a session,
choosing an image that represents the issue, identifying negative and positive cognitions, establishing the validity of the positive cognition, identifying the emotion
connected with the negative cognition and the image and level of disturbance, and
finding where the disturbance is felt in the body.

4 Desensitization, wherein the client processes the representing picture,
emotion, and physical disturbance.

5 Installation, in which the positive cognition is revised (if the client so
decides), installed, and strengthened.

6 Body scan, wherein the client is asked to think of both the original picture and the positive cognition and to scan her or his entire body for any sensations. Eye movement is done on any reported sensations.

7 Closure, the point at which a client needs to be returned to a state of
emotional equilibrium.

8 Initiation of next session, when the prior presenting issue is reevaluated
to determine whether any further work needs to be done.

Basic Assumptions of the Approaches

Both TIR and EMDR assume that all people have the innate ability to heal themselves (Shapiro, 1995; Gerbode, 1989). Both approaches hold that a client will be able to process a traumatic event only a safe environment. TIR training specifically directs a clinician as to how to create a safe environment by describing a set of rules that must be adhered to and a communication discipline that must be followed in order for a client to feel empowered enough to process painful material. Both TIR and EMDR are possible only when a clinician creates an environment wherein a client feels completely safe to access traumatic material. It has been noted that "trauma victims face two major obstacles in their efforts to express their trauma-related emotions; their own reluctances to revise fundamental world assumptions, and other people's resistance to hearing about traumatic events" (Harber & Pennebaker, 1992). Since trauma is so commonplace, all clinicians should be prepared to listen without resistance and for as long as it takes for resolution to occur.

Clinical Traumatology Rules (Gerbode, 1989; Moore, 1993, Descilo, 1996) The rules involved in clinical traumatology are as follows:

1 Ensure that the client is in optimum physical condition for the session. Processing painful material requires that a client be well rested and fed and not under the influence of drugs or alcohol.

2 Ensure that the session occurs in a suitable place and at a suitable time. A suitable place means that there will be no interruptions from other people, phones, or pagers. A suitable time means that both clinician and client have at least a 2-hour block set aside to ensure that an end point is reached.

3 Do not interpret for the client. This is one of the hardest points for someone trained in traditional therapy to practice. A client is the ultimate authority on his or her experiences. TIR and EMDR are empowering approaches in that they allow clients to come to their own conclusions.

4 Do not evaluate for a client. This approach requires that the clinician not tell clients whether they are right or wrong. "Do not judge, criticize, disparage, or invalidate the client or client's perceptions, assumptions, conclusions, values, reactions, thoughts, feelings or actions" (Moore, 1993).

5 Control the session and take complete responsibility for it without dominating the client. This allows clients to concentrate on the difficult material they are confronting.

6 Be sure to comprehend what the client is saying. We all know when we are not really understood. A client will feel alone and unsupported if he or she is not understood. Also, ask for clarification without feedback or active listening. Simply tell the client that you do not understand and would like clarification.

7 Be interested in the client and in what the client is saying instead of being interesting to the client. A clinician's interest supports the client's willingness to view and report on the material being viewed.

8 Act in a predictable way so as not to surprise or distract the client.

9 Do not try to work with someone against that person's will or in the presence of any protest. Trauma resolution can occur only when a person is fully willing to participate in the process.

10 Carry each session to success for the client. Trauma resolution cannot occur in the context of a 50-minute hour. TIR and EMDR sessions must be open ended to allow a client to reach a point of resolution.

11 Maintain a firm and primary intention to help the client. While this may seem obvious, if a clinician's primary intentions are to make money or improve skills, a client will perceive this and be less willing to trust the clinician.

Clinical Traumatology Communication Skills   The purpose of communication can be stated as follows: to have a desired idea, experience or feeling fully understood. The components of communication include a point to communicate from, a point to communicate to, something to communicate, an intention to give or receive the communication, attention on the part of the recipient and originator of the communication, acknowledgment of the concept, and comprehension on the part of the recipient.

The ability to control one's attention and intention unlocks personal power and success in any endeavor. The success of any approach depends on the attention and intention of the clinician. According to Chopra (1994):

> Attention energizes, and intention transforms. Whatever you put your attention on will grow stronger in your life. Whatever you take your attention away from will wither, disintegrate, and disappear. Intention, on the other hand, triggers transformation of energy and information. Intention organizes its own fulfillment.

The drills described in the sections to follow teach the underlying communication microskills that are vital to obtaining results with traumatized clients. There are seven drills in total. Each drill addresses one of the components listed earlier. The first two drills will be run by the instructor. The five remaining drills require that students work in teams of two, reversing the roles of "student" and "trainer." These roles are fully defined later in the chapter.

Focusing Drills   The first three drills teach the ability to focus. While this may sound like a simple task, think of all the times during a workshop that your attention wandered to another topic. Now think of a time in the last week when you had something to communicate to someone, who reacted to what you said, which in turn caused you to react, with the result that the original communication was never resolved. These are examples of losing focus. Unfortunately, we are not in total control of parts of our minds. Others' actions or inaction and words can cause a reaction on our part that we would not give in to, given a conscious choice. The purpose of the first three drills is to develop the awareness of how it feels to trigger and lose focus and then gain mastery of one's attention. Mastery of one's attention would manifest in the ability to not react or, at the very least, to not transmit a reaction to what has been said or done. Attaining the ability to control one's attention is no small accomplishment. A person who is able to keep his or her attention focused and not react to a situation is a person in control. In a therapeutic context, controlling one's attention safeguards against countertransference issues. When a clinician is able to continuously direct his or her attention outward, no matter what content is being presented, personal material is less likely to be triggered. Have you ever had the experience of listening to the grisly details of a traumatic event and being completely interested and immersed in the story? Did you feel triggered by the experience?

Maintaining focus is the secret to not accumulating trauma or, at the very least, remaining functional in the wake of trauma. A traumatic event is able to complete itself if one is able to maintain focus throughout the event. It is only what we allow ourselves not to know, not to focus on, not to complete, that can harm us. In support of this view, Herman (1992) reports:

> A study of ten Vietnam veterans who did not develop post-traumatic stress disorder, in spite of heavy combat exposure, showed once again the characteristic triad of active, task-oriented coping strategies, strong sociability, and internal locus of control. These extraordinary men had consciously focused on preserving their calm, their judgment, their connection with others, their moral values, and their sense of meaning, even in the most chaotic battlefield conditions.

Each of the following drills build on the skills of the preceding drill.

Focusing Drill 1   All of the drills are performed sitting face to face with a partner, knees almost touching. The purpose of the first drill is to become comfortable sitting in front of another person with eyes closed, maintaining awareness of the other person and controlling body movements. Each student sits with feet flat, hands on lap, with no fidgeting, laughing, or mental wandering. Ideally, we could disengage from all thoughts in our minds and be totally aware of the person in front of us. However, gaining an ability to not engage in the thoughts that our minds present is a more likely goal.

Focusing Drill 2   The purpose of the next drill is to feel comfortable facing another person, while remaining still, attentive, and not caught up in personal thoughts or physical discomfort. The idea is to maintain the ability to be an interested point to communicate to or from regardless of what mental or physical phenomena are occurring. It is this part of communication that most people have difficulty with.

In doing trauma work, it is necessary for a clinician to feel comfort with discomfort. In fact, in any process that will result in a higher level of resolution or understanding, it is necessary that one not resist unpleasant emotions or situations that may be evoked as the process is begun. It is impossible to reach a higher level of resolution or understanding in any area of life if one is unwilling to experience giving or receiving discomfort.

Mastering this drill also helps build true empathy. Only when we can put our own agendas aside and completely attend to another person are we capable of fully understanding the motives and feelings of another.

This drill is complete when one is able to sit comfortably for some time, facing and focusing on another.

Focusing Drill 3   For this drill, a new role is added, that of trainer. Each student will take turns being a trainer. The trainer is the one who is running the drill. The student is the one learning the drill. The trainer has the task of helping the student master the purpose of the drills that follow. There are certain guidelines for the trainer to follow:

1   Begin a drill by telling your partner to "start." If the student reacts or needs correction for an error, give a time out signal, saying "Time out" and telling the student what the mistake was. Then tell the student to "start."
2   Repeat whatever caused the reaction. Or, in later drills, have the student repeat a phrase that caused her or him to react.

Always begin training with simpler, less difficult material. The idea is to build skills, giving a gradient of success.

Only correct one mistake at a time, concentrating first on the more obvious ones and then working on more subtle errors.

Keep working at the drill until it is mastered. Be responsible for ensuring that time is spent on drilling, not talking about it.

The last of the focusing drills requires that a student maintain focus no matter what the trainer says or does. The purpose of the drill is for the student to gain a mastery over the mind and body's reaction to an outside stimulus.

The trainer starts the drill by saying "Start" or "Begin." The trainer "baits" the student by doing or saying some simple thing (e.g., sticking his or her tongue out at the student). If the student laughs, the trainer gives the time out signal, saying "Time out, you laughed. Begin." Once the student has completely composed her- or himself, the trainer will again stick his or her tongue out. If the student again laughs, the trainer will again give the time out signal and message. The trainer will continue to stick his or her tongue out at the student until the action no longer provokes laughter.

The material used to bait can be incidental, personal, nonsensical, or rude. The only thing the trainer cannot do is leave her or his chair.

Gaining mastery over one's reactions to an outside stimulus is accomplished by finding control over situations that evoke laughter. The mechanism that allows us to control our reaction to humor seems to be the same mechanism that allows us to control our reactions to unpleasant material. Once mastery is gained in directing attention while being baited, one will then be able to direct attention in other situations.

Attitude Adjustment Drill   This drill has the dual purposes of learning to clearly communicate a phrase or question and to do so without expressing any type of judgment or secondary meaning through body language or tone of voice. Herman (1992) notes that "chronically traumatized patients have an exquisite attunement to unconscious and nonverbal communication. Accustomed over a long time to reading their captors' emotional and cognitive states, survivors bring this ability into the therapy relationship. . . . The patient scrutinizes the clinician's every word and gesture, in an attempt to protect herself from the hostile reactions she expects" (p. 139).

An important component needed to create a safe therapeutic environment is refraining from communicating any evaluation or judgment in response to what a client says during a session. We are all familiar with the meaning of "body language" and know that if someone is saying words that his or her body language contradicts, it is wise to believe the body's communication and not the words.

We are not always aware that we are communicating through our facial expressions and tone of voice. This drill is done to become aware of and eliminate any attitudes that may be expressed through physical mannerisms or tone of voice. While in most social communication, we can just "be ourselves" and not edit our body expressions and voice tone, there are many situations in which having control of our output would be in order. Since this entire discipline requires that a clinician never evaluate or judge a client, having awareness and control over body language is vital. Another situation that would require awareness of body language and voice expression is a potential conflict. A raised eyebrow or a condescending tone of voice could certainly escalate a situation that is already precariously balanced.

This drill, as well as all of the others that follow, is done in the trainer/student dyad. The trainer, as outlined earlier, will tell the student "begin," at which point the student will read a phrase from the indicated prepared sheet, memorize it, look at the trainer, and say it as though it were the student's own phrase. In the beginning of the drill, the trainer allows the student to say a number of phrases without correction, to become accustomed to executing the drill. Once the student has provided a few phrases, the trainer will begin to point out any facial expressions or tones of voice that convey secondary meaning. The student will then repeat the phrase that evoked the expression until he or she can do so naturally without any physical or vocal additions.

When the student can deliver a phrase that consistently sounds natural, without any additional body language or vocal attitude, the drill is complete.

Acknowledgment Drill   The purpose of the next drill is to learn to acknowledge communication. An acknowledgment is an indication that a communication has been heard and understood. It is a method of ending and controlling communication. While acknowledgment conveys understanding, it does not mean one agrees with what was said.

Have you ever had the experience of explaining the same idea more than once to a person? The person probably did not acknowledge you the first time.

Have you ever felt as though someone was not interested in what you had to say because the person cut off your communication before you were finished? The person probably acknowledged you prematurely, which is what left that impression with you. Have you ever become exasperated with someone who you knew was willfully not acknowledging you? (Were you telling that person to perform a task that he or she did not want to do?) Now think of someone with whom you enjoy communicating. What part does acknowledgment play in his or her communication with you?

Acknowledgment also should not express judgment or evaluation. Simple statements such as "Fine," "Thank you," "I hear what you're saying," "Good," and "OK," are all that are needed to convey understanding.

This drill is done in the following manner: the trainer tells the student to "begin." The trainer then reads a line from a prepared list as her or his own. The student uses one of the preceding acknowledgments to let the trainer know he or she was understood. The trainer corrects the student for any of the following: attitude conveyed by voice or mannerism, use of an inappropriate acknowledgment, incorrect timing (either too soon or too late), or any break in focus.

The drill is complete when the student can naturally acknowledge a communication without using body language.

Closure Drill   From the theory on trauma previously described, any intention not completed through the desired activity being done or by a conscious decision to end it continues into the present. At any given time, one has only so much energy to intend activities. At best, the result of having incomplete intentions is feeling tired and less energetic to participate in new communication or activities. At worst, having too many incomplete intentions and activities is a cause of burnout and all of its implications. After Hurricane Andrew, a favorite T-shirt of mine read "I survived Hurricane Andrew, but the recovery is killing me."

When working with clients, and especially with trauma clients, it is vital to complete a communication. (It is vital to complete communications in any area of life.) Specifically, if a question is asked or a particular topic is chosen for resolution, it is vital to bring closure to that question or topic. The next two drills address the topic of bringing a question to a point of closure.

When any question is asked, there are four different responses possible. One is an answer to the question, which deserves an acknowledgment. The second is a comment, which is defined as a social response to a question that does not answer the question but requires a brief, polite response. The third is an evasion, which is an attempt to misdirect another from the issue that was raised. Evasions are ignored. The fourth possible response to a question is what is described as a concern. A concern is a subject or situation that so holds a person's attention that the concern must be addressed before the person can answer the question asked. Examples of these responses and how each would be completed are as follows:

1. An answer:

    Mother: "Did you do your homework?"

    Child: "Yes, Mom, I did."

    Mother: "Great."

2. A comment:

    Mother: "Did you do your homework?"

    Child: "Your hair looks really nice."

    Mother: "Well, thank you! Did you do your homework?"

3. An evasion:

    Mother: "Did you do your homework?"

    Child: "It's time for my favorite TV show!"

    Mother: "You didn't answer my question: Did you do your homework?"

4. A concern:

    Mother: "Did you do your homework?"

    Child: "I have a terrible headache."

    Mother: "I'm so sorry to hear that. When did it start?"

    Child: "Around lunch time."

    Mother: "Would you like a painkiller?"

    Child: "I took one about 20 minutes ago."

    Mother: "All right. Were you able to do your homework?"

    Child: "No, not yet. I was waiting for the pill to kick in."

    Mother: "OK. Let me know how you're doing later."

These are simple examples of each. Answers are not always so clear cut. Sometimes they are buried in long explanations. Some people are quite expert at giving "almost answers" that are in fact evasions. Or they are very skilled at directing attention to some other topic with the result that the original question is left incomplete. Politicians are usually expert at this. Concerns can take an entire session to resolve. However, it is always important to remember to return to the original question or topic and bring closure to the communication.

This drill is broken down into two parts. In the first part, the purpose is to learn to distinguish among answer, evasion, and comment.

The drill is completed as follows. The trainer, as before, will start the training period with "Start" or "Begin." The student asks an insignificant, nonpersonal question, such as "Is the earth round, is the grass green, are birds blue?" Once the student chooses a question, it is not changed. The same question is asked over and over again as though it had never occurred before. The idea of the drill is to master the mechanics of bringing closure to a topic or question, not to have to think about new and interesting questions to ask. After the student has asked a question, the trainer has three choices: He or she can answer it, make a comment, or give an evasion. If the trainer answers the question, the student gives a simple acknowledgment. If the trainer offers a comment, the student gives it an appropriate acknowledgment and then says, "I'll repeat the question, Is the earth round?" In sessions and in life, one does not necessarily use a "repeat" statement. However, for purposes of the drill, this statement is used to indicate to the trainer that the student knows that the question was not answered. If the trainer answers with an evasion, the student only says, "I'll repeat the question, Is the earth round?"

In this part of the drill, the trainer may bait the student in an attempt to make the student lose focus. If the student loses focus, does not acknowledge an answer, does not correctly handle a comment, does not ignore an evasion, or communicates with any mannerism or attitude in her or his voice, the trainer gives a "time out," tells the student what needs to be corrected, and repeats whatever was done that threw the student off.

When the student can consistently distinguish among an answer, an evasion, and a comment, the next part of the drill is initiated.

Closure Drill Part 2   The purpose of this part of the last drill is to teach a student how to recognize and effectively deal with a concern and then reach closure on the original topic.

The instructions for this drill are the same as those for the preceding drill except that no baiting is involved. Occasional concerns are voiced by the trainer that the student needs to effectively handle before a return to the original question. An example of this drill is as follows:

Student: Is the earth round?

Trainer: I am feeling extremely tired.

Student: When did this feeling start?

Trainer: About five minutes ago.

Student: How many hours of sleep did you get last night?

Trainer: About seven.

Student: It's not unusual in doing this kind of work for tiredness to start like this. Let me know how it goes as we continue with the question we were on: Is the earth round?

The student must indicate in some way that he or she is repeating the question that was not answered before.

This drill is complete when a student can distinguish among an answer to a question, an evasion, a comment, and a concern and effectively bring closure to each.

End Points   While training in TIR includes specifically identifying an "end point," the assumption that the end point occurs as a result of processing trauma is also manifest in EMDR. Gerbode (1989) defines an "end point" as "the point at which an activity has been successfully completed. This is the point at which the activity should be ended. It is manifested by a set of phenomena that indicate the successful termination of the activity" (p. 513). An end point includes the following: A client extroverts from the subject being addressed to a greater or lesser extent, feels and looks better, and has some sort of insight regarding the area being addressed. It is vital to recognize and stop a procedure at an end point. Continuing past an end point can cause a client to engage in a number of undesired outcomes: continuing to create the material that had been resolved, which will result in a client experiencing self-doubt and uncertainty about his or her ability to unravel issues; becoming immersed in different, unidentified material that the client now misassociates with the subject originally addressed; and creating new and uncharged material related to the original subject.

Herman (1992) in describing the following, also describes what is referred to as an end point:

> After many repetitions, the moment comes when the telling of the trauma story no longer arouses quite such an intense feeling. It has become part of the survivor's experience, but only one part of it. The story is a memory like other memories, and it begins to fade as other memories do.
>
> The major work of the second state is accomplished, however, when the patient reclaims her own history and feels renewed hope and energy for engagement with life. Time starts to move again. When the "action of telling a story" has come to its conclusions, the traumatic experience truly belongs in the past. (p. 195)

Another specific assumption in the theory of TIR is that traumatic events and issues need to be addressed from different "causal directions" (CDs). A CD is defined as the direction of an activity as observed by an individual. There are four basic CDs: something that has been caused by an outside source that we experience personally, those things that we cause another to experience, what we observe another or others cause for another or others, and what we directly cause ourselves to experience. For example, if a client resolved the traumatic event of a car accident wherein another was at fault, the next series to ask about (and apply TIR to) would be any time or times the client caused a car accident, followed by any incidents wherein the client observed a car accident, and finally any car accidents that the client caused and solely experienced.

Although causal directions have been specific to the practice of TIR, they can and should be applied to the practice of EMDR.

The Emotional Scale (Gerbode, 1989; Descilo, 1996)   A final assumption taught as part of TIR, but that is also evident in practice with EMDR, involves the role emotions play in processing and assessing client progress.

The word *emotion* is defined in the *World Book Dictionary* as "a strong feeling of any kind," which really does not say much. A far better definition is given by Goleman (1995):

> All emotions are, in essence, impulses to act, the instant plans for handling life that evolution has instilled in us. The very root of the word *emotion* is *motere*, the Latin verb "to move" plus the prefix "e-" to connote "move away," suggesting that a tendency to act is implicit in every emotion. (p. 6)

Building upon this definition, the emotions seem to fit in a hierarchy based on the degree of *conscious, self-determined* motion possible. Bower (1992) observed that "very depressed or anxious people are usually poor learners because their working memory is so preoccupied or 'filled' with ruminations associated with their emotions." While his example applies to the ability to learn, the concept also supports the idea that negative emotions make one less conscious of one's environment as a result of the preoccupation of attention that is normally accompanied by the emotion. I think we have all seen that people who are grief stricken are less able to control their attention and so motivate themselves or engage in activity, whereas enthusiastic people are far more able to direct their attention and to motivate themselves easily and engage in any activity that interests them. It appears that where a particular emotion fits on the hierarchy correlates with consciousness, awareness of self and environment, ability to choose, and degree of control of one's life. Support of the view that different emotions affect our consciousness, awareness, and ability to learn can be found in Bower (1992); Leichtman, Ceci, and Ornstein (1992); and Nilsson and Archer (1992).

Any one of the emotions in the hierarchy can be either acute or chronic. A chronic emotion colors and eventually structures the world that is seen and lived in. For example, a person who has been mugged can continue to manifest the emotion of fear beyond the duration of the event. Fear can manifest by an unwillingness to drive at night, needing a companion every time one leaves the house, or refusing to allow one's children to walk to the store.

We also experience acute emotions. Even someone who is chronically sad can receive news that would make him or her at least momentarily happy. A usually happy person can experience an event that can leave her or him temporarily angry.

The various emotions and their proposed order are as follows (Gerbode, 1989):

Elation

Enthusiasm

Cheerfulness

Strong interest

Conservatism

Boredom

Antagonism

Anger

Hatred

Hidden hostility

Fear

Grief

Apathy

The Role of Emotions in Processing Traumatic Events   Emotions play an integral role in the process and outcome of resolving trauma. Understanding how each emotion manifests, where each emotion stands in relationship to the others, and accurately assessing the chronic emotional state of a client are observation skills that need development to successfully apply TIR and EMDR.

Affect is a major indicator that a primary trauma has been found. Most of us have been socially trained to balk at affect, change the subject, direct the person's attention elsewhere. If any of the preceding were done when a client was manifesting affect during a session, it would result in the client being stuck in the affect. Also, in any subsequent session, the client would be less likely to feel safe enough to connect with the affect again.

> As Breuer and Freud noted a century ago, "recollection without affect almost invariably produces no result."... As the patient explores her feelings, she may become either agitated or withdrawn. She is not simply describing what she felt in the past but is reliving those feelings in the present. The clinician must help the patient move back and forth in time, from her protected anchorage in the present to immersion in the past, so that she can simultaneously reexperience the feelings in all their intensity while holding on to the sense of safe connections that was destroyed in the traumatic moment. (Herman, 1992)

The importance of contacting and relieving emotion during trauma work is also supported by Harber and Pennebaker (1992): "The problems of post-traumatic thought intrusion lie not so much with the memories themselves, as with the unassimilated emotions that drive these memories to the surface of consciousness."

Ultimately, a client's chronic emotional state will improve as traumatic events are resolved. A client who has been locked in an emotional state of grief can be expected to cycle through the emotions above grief, until, ideally, he or she is closer to a "cheerful" outlook on life. In the case of single-incident trauma, this change can happen over the course of one session. For clients who have suffered multiple traumas throughout their lifetime, this change of emotional outlook will take a number of sessions.

Whenever a client is manifesting change while reviewing a trauma, it is considered a positive indicator. Change can mean a change in affect or a change in content. The content of a traumatic event often changes as the client gets a clearer picture of the event. The material also changes as a client manifests different emotions experienced during the event. Different emotional states will seem cued to different memories within the same traumatic event. In both EMDR and TIR, change means that you are on the right track and should continue with what you are doing. The change will eventually taper, and the client will reach an end point.

During the process of resolving a trauma with TIR or EMDR, clients will often manifest acute emotional changes. It is not unusual for a client to begin a session with no emotion, and during the course of a session cry, express anger, experience fear, cry again, feel hateful, and so on, until the trauma and all of its content have been fully confronted. At this point, a client will usually express relief and, in most cases, manifest an emotional level closer to that of cheerfulness.

ISSUES OF ASSESSMENT

In the case of the loss of a loved one, whether or not TIR or EMDR should be used would be determined by the following:

1   If a client presents him- or herself for treatment because of a death, use either TIR or EMDR as indicated by other factors pertaining to the client's mental status. In other words, no other assessment is needed. The client, by presenting him- or herself for treatment, has assessed that intervention is required.

2   If a client in a long-term therapeutic relationship still manifests undesired emotions, thoughts, or behaviors following any death that occurred during the client's lifetime, the clinician would ask the client whether she or he had interest in addressing the loss with one of the preceding approaches.

Determining which approach to use is covered in the following section.

TIR APPROACH METHODOLOGY

The following are the steps for preparing a client for TIR and a description of the protocol.

The first step is education. Give an explanation of trauma that "trauma occurs when an actual or perceived threat of danger or loss overwhelms a person's usual coping ability" (James, 1994). Go over the rules concerning being well rested and fed, no alcohol for a 24-hour period before a session, no recreational drugs for two to four weeks before a session, and being on time for appointments. A client will need to concentrate on elusive material and needs to be in good physical and mental shape to do so.

The second step is to explain to clients how the technique works and what is expected of them. (Explain how we all have a natural defense mechanism called "repression" that can kick in when we are traumatized. When something gets repressed, one cannot remember all or parts of the event. And because an event is repressed, it never is allowed to end. That a trauma is never ending is seen by the fact that people continue to have symptoms as though the trauma were still occurring. Another point that prevents a trauma from ending is that most times a person will make a decision at the time of the incident. Any decision made at that point also continues on into the present, unknown to the person.

TIR helps a person "unrepress" traumas and find the forgotten decisions. When this is done, the trauma becomes a harmless memory, and a person is no longer affected by it. Sometimes while doing TIR, unpleasant emotions stir up. While it may feel terrible for awhile, it means stable relief is on the way. The end point is always worth the journey.) Ensure that the client understands the basic terms and procedure. Cover the following points:

1 No interpretation or evaluation.
2 Unfixed session lengths.
3 Sleep, food, no drugs or alcohol.
4 Go over the procedure, explaining each part.
5 Why repetition.
6 Expect affect (really prepare them for this).
7 Answering with whatever comes up. Ensure clients know not to edit the material that entered their mind.
8 Run a dummy sequence, such as "the time you ate breakfast."

Third, make up the charged areas list (Bisbey, 1995) as follows:

1 Cull the intake taken in the first session and make a list of all traumatic incidents and emotionally charged persons and areas.
2 Show the list to the client. Get him or her to add anything to the list that may have been left off. If any items on the list are broad emotions such as fear or anger, have the client reword them to something more specific, such as fear of the dark.
3 Read the items on the list to the client, asking the client to assign a number between 0 and 10 to the item as follows: 0 = not at all emotionally charged, 10 = completely emotionally charged (this is referred to as a SUDS rating—subjective units of distress).
4 Once this is done, show the client the list and ask "Which item on this list most holds your attention?"
5 Take up whatever the client gives you, whether it is a 10 or not. Note that a client may not choose the issue brought to the session. However, start with where the client is at. With some clients, it may be appropriate to ask them to choose something that is less than a 10 if there are indicators that they need to build ego strength.
6 If it is a traumatic incident, or some feeling, emotion, attitude, or pain, use TIR. (See following description.)
7 If it is a person, place, or subject, explore the subject with the client. Ask what unwanted emotion or feeling is connected with the subject and then address that emotion or feeling with TIR.
8 At the beginning of each session, ask the client whether he or she has had sufficient sleep and food. Ask whether she or he has consumed any drugs or alcohol since the last session.
9 Address any CD not completed in the last session. Once this has been done, hold up the charged area list and ask which item most holds the client's attention.

10 Take the item the client chooses and proceed as before.

11 At the beginning of the session *after* the session in which the client has run the crime incident for which he or she was referred, ask for feelings, emotions, sensations, attitudes, or pains (FESAPs) connected with the incident, add them to the charged items list, and do a rating of them.

Finally, repeat Steps 7–9 until the client appears to have changed dramatically or expresses no interest in any remaining items on the list.

Summary of TIR Steps

For the first incident and any time a new incident is encountered:

A1. Locate the incident or locate the time when the incident occurred.
A2. When was the incident? or When did it happen?
A3. How long does the incident last?
A4. Where did the incident take place?
A5. If not already closed: Close your eyes.
A6. Go to the start of the incident.
A7. What are you aware of? or What are you aware of at the beginning?
A8. Move through to the end of the incident.
A9. Tell me what happened.

The second and subsequent times a client is asked to review the incident:

B1. Go back to the beginning of the incident. Tell me when you are there.
B2. Move through to the end of the incident.
B3. Tell me what happened.
B4. Discretionally: Is the incident getting lighter or heavier?

If the client says heavier, then do the earlier beginning/earlier incident procedure (described subsequently). Otherwise, repeat B1 to B4.

Earlier Beginning Procedure   Is there an earlier beginning to the incident? If there is an earlier beginning, then do the second run-through procedure (B1–B4), but instead of "Go back to the beginning of the incident" use "Go back to the *new* beginning of the incident." If there is no earlier beginning, complete the earlier incident procedure (described next).

Earlier Incident Procedure   Is there an earlier similar incident? If yes, use the first run-through procedure (A2–A8). If there is no earlier incident, redo the second run-through procedure (B1–B4).

End Point   End when the client has had a realization, is extroverted, and has brightened up.

Checking Other Causal Directions (CDs)   After completing the first CD, check the other CDs as follows:

> **CD2.**   Locate an incident when you caused another _____.
>   E2. Is there an earlier incident when you caused another _____?
> **CD3.**   Locate an incident when another caused others _____.
>   E3. Is there an earlier incident when another caused others _____?
> **CD4.**   Locate an incident when you caused yourself _____.
>   E4. Is there an earlier incident when you caused yourself _____?

Repeat Steps A2 through B4 on any flow as indicated.

Questionable End Points   At any point that an incident seems to have reached an end point but all indicators are not present, ask either How does the incident seem to you now? or Did you make any decision at the time of the incident?

EMDR Protocol (Shapiro, 1995)

First, set up your chairs in the necessary positions. If you will be using eye movement to process, you will need to set up your chair either to the right or left of your client so that when you move your arm back and forth, the client is not looking at your face.

Second, explain EMDR to your client. How much you explain will depend on your client. The following explanation is from the EMDR training materials (Shapiro, 1996):

> When a trauma occurs it seems to get locked in the nervous system with the original picture, sounds, thoughts and feelings. (This material can combine factual material with fantasy and with images that stand for the actual event or feelings about it.) The eye movements we use in EMDR seem to unlock the nervous system and allow the brain to process the experience. That may be what is happening in REM or dream sleep—the eye movements help to process the unconscious material. It is important to remember that it is your own brain that will be doing the healing and that you are the one in control.

> What we will be doing often is a simple check on what you are experiencing. I need to know from you exactly what is going on with as clear feedback as possible. Sometimes things will change and sometimes they won't. I'll ask you how you feel from 0–10—sometimes it will change and sometimes it won't. I may ask if something else comes up—sometimes it will and sometimes it won't. There are no "supposed to's" in this process. So just give as accurate feedback as you can as to what is happening, without judging whether it should be happening or not. Let whatever happens, happen. We'll do the eye movement for awhile, and then we'll talk about it.

Third, establish the stop signal. Some clients can't always articulate when they are abreacting, or we may misinterpret their need to stop as part of the abreaction. Agree, before beginning processing, on a physical sign (e.g., the time out signal) to indicate that the client needs to stop the processing.

Fourth, establish a metaphor for any time a client needs some encouragement to get through an abreaction. An example of a metaphor that is commonly used is to tell clients to imagine that they are on a train and that the material they are viewing is just scenery that is passing them by.

Fifth, establish whether you will use eye movement or some other method to process, such as a sound device or tapping on the client's knees. Work out a comfortable distance and speed, or volume and speed if using a sound device. (To do eye movement with a client, hold your hand up as though you are giving someone the "peace" sign, but hold your fingers together. Extend your arm so that your elbow is almost straight and then bring your hand back so that it is almost touching your head. Be sure not to point your fingers at the client. The faster the eye movement, the faster the material processes, but you must establish what is comfortable for the client. Each client will require a certain number of eye movements before taking a break. However, start with at least 24 repetitions until you observe what your client needs. Also, when a client is processing more distressing materials, more eye movement will be necessary. When stopping your fingers, do so slowly, not suddenly, returning your fingers to the client's center of vision.)

Sixth, create a safe space. Ask the client for some real or imagined place where he or she feels safe. Have the client picture it, remember what it feels like. Use the safe space if a client needs a break during a session or if a session does not reach a full end point.

1   Ask the client for the issue or memory she or he would like to address.
2   What picture represents that issue or memory?
3   When you look at that picture, what negative belief do you have about yourself now?
4   When you think of that picture, what positive belief would you like to have about yourself now?
5   Validity of cognition: When you think of that picture, how true does [the positive belief] feel to you now on a scale of 1–7, where 1 feels completely false and 7 feels completely true?
6   When you look at the picture, what emotions or feelings do you get now?
7   How intense are those feelings/emotions on a scale of 0 through 10, with 0 being no disturbance and 10 being complete disturbance?
8   Where do you feel the disturbance in your body?
9   Look at the original picture, the feelings of _____, and the [negative belief]. Hold these things together as best you can and follow my fingers. Use eye movement (EM), tapping, or sounds as previously established. Take a deep breath. What do you notice now? Go with that. EM. Deep breath. Tell me what happened, what do you notice now? (Continue until there is no change, negative or positive, for two sets. If the client abreacts, do longer EM sets.) After two sets of no change, ask the client to think of the original picture. Ask "How disturbing

is that image now to you on a scale of 0–10?" If 2 or more, have the client focus on the disturbance and do EM as before. If the SUDS is at 0 or 1, continue.

10   Do the words _____ [positive belief] still fit or is there another positive statement that you feel would be more suitable?

11   Think about the original picture and _____ [positive belief]. On a scale of 1–7, with 1 being completely false and 7 being completely true, how true does that belief seem now?

12   Have the client hold the statement and the original picture together. Do EM. Check for how true it feels again. Repeat doing EM until it no longer strengthens.

13   If the positive belief does not move above a 5, check to see if it is appropriate. If not, have the client change the belief and do EM. Or check whether there is a blocking belief. Establish the blocking belief and do EM.

14   Body scan: Close your eyes. Concentrate on the picture, the positive belief, and mentally scan your entire body. Tell me if and where you feel anything. Focus on that. EM. Repeat this step until there are no more body sensations.

15   Closure/debriefing. Sometimes things will emerge between sessions. Please note them down so that we can take them up in our next session. (If this session did not close on an end point, use a visualization or anchoring technique to bring the client back into the here and now and then let the client know that she or he can call you between sessions if needed.)

Instructions and Observations Regarding EMDR   Regarding abreaction, if a client begins to manifest affect, continue with the EM until they subside. For purposes of arm comfort, you may need to take a change in the affect as a point to lower your arm and have the client pause. Continue with the EM as soon as possible, because it is important to get the client through this period. It will end! While it may be necessary to encourage a client to continue through an abreaction, I keep comments at a minimum so as not to distract the client from getting through. I do not use a metaphor at this point to keep the client going.

Each client needs a different length of EM. Some clients will noticeably brighten up after 18 EMs. Notice your client. Look at his or her facial expressions. Use your judgment.

After completing EMDR on a target area, ask the client for the other causal directions regarding the area. For example, if the client's presenting issue was fear of the dark, ask if she or he has ever caused another to be afraid of the dark. Ask for the picture that represents that, and continue with the procedure. When CD2 is complete, check to see if the client also has CD3 and CD4 on the same presenting issue (a time when another caused another to be afraid of the dark and a time the client caused her- or himself to be afraid of the dark).

While EMDR training tapes showed the clinician making encouraging comments during eye movement, the approach works well with the clinician silent during EM and only making an encouraging comment if the client is hesitant during an abreaction.

For overwhelming or repeated trauma, after addressing the trauma with EMDR or TIR, ask the client to think of the event and notice what unwanted emotions or feelings are present. Address one emotion or theme at a time with EMDR (or TIR).

While I was trained in the first EMDR training to go through all of the steps with a client, Shapiro indicated, in the second training session I attended, that if a client extroverts completely, she would end the session at that point. When I use EMDR, I recognize and stop the session when the client manifests an end point, as described previously.

One of the reasons the approach is so powerful has to do with asking for the basic beliefs connected with the incident. This speaks to a person's basic identity and is very effective in bringing about desired change when done correctly. It is also a point where one needs to be cautious. The basic beliefs must be ones that completely feel right to a client. While it is acceptable to help a client identify the exact wording of a negative or positive belief, the final statement must completely fit for a client. There have been reports of client distress between EMDR sessions. While this distress could be the result of more memory processing, it could also be caused by a positive or negative belief that was not completely correct for the client. If a client ever becomes very upset or apathetic between sessions, first check the negative and positive beliefs for correctness. If either or both beliefs are not correct for the client, find out what wording or belief is right and then continue with EMDR. If they are correct, continue processing what emerged during the week.

What Can Go Wrong in TIR   Given that TIR is appropriate for the client, the two most common reasons why a TIR session does not reach an end point are that there was an earlier similar incident or an end point was missed.

Sometimes a clinician will accept an earlier similar incident that is not similar at all. At other times a client has a pressing problem that prevents him or her from being able to focus on a traumatic event. These situations will also prevent an end point from occurring.

If you suspect one of the preceding to have occurred, ask the client the following:

1   Is there an earlier similar incident? If so, proceed with the protocol.

2   Was there some point when you felt better about this event (or theme)? If so ask, when did that occur? Then ask, What happened at that point?

3   Did we take up an unrelated trauma? If so, tell them so. And then ask for the last trauma addressed that was related to the original theme or event. Return them to it and continue with the protocal.

4   Is there some other situation that is holding your attention? Is so, gather all of the information pertaining to the situation and do whatever is necessary for a resolution.

Sometimes, none of the preceding will "bring a client out of it," and the client may still seem emotional or out of the present at session end. If this occurs, use a technique to bring a client back into the "here and now."

An anchoring technique simply consists of repretitively telling a client, for example, to look at a room object. The clinician would pick 10 to 15 different room objects. Other anchoring techniques, which can be done while walking about, are as follows:

- Point out something that you haven't noticed before.
- Touch that [room object].
- Look around here and find something that isn't reminding you of [someone the client lost].

After using one of these techniques, ask the client how he or she is doing now. Any coping technique that relaxes a client or brings the client into the here and now would be appropriate at the end of any session that does not reach an end point.

What Can Go Wrong With EMDR   Some of the difficulties encountered with EMDR include the following:

1   A client is unable to find a picture to represent the trauma or issue. Do not attempt EMDR. TIR may be effective in this case, or other approaches that build awareness and strength.

2   A client cannot easily formulate a positive or negative belief. Again, EMDR should not be pursued.

3   There is no change of affect or content during reprocessing. The client requires another approach.

4   The client loops with the material. In other words, the same material presents itself during EM, and the SUDs rating does not diminish. Change the direction of the EM if that is the method of reprocessing. Otherwise, ask the client whether there is an earlier beginning to the material being addressed or for an earlier similar incident.

5   The abreaction does not subside or a client wants to stop at any point. First try sending the client to her or his safe space. I would then use an anchoring or relaxation technique. Supervision would be advised. At the very least, I would not attempt EMDR until less traumatic issues had been resolved and ego strength had increased.

When to Use TIR and EMDR   If a client needs to build ego strength, start with TIR. Some of the indicators that a client needs to build ego strength are as follows: The client has attempted or seriously considered suicide, the client is not functioning well in life, and the client has no support system and cannot build one. However, when in doubt, use an appropriate scale that measures ego strength, such as the Minnesota Multiphasic Personality Inventory (MMPI). If a client is unable to find a target or has trouble formulating a negative or positive cognition, use TIR instead. If a client has an intense interest in recovering forgotten pieces, use TIR.

One of the easiest ways to determine which approach to use is to ask your client. Let the client experience both approaches and determine which one addresses issues best for her or him.

I encourage you to include more than a weekly session when working with a client who has an extensive trauma history or the identifying factors for complicated mourning (Rando, 1996). With both approaches, a fragile client will have a difficult time between sessions. It is far better for the client's well-being to have more frequent sessions until the majority of the trauma work is done.

When TIR and EMDR Cannot Be Used   There are certain situations wherein these approaches are not appropriate. These circumstances include the following:

- If a client is currently abusing drugs or alcohol
- When a client is taking certain psychotropic medications that prevent him or her from accessing memories
- Any client who is psychotic
- A mandated client, whether the mandate is from the court or a parent (unless a client agrees to the treatment, it is not likely to be effective)
- With EMDR, any client who has a dissociative disorder
- With TIR, a client who is too young to understand the process or to focus long enough for a resolution to occur
- With a clinician who does not apply the microskills and rules described in this chapter

Further Cautions Regarding EMDR (Shapiro, 1995)   Do not use eye movements with someone who has epilepsy or eye problems. Use an alternate method such as tapping the client's knees or hands or a sound device.

Do not use EMDR with clients who have dissociative disorders. A client with a dissociative disorder can become stuck in a high level of disturbance with EMDR. Consult the *DSM-IV* for the indicators of this disorder. (TIR may be more appropriate to use with these cases because the approach narrowly focuses on one type of affect or traumatic event. However, if in doubt, seek supervision.)

If you have no previous experience with a trauma approach, it is strongly recommended that you begin by using TIR. Because of its narrower focus, both client and clinician have more control of the process. Once certainty is gained with TIR, use EMDR. In the best of all worlds, learning both approaches would be done under supervision.

Additional Steps for Dealing With a Death

Sometimes a death will have no earlier beginning and there will be no earlier incident, yet the incident does not reach a point of desired relief. In this case, complete the following steps:

1   If the full end point is still not present, have the client run the death from the deceased person's point of view. Many times, when a deep empathy bond has existed between two people, it is not unusual for a person to have fully imagined the death through the eyes of the deceased.

2   Use TIR or EMDR to address the loss of the future one had planned with the deceased.

3   Tell the client to imagine that the deceased person is in the room. Direct clients to talk to the person as though he or she were there, telling the person all of the things that they had meant to say, wanted to say, and needed to say. Tell the client to imagine that the deceased person acknowledges all of his or her communications.

4   Next, have the client imagine that the deceased person is communicating what was left incomplete for her or him. Have the client report to you what is being said, and tell the client to acknowledge the communication received.

5   Ask the client how distressed he or she feels about the death now, giving a SUDS rating as described previously.

6   If the client has not reached a point of relief, ask what unwanted emotions or feelings the client experiences when he or she thinks of the death now. Write the emotions and feelings on a charged areas list and ask the client to assign points to each. Next, ask which item most holds the client's attention. Use thematic TIR on these items, making sure to ask the client whether an incident exists for each CD.

EVIDENCE OF EFFECTIVENESS

A large body of literature supports the efficacy of EMDR. Some of the research conducted with EMDR includes Tinker, Wilson, and Becker (1995), on traumatized individuals; Solomon and Shapiro (in press), on bereavement due to loss of a loved one or to line-of-duty deaths, and Levin, Grainger, Allen-Byrd, and Fulcher's (1994) controlled study of 45 Hurricane Andrew victims.

There is a growing body of research with regard to the efficacy of TIR. The most recent work completed using TIR is an impeccable outcome study of 123 female inmates at Federal Correction Institution Tallahassee. Valentine (1997) used a single session of TIR, given after a brief intake and followed by a session for closure and posttesting, versus a waiting list control group. She included measures for depression, anxiety, and learned helplessness, which are primary symptoms of posttraumatic stress. The improvements in all measures following treatment were statistically significant. Furthermore, at a 3-month follow-up, all measurements showed a significant improvement for the treatment group from the first posttest.

Bisbey (1995) completed the first experimental study using TIR on 64 crime victims in England. She compared TIR with direct therapeutic exposure and a waiting list control group. All subjects were screened for a positive diagnosis of PTSD. Bisbey (1995) reported:

> In this study, as hypothesized, both treatment groups experienced a significant decrease in trauma symptoms while the control group did not. In fact, most of the members of both treatment groups no longer qualified for a diagnosis of Post-traumatic

Stress Disorder at the conclusion of the study. It was hypothesized that the Traumatic Incident Reduction group would show a larger decrease in incident specific symptoms than the Direct Therapeutic Exposure group. This turned out to be correct.

Coughlin's (1995) quasi-experimental design study looked at the efficacy of TIR in treating 20 subjects diagnosed with panic and anxiety symptoms. She wrote:

> Clinical and statistic differences post-treatment have been confirmed. Yeaton and Sechrest (1981) define "cure" as the point "when the deviation from the norm has been eliminated (p. 163)." Fourteen participants had state anxiety scores more than one standard deviation above the mean on pretest. Deviations from the norm ($\pm$ one standard deviation) were eliminated for eleven participants at one-month follow-up and nine participants at three-month follow-up. Thirteen participants had trait anxiety scores more than one standard deviation above the mean on pretest. Deviations from the norm were eliminated for ten participants at one-month follow-up and nine participants at three-month follow-up. The data supports the effectiveness of TIR. 64% of participants with clinically significant state anxiety remained "cured" at three month follow-up and 69% of participants who had clinically elevated trait anxiety remained "cured" at three month follow-up. TIR satisfies Yeaton and Sechrest's definition of a successful treatment. (pp. 64–65)

Case Example

The case example I give to demonstrate various aspects of both approaches is one from a workshop wherein both EMDR and TIR were taught. I usually give live demonstrations of both techniques. My experience has been that if someone self-selects, she or he will be ready for the experience.

TIR is taught first in the course of the workshop. The volunteer wanted to address the death of her mother. I normally do not address deaths in this forum, but after interviewing the participant, I decided that it would be appropriate to pursue. Her mother had died 6 months earlier in a car accident. The client, who was in her 40s, had not stopped crying since then.

I began the approach by asking her when it happened, along with the questions given earlier when one is addressing a new incident. I then had her return to the beginning of the incident, move through the incident and tell me what happened. During the second recounting, the client began crying. I had the client review the incident 37 times in total. The client recounted different aspects to the event most times. Her sadness peaked and waned. She became angry. She began to present the theme that because of what she was taught in her upbringing, it was not okay to cry and be weak. After the 15th recounting, the client gave her first smile and laugh. However, during the next time through, she began crying. But from this point, the grief was less frequent and less intense. When she indicated that the incident felt the same at Point 19, I asked her whether the incident was getting lighter or heavier. From her indication, I continued to cycle her through the incident. Her recounting of the incident continued to change in content and emphasis until the 33rd time through, at which point her affect improved and the content remained the same. After the 37th recounting, I asked her whether she made any decision at the time of the incident. Her reply was "That was a sad time, but that's what it was—that was then and this is now." She had successfully completed the trauma, and I ended the session there. The entire session lasted a little more than an hour.

The next day, I asked her how she was doing. She said she felt better but that she was still crying frequently. I arranged to give her another session that day. This session began with an exploration to determine whether the TIR we had done the day before was incomplete. She felt that the traumatic aspects of the death had resolved. I continued to explore and discovered that she had many unresolved issues with her mother, with the primary issue at this point being her mother's edict to always be strong and never to cry. It was an idea that had permeated her life. I decided to use EMDR for this issue.

After completing the initial EMDR steps, I asked her for the presenting issue. Her answer was her mother enforcing the idea to be strong and never to cry. I asked her "What picture represents this issue?" and she immediately responded with an incident that happened when she was 4. She threw her first and only tantrum; her parents' response was so swift and forceful that she never attempted to show that type of emotion again. When asked for her negative belief about herself now when she looked at that picture of herself at 4, she replied, "I must not be very strong." When asked what positive belief she would like to have about herself now when looking at that image, she said, "I'm very strong." I then asked her "When you think of that picture, how true does 'I'm very strong' feel to you now on a scale of 1–7, where 1 feels completely false and 7 feels completely true?" Her answer was 1. When next I asked her what emotions or feelings she experienced when she looked at the picture, she replied, "Anger and helplessness." When asked to rate how strong the feelings were, she rated them with a SUDS of 10. She felt the disturbance in her solar plexus.

Next I directed her to hold the image, the negative belief that "I must not be very strong," and the feelings of anger and hopelessness together the best that she could and to follow my fingers. I initially started with 24 eye movements. During the course of the next hour, I used longer or shorter EM sets depending on her affect. She cried less during the EMDR. She brought up information from all parts of her life that had to do with the themes of being strong and not showing emotions. Three times during this stage, when the client had no change of content or affect for two sets of EMs, I asked her to look at the original image and give me a SUDS rating. The first time her response was 3, the second was 1–2, and the last was 0–1. The client said, referring to the original picture, "It's funny." I ended the EM phase there. When asked if the positive belief "I'm very strong" still fit or if there was another positive statement she felt would be more suitable, she responded with "I'm as strong as I need to be." I had her think about the original incident and the new positive belief and asked her how true the belief seemed to her now. She replied, "7." I installed it once with EM, and it remained at 7. The final step entailed the body scan. She did not feel anything, so we ended there. I let her know I would be available for another session if she needed it and that I would refer her to someone in her home town for follow-up. She was bright and smiling at the end of the session, which had lasted an hour and 30 minutes.

I called her three months after these sessions to ask for permission to use her case here. She told me our work had "opened the door and helped me through the trauma part of it."

CONCLUSION

While there is no panacea for all levels of suffering in all situations, TIR and EMDR have proven to be very effective tools for relieving trauma-related symptoms in many different populations. These approaches require practice and, ideally, supervision for mastery. When first beginning to use these approaches with clients, follow the directions. Both approaches have been developed over years, and the form they have evolved to represents thousands of hours of clinical trials.

When applying these techniques to those who have lost loved ones, if you can open the door and help them through the trauma part of it in the brief time it takes to apply one of these approaches, you will have accomplished more than has been the norm in the past.

REFERENCES

Barnhart, C. L., & Barnhart, R. K. (Eds.). (1977). *The World Book dictionary*. Chicago: Doubleday.

Barrionuevo, G., Schottler, F., & Lynch, G. (1980). The effects of repetitive low-frequency stimulation on control and "potentiated" synaptic responses in the hippocampus. *Life Sciences, 27*, 2385–2391.

Bisbey, L. B. (1995). *No longer a victim: A treatment outcome study for crime victims with posttraumatic stress disorder*. Unpublished doctoral dissertation, California School of Professional Psychology.

Bower, G. H. (1992). How might emotions affect learning? In S. I. Christianson (Ed.), *The handbook of emotion and memory: Research and theory* (pp. 3–32). Hillsdale, NJ: Erlbaum.

Cable, C. G. (1996). Grief counseling for survivors of traumatic loss. In K. J. Doka (Ed.), *Living with grief after sudden death* (pp. 117–126). Washington, DC: Hospice Foundation of America.

Chopra, D. (1993). *The seven spiritual laws of success*. San Rafael, CA: Amber-Allen.

Coughlin, W. E. (1995). *TIR: Efficacy in treating anxiety symptomology*. Unpublished doctoral dissertation, Union Institute.

Descilo, T. (1996). *Clinical traumatology workshop*. Unpublished manuscript.

Everstine, D., & Everstine, L. (1993). *The trauma response: Treatment for emotional injury*. New York: Norton.

Figley, C. R. (1996). Traumatic death: Treatment implications. In K. J. Doka (Ed.), *Living with grief after sudden death* (pp. 91–102). Washington, DC: Hospice Foundation of America.

Figley, C. R., Bride, B., & Mazza, N. (Eds.). (1997). *Death and trauma: The traumatology of grieving*. Washington, DC: Taylor & Francis.

French, G. D., & Gerbode, F. A. (1995). *The Traumatic Incident Reduction Workshop*. Menlo Park, CA: IRM Press.

Gerbode, F. A. (1989). *Beyond psychology: An introduction to metapsychology* (2nd ed.). Palo Alto, CA: IRM Press.

Gerbode, F. A., & Moore, R. H. (1994). Beliefs and intentions in RET. *Journal of Rational-Emotive & Cognitive-Behavior Therapy, 12*, 27–46.

Goleman, D. (1995). *Emotional intelligence.* New York: Bantam Books.

Goodwin, D. W., Powell, B., Bremer, D., Hoine, H., & Stern, H. (1969). Alcohol and recall: State-dependent effects in man. *Science, 163,* 1358–1360.

Harber, K. D., & Pennebaker, J. W. (1992). Overcoming traumatic memories. In S. I. Christianson (Ed.), *The handbook of emotion and memory: Research and theory* (pp. 359–388). Hillsdale, NJ: Erlbaum.

Herman, J. (1992). *Trauma and recovery.* New York: Basic Books.

James, B. (1994). *Handbook for treatment of attachment-trauma problems in children.* New York: Lexington Books.

Janoff-Bulman, B. (1992). *Shattered assumptions.* New York: Free Press.

Larson, J., & Lynch, G. (1989). Theta pattern stimulation and the induction of LTP: The sequence in which synapses are stimulated determines the degrees to which they potentiate. *Brain Research, 489,* 49–58.

Leichtman, M. D., Ceci, S. J., & Ornstein, P. A. (1992). The influence of affect on memory: Mechanism and development. In S. I. Christianson (Ed.), *The handbook of emotion and memory: Research and theory* (pp. 181–200). Hillsdale, NJ: Erlbaum.

Levin, C., Grainger, R. K., Allen-Byrd, L., & Fulcher, G. (1994, August). *Efficacy of eye movement desensitization and reprocessing (EMDR) for survivors of Hurricane Andrew: A comparative study.* Paper presented at the annual convention of the American Psychological Association, Los Angeles, CA.

Levine, P. A. (1997). *Waking the tiger.* Berkeley, CA: North Atlantic.

Lewis Herman, J. (1997). *Trauma and recovery.* New York: Basic.

Moore, R. H. (1993). Cognitive-emotive treatment of the post-traumatic stress disorder. In W. Dryden & L. Hill (Eds.), *Innovations in rational-emotive therapy.* Newbury Park, CA: Sage.

Nilsson, L. G., & Archer, T. (1992). Biological aspects of memory and emotion: Affect and cognition. In S. I. Christianson (Ed.), *The handbook of emotion and memory: Research and theory* (pp. 289–307). Hillsdale, NJ: Erlbaum.

Potocky, M. (1993). Effective services for bereaved spouses: A content analysis of the empirical literature. *Health Social Work, 18,* 288–301.

Prigerson, H. G., Shear, M. K., Frank, E., Beery, L. C., Silberman, R., Pilgerson, J., & Reynolds, C. R. (1997). Traumatic grief: A case of loss-induced trauma. *American Journal of Psychiatry 154*(7), 1–6.

Rando, T. A. (1996). Complications in mourning traumatic death. In J. K. Doka (Ed.), *Living with grief after sudden death* (pp. 139–160). Washington, DC: Hospice Foundation of America.

Raphael, B., & Martinek, N. (1997). Assessing traumatic bereavement and posttraumatic stress disorder. In J. P. Wilson & T. M. Keane (Eds.), *Assessing psychological trauma and PTSD.* New York: Guilford.

Shapiro, F. (1989a). Efficacy of the eye movement desensitization procedure in the treatment of traumatic memories. *Journal of Traumatic Stress Studies, 2,* 199–223.

Shapiro, F. (1989b). Eye movement desensitization: A new treatment for post-traumatic stress disorder. *Journal of Behavior Therapy and Experimental Psychiatry, 20,* 211–217.

Shapiro, F. (1995). *Eye movement desensitization and reprocessing.* New York: Guilford Press.

Solomon, R., & Shapiro, F. (in press). Eye movement desensitization and reprocessing: An effective therapeutic tool for trauma and grief. In C. Figley (Ed.), *Death and trauma.* New York: Brunner/Mazel.

Valentine, P. (1995). Traumatic incident reduction: A review of a new intervention. *Journal of Family Psychotherapy, 6,* 79–85.

Valentine, P. V. (1997). *Traumatic incident reduction: Brief treatment of trauma-related symptoms in incarcerated females.* Unpublished doctoral dissertation, Florida State University.

Weil, A. (1995). *Spontaneous healing.* New York: Knopf.

Wilson, S. A., Becker, L. A., & Tinker, R. H. (1995). Eye movement desensitization and reprocessing (EMDR) treatment for psychologically traumatized individuals. *Journal of Consulting and Clinical Psychology, 63,* 928–937.

Chapter 10

Death-Related Treatment Applications for the Elderly

Michael McGee

The death of a spouse or a child is considered to be the most traumatic stressor one can experience (Holmes & Rahe, 1967). The elderly are no exception in experiencing stress (Kiyak & Kahana, 1975). Loss of close family members, friends, and cohorts and their own demise affect seniors. These major stressors can effect the elderly in such a way that their reduced coping skills can result in trauma. As such, there are a number of psychological and cognitive issues associated with stress that need to be addressed if seniors are to complete their normal daily activities. The loss of a spouse or other family member was reported by Holmes and Rahe (1967) to be almost overwhelming; however, an older person who has previously experienced the loss of family or friends may be less stressed at another's dealth (Hooyman & Kiyak, 1996). Regardless of degree of intensity, major stress is significant. Addressing this stress is critical to the elderly in terms of maintaining psychological well-being, accomplishing daily functioning activities, and completing developmentally appropriate tasks (Phifer, 1990).

Senior citizens are often thought of as a group. They are frequently described as being at least 65 years of age. This is not the case. As Riley and Riley (1986) noted, there are significant differences among the "young-old" (65 to 74 years), the "old-old" (75 to 84 years), and the "oldest-old" (more than 85 years). These differences can include physical health, economic resources, social supports, work status, socioeconomic class, gender concerns, and ethnic beliefs (Hooyman & Kiyak, 1996). Such differences are critical in terms of understanding how stress may affect the elderly. Most gerontologists no longer classify elders solely on how many years they have lived. Elders are now viewed in regard to four distinct processes:

> 1) Chronological aging (aging on the basis of a person's years from birth); 2) Biological aging (referring to the physical changes that reduce the efficiency of organ systems); 3) Psychological aging (including the changes that occur in sensory and perceptual processes, mental functioning, adaptive capacity, personality, drives, and

motives); and 4) Social aging (referring to an individual's changing roles and responsibilities in the social structure). (Hooyman & Kiyak, 1996, p. 2)

These aging concepts are reviewed and discussed here as they affect a senior's
ability to cope with a major stressor (the loss of life). As a means of most clearly
specifying what is appropriate, a new, senior-specific developmental model is
desribed. This model, the Senior Life Span Developmental Model (SLSDM), is
then used to explain and predict the impacts of major stressors on seniors during
different phases of their developmental process. Coinciding with this discussion
of developmental stage is a presentation on how to assist seniors. The model is
introduced with specific and unique methods of therapeutically treating phase-
specific populations.

BACKGROUND

Even though we know a great deal about stress and human responses to it, our
understanding of the facets of gerontological reactions to trauma is limited. In
fact, the entire field of gerontology and the relevance of varying psychological
or social theories are evolving (Hooyman & Kiyak, 1996). This process should
not be unexpected. In reviewing the population trends for the past 100 years,
it is clear that the segment of our population over the age of 65 has increased
dramatically (in terms of both numbers and level of economic influence). Seniors
now constitute 13% of our total population (vs. 4% in 1900), and this figure is
expected to grow to 22% by the year 2050 (U.S. Senate, Special Committee on
Aging, 1991). Additional figures support this shift in our population mix. In 1900,
the average life expectancy was 47 years; by 1920, it was 54 years; and, as of
today, females born in 1993 can expect to reach the age of 79.5 years and males
72.5 years (U.S. Bureau of the Census, 1993). These changes highlight the fact
that our nation's concept of, knowledge about, and expectations for those over 65
years of age are undergoing change.

Research has shown that seniors experience the same reactions to death as
younger persons. These reactions were described by Kubler-Ross (1969) as five
distinct phases: denial, anger, bargaining, depression, and acceptance. In studying these phases, Kubler-Ross noted that one may shift between stages but that
acceptance of one's, or a spouse's, death is necessary for one to die with dignity.
In Erik Erikson's psychological stages of life, the last stage is ego integrity versus
despair. This stage focuses on establishing a sense of meaning in one's life, accepting oneself and one's life without despair. Kubler-Ross concurred and noted
that this acceptance is critical if one is to accept one's infallibility.

With the death of a loved one, all family members generally experience shock
and denial. All individuals struggle to cope with the terror and loss they are experiencing. Some researchers believe that seniors are particularly vulnerable to loss
of the wherewithall to live and often realize a loss of coping resources that creates
psychological distress (Freedy, Saladin, Kilpatrick, Resnick, & Saunders, 1994;

Hobfoll, 1989). Others state that there are no emotional differences in terms of older and younger generations' reactions to a stressor such as death (Nadler & Ben-Shushan, 1989).

Extensive research and practical experience indicate that coping with the psychological consequences of a major stressor is difficult (Figley & McCubbin, 1983). If the stressful event is of sufficient magnitude, it can (a) disrupt the routines and problem-solving patterns of survivors, (b) cause a sense of disruption and loss for the survivors and their families, and (c) be recalled voluntarily or involuntarily, such that the event often influences future situations (Burgess & Baldwin, 1981; Figley, 1978, 1982; Figley & McCubbin, 1983; Horowitz, 1976). After much analysis, it is apparent that a majority of individuals who experience a stressful event such as the death of a family member are affected for a period of time (Greene, 1994) and that the victim's family support is the most effective defense against the unwanted consequences of the associated stress (Figley & McCubbin, 1983; Solomon, 1988; Boss, 1988). The goal is to help elderly people reduce their level of stress and relieve their emotional suffering. For many seniors who have lost a spouse or are terminally ill themselves, this means addressing the concept of death and resolving unsettled issues.

Stress consequences have been identified as flashbacks, sleep disturbances, hyperanxiety, and depression (Figley, 1978; Solomon, Mikulincer, Fried, & Wosner, 1987). While familial social support is a powerful force in alleviating stress, it may be insufficient to handle the impact of a major stressor (Levitt, Antonucci, Clark, Rotton, & Finley, 1985). Hagstrom (1995) reports that seniors' reactions to a traumatic event are more likely to include higher stress symptoms of intrusiveness and preoccupation. Other researchers note that elders need to reestablish a sense of control and predictability as well as restore feelings of confidence and self-worth after a traumatic event (Department of Aging, 1994). Yet, the current state of gerontological research on stress resulting from loss of life cannot confirm or deny this; the existing research base may be described as being in its infancy stage. Dwyer and Coward (1992) noted that there are multiple research needs in gerontology: cultural comparisons, disentangling the effects of gender from other covariants, and the inclusion of families rather than simply caregiving dyads. A family's social support in helping seniors address their experience(s) of death and dying does not appear to be sufficiently well documented to make a definitive statement in terms of its influence.

THEORETICAL PERSPECTIVES

There are a variety of theories on how stress affects seniors, including early research by Lawton and Nahemow (1973) that studied individuals' relationships with the elements in their social and physical environments (and their abilities to adapt and respond or to change). Other models, such as the sociocultural model developed by Anderson and Newman (1973), focused on environmental conditions and physical well-being. These models attempted to explain and predict seniors' use of services and the degree to which they employ internal and external resources to manage stress. A general conclusion of these models was that the probability of a senior using a needed service is predicated on (a) predisposing variables (demographic factors, sociological structure, and health beliefs), (b) enabling conditions (those elements that make the service most accessible, such as income, insurance, and type and source of health care), and (c) need factors (perceived health, functional abilities, and physical rating) (Wister, 1992).

After reviewing a series of stress-related research material, Smith (1985) suggested five hypotheses for why the elderly may be particularly vulnerable to stress. These hypotheses, as noted by Kahana (1992), are as follows:

* The victimization hypothesis refers to the selective nature of certain forms of trauma in preying on older persons.
* The differential exposure hypothesis implies that older persons have an increased risk of exposure to certain forms of extreme stress (e.g., bereavement).
* The vulnerability hypothesis suggests that stress, which has a more limited impact on younger persons, may have a more adverse effect on older people who may have reduced adaptive capacities (Rosow, 1967).
* The additive burden hypothesis suggests that the elderly have accumulated many more stressful life experiences than their younger counterparts and that additional negative life events place them at a greater risk for negative outcomes.
* The chronic burden hypothesis refers to the long-term effect of extreme stress that was experienced earlier in life. (p. 155)

Kahana (1992) concluded that a key concept in each of the senior stress hypotheses identified by Smith is vulnerability. Vulnerability in seniors may be a function of many factors, from such diverse situations as increased exposure to multiple traumatic events to diminishing resources in managing the emotional consequences of the traumatic event. Vulnerability, therefore, appears to be a critical component and needs to be addressed. As Aldwin (1992) points out, vulnerability and resources are accumulated over a life span, and their interaction at key points is often helpful in inducing development.

SENIOR DEVELOPMENTAL ACTIVITIES

Newman and Newman (1995) described senior developmental activities as promoting intellectual vigor, redirecting energy to new roles and activities, accepting one's life, and developing a point of view about death. Steinglass (1987) added the processes of distillation and clarification of the family legacy and transmission of this legacy to the next and future generations. Aarts and Op den Velde (1996) suggested combining the research of Coleman (1986), Schmidt (1991), and Erikson (1965) to clarify the developmental issues for successful adaptation to aging: (a) mourning for losses, (b) giving meaning to past and present experiences, (c) accepting one's past and present state, (d) (re)establishing self-coherence and self-continuity, and (e) achieving ego integration. These varying concepts of developmental activities, however, do not account for developmental differences amomg elderly age groups.

In evaluating how a senior will react to death, it is essential to recognize the relationship between physical and emotional well-being. Knight (1992) notes that the increased proportion of chronic illness and disability with each decade of life correlates with an elder's psychological state. In later life, seniors go through a dependency process. For those in the 65–74-year age group, physical activities, independence, and cognitive functioning are beginning to decline, yet they are often still operating close to their pre-65 lifestyle level. Nelson (1995) reports that only 8% of seniors in this age group are impaired in carrying out activities of daily living (self-care, eating, bathing, moving from bed to some other location, and using the toilet). Longitudinal research completed by K. Warner Schaie (1989) identified six factors that help explain the energetic lifestyles of many individuals in this age group (this list highlights the interplay of the biological and social systems): (a) absence of cardiovascular and other chronic diseases, (b) favorable environment linked to high socioeconomic status, (c) involvement in a complex and intellectually stimulating environment, (d) flexible personality style at midlife, (e) high cognitive functioning of spouse, and (f) maintenance of level of perceptual processing speed. Fozard, Vercruyssen, Reynolds, Hancock, and Quilter (1994) note limited changes in reaction time to varying stimuli for this group as compared with men and women at age 50. In addition, as many as 40% of these individuals are either employed or actively volunteering in a nonretirement activity (Hayward, Crimmins, & Wray, 1994).

Elders in the old–old category (75–84 years of age) are more likely to be widowed (61% vs. 36%) and female (62 men per 100 women) than those elders over 65 and under 74 (U.S. Bureau of the Census, 1989). It has been estimated that losses as great as 20% in hearing (Ordy, Brizzee, Beavers, & Medhart, 1979) and 25% to 40% in response time (Fozard et al.) develop during these years. Major diseases of the eyes affect as much as 45% of the population (vs. 18% in the 65–74-year age group and 4% in those 52–64 years of age) (Kini et al., 1978). In a study of this age group completed in Framingham, Massachusetts, 39% were unable to stand for a 15-minute period, 23% were unable to walk one half of a mile, 15% could not climb stairs, 24% were unable to lift small items weighing less than 10 pounds, and more than 50% were unable to lift heavier items or to stoop, crouch, or kneel without difficulty or assistance (Hickey, Wolf, Robbins, Wagner, & Harik, 1995).

Jarvik, Lavretsky, and Neshkes (1992) report that while only 8% to 10% of the population over the age of 65 is considered to have some form of dementia, this figure increases to 30% or more starting at the age of 80. Crystallized intelligence (learning and acculturation over a lifetime) is maintained at this stage, but fluid intelligence (neurological and physiologic functioning: information processing, reasoning, perceptual and spatial relationships) begins declining very rapidly (Horn, 1985). Those employed or actively volunteering drop to less than 5% and financial security is closely tied to social security payments (Hayward et al., 1994). In general, a deterioration or loss of health, mobility, and independence issues affect these individuals' well-being and their ability to cope with their environment (McGee, 1996a).

In the 85+ age group, the statistics regarding male–female ratios worsen (40 men per 100 women) (U.S. Bureau of the Census, 1989), and major health problems affect more than 50% of those in this category (Hooyman & Kiyak, 1996). Twenty-three percent of this age group live in nursing homes, 75% of them without spouses (U.S. Senate, Special Committee on Aging, 1986). Serious mental (dementia and forms of delirium) and physical (wheelchairs, walkers, hearing aids, and eyesight) health issues appear to affect this group. Roberts, Dunkle, and Haug (1994) indicate that deterioration of health and increased dependence in assisted daily living activities may restrict the abilities of this age group to control many aspects of their lives; they are generally dependent on others.

DEVELOPMENTAL ACTIVITIES AND MAJOR STRESSORS

Seniors' responses to a major stressor such as the death of family or friends can be evaluated in terms of their abilities to complete tasks and processes that are typically completed in their stage of the life cycle. Steinglass and Gerrity (1990) believe that these impacts can be surveyed from a position of psychosocial well-being or developmental functioning. While seniors may appear to be operating effectively, many of their daily functioning activities may suffer because of "environmental docility" caused by extreme stress (Lawton & Nahemow, 1973). In terms of the issue of impending death of a spouse, Aldwin (1992) describes how this critical life situation frequently creates depression. A consequence of this depression, he notes, is deterioration of mental and physical well-being. A model developed by Levinson (1986) addresses this problem by examining developmental stages in terms of life structures at varying points of adult life. These life structures include sociocultural features (e.g., social class, ethnicity, and occupation), one's personal self (e.g., conflicts, fantasies, and anxieties), and participation in society (e.g., interaction between self and society). If one is sensitive to change (psychologically and biologically) and the environment is supportive of this change, then the individual can respond accordingly. However, if these structures are "out of synch," individuals are unable to establish equilibrium within their environment. Older persons who deny biological or physiological changes are more likely to experience problems at their developmental stage. As such, death or loss of life would likely present such a problem.

Kahana (1992) noted that older individuals' reactions to a trauma often go beyond the event itself, and these reactions frequently have negative impacts on their ability to hold jobs or form intimate relationships. Other researchers believe that the trauma may alter an elder's psychological completion of such development processes as consolidation of life themes or reviews (Butler, 1968). This developmental task completion research seems to imply that successful resolution of the trauma's crisis is needed for an individual's development. If this resolution is successfully accomplished, then a sense of efficacy and ego integrity is obtained in later life (Billings & Moos, 1981).

ELDER INTERVENTION ISSUES

Current research on death's traumatic effects on the elderly has only a limited base of knowledge; the crisis-response research base is almost nonexistent. As a result, elderly crisis-related process concerns have not been established, and a generalizable mental health model has not been developed. To properly complete such a task, information on senior family support, social networking among elders, the role of the nursing home or assisted care facility in resolving senior stressors, mental and physical health conditions, and the identification of late phase process distortions affected by a traumatic event need to be understood.

Current intervention actions by mental health professionals for the elderly evolve around physical health concerns and social networking with the following foci: (a) Counseling efforts for seniors are primarily completed in residential facilities; (b) elders' well-being is defined as a function of their physical health; (c) elder social networks are not used by counselors to assist the elderly in coping with trauma; (d) almost all existing research on older adults' responses to trauma focuses on posttraumatic stress rather than the acute stress syndrome that is associated with death or bereavement (symptom elimination in less than 6 months); and (e) research and counseling efforts group elders homogeneously (as a function of age rather than developmental, mental, physiological, or psychological levels) (McGee, 1996b).

From these foci, intervention efforts in understanding about and responding to senior reactions include contacting seniors and providing them with "physical" assistance or help in completing a life review. These intervention actions appear to have their origins in a physical recovery model (and not in a psychologically based model). It is therefore no surprise that many, if not most, senior crisis counseling programs are based on little or no trauma reduction research. Individual and family life cycle developmental issues, social functioning, and emotional well-being are generally not addressed or included in an intervention approach for seniors. Zarit (1980) hypothesizes that this reaction should not be unexpected:

> Because of the tendency to view old persons as impaired due to their age, excessive use of the medical model and its variants reinforces the likelihood that one will blame a problem on something inside the person and miss those factors in the individual's environment that are influencing or controlling the disturbed behavior. (p. 117)

ASSESSMENT MODELS

Assessment models review an event, assess its influence, evaluate individual or group coping abilities, and make a prediction as to the likely outcome. Parad and Parad (1990) suggest the following criteria for evaluating assessment models: (a) Start with a specific and identifiable stressful precipitating event; (b) perceive the event as meaningful and threatening; (c) note disorganization or disequilibrium resulting from the event; and (d) identify the coping and intervention tasks involved in resolution, which may be adaptive or maladaptive. Many of the better known models have been in existence for several years, yet their adaptation to the elderly is limited.

A commonly used model in crisis assessment was developed by Naomi Galon (1978). This model has five primary components that survey the degree of a crisis's turbulence: (a) hazardous event (specific stressful occurrence that could be anticipated, unanticipated, or unheralded), (b) vulnerable state (one's reaction to the hazardous event), (c) precipitating factor (what converts one's state into a crisis situation), (d) state of activity (exhaustion or shock), and (e) reintegration (return to equilibrium, with associated correct cognitive perceptions, management of affect, and development of coping mechanisms).

Aguilera and Messick (1982) developed a similar assessment approach. Their model incorporates and compares reactions and balancing factors between the individual and the crisis-provoking stressor over a specified time frame. Balancing factors are internal and external elements that assist one in coping with a crisis. These include factors perception of an event, degree of situational support, and type of individual coping skills. Each of these balancing factors (or lack thereof) helps the individual regain his or her equilibrium and avoid (or go into) a crisis. Balancing factors represent Aguilera and Messick's effort to include systemic and individual coping components with an individual's developmental stage in dealing with the crisis event.

From this review of trauma assessment models and senior deveopmental issues, it appears that an approach to help seniors cope with death encompassing both individual developmental concerns and systemic influencing components is most appropriate. Many of the social gerontological models identify the environment in which the senior operates as having a significant impact on his or her ability to adapt and respond to the impact of stressors (Kahana, 1975; Lawton & Nahemow, 1973). Developmental concerns include the individual aging concepts noted at the beginning of this chapter: chronological aging, biological aging, psychological aging, and social aging.

SENIOR TRAUMA METHODOLOGICAL APPROACH

A model for evaluating and predicting seniors' responses to a traumatic event such as death and loss of life needs to build upon newly developed data that are senior specific for developmental stages. Much of the previous research relied on assumptions regarding the stress of death and its effect and did not account for developmental changes. Chief among these assumptions is the belief that all seniors exhibit the same symptoms and that these symptoms may uniformly inhibit wants, needs, concerns, and emotional well-being. That would be similar to say-

Table 10.1 Senior Developmental Phases Applicable for Trauma Issues

Developmental issues	Developmental phase		
	Moderation of abilities	Loss of independence	Dependent

Biological aging
  Physical health
    Self-rating
    Mobility
  Number of
  activities of
  daily living
	Generally in good physical condition; some reduction in mobility; frequently participate in golf, tennis, and other activities	Hearing loss and eyesight deterioration begin to accelerate; number of activities of daily living problems increase	More than 50% have major health problems; mobility very limited

Psychological aging
  Mental health
    Memory
    Intelligence
  Adaptability
  Self-esteem
	Cognitive functioning generally at pre-65 level; flexible personality similar to midlife; slight loss of perceptual processing speed	Crystallized intelligence still intact, but less concentration, attentiveness, and adaptability in thought process; probability of dementia increases from 10% to 30%	Mental disorders such as dementia affect more than 30% of population; reaction time is 10 times longer for problem solving than at age 50

Social aging
  Size of social
  network
  Cohort norms
  Family within
  10 miles
  Marital status
	Many cohorts still alive; social networks (formal and informal) large; most married; other family not necessarily near	Cohorts dying at an increasing rate; 61% of women are widowed; begin the process of moving closer to family	Cohorts continue dwindling, now only 40 men to each 100 women; 75% are widowed females

Additional resources
  Independence
    Drive auto
    Financial
    Outside
    employment
  Medical
  insurance
	Most still drive a car; about 40% work or volunteer their time; many have stable financial worth	Few still drive; only 46% have a high school education; less than 5% work or volunteer; most rely on Social Security and Medicare	Almost 25% live in nursing homes; few are employed or perform volunteer work; generally dependent on others

ing one can predict a small child's responses to death based on an adult model of development.

The model postulated in this chapter includes individual developmental considerations as well as resources available to seniors. Furthermore, from this point in the chapter, seniors are referred to by developmental phases rather than their chronological age. The basis for these phases evolved from the gerontological age groupings, but they are not "wedded" to a specific chronological time frame. This model recognizes that seniors progress through a series of changes that alter their abilities to respond, react, and cope with stimuli as they had when they were middle-aged adults. As seniors' ability to adapt deteriorates, they become less independent and rely on others. The SLSDM is based on this premise. The model's phases include moderation of abilities, loss of independence, and dependent (see Table 10.1).

Most geriatric models discuss the impacts of aging but do not fully integrate these concepts into their theory of stress management. Seniors who are in excellent health, continue to work, enjoy recreational activities, and are active in the community would be classified as being in the moderation of abilities phase. Their adaptive abilities and their coping systems are largely intact. As such, their stress management process would be different from one developed for seniors in later phases. Their age, be it 65 or 80, is not as significant as their ability to cope with and adapt to their environment.

When an elder is no longer able to drive an automobile or walk to a friend's house, he or she has entered the loss of independence phase. These seniors are relying on others for selected services to meet their needs. From a developmental perspective, they are in need of assistance. When seniors enter the last developmental phase, they are reliant on others for most, if not all, of their daily needs. They are dependent.

An example of a recent attempt to integrate developmental issues into gerontological stress issues was that of Roberts et al. (1994). They studied the degree to which seniors' (85+ years) functional abilities (physical resources and independence in daily living activities), psychological resources (mastery, self-esteem, and coping), and social resources (frequency of social interaction and size of network) could alleviate the adverse effects of moderate levels of stress on mental health. Their findings indicated greater independence in activities of daily living and greater perceived control of events, which significantly attenuated the adverse effects of strain on psychological well-being (this coincides with the less independent and dependent developmental phases and represents a key component for a trauma response approach). This study also noted that, contrary to the authors' expectations, self-esteem, coping, and general health had only a minimal impact in alleviating the effects of stress (which makes sense given the subjects' dependent status; these concepts would, however, be of importance to seniors in an earlier developmental phase).

A broad-based geriatric stress reduction model that has been used for bereavement is one developed by Miller and Jay (1989). This approach identifies

Table 10.2 Stress Management Model for Geriatric Patients

Module	Therapeutic task	Expected outcome
Behavioral assessment	Assess the components of stress experienced by the person as they relate to life events	Patient understands elements of stress and specific factors that trigger anxiety and result in stress
Cognitive appraisal	Appraise the manner in which the patient perceives and communicates stress behavior in life stress events	Patient understands how he or she processes the perception of stressful situations and uses this information to control stress-producing experiences
Education and training	Educate and train the patient to use a four-step model in dealing with stress and its associated pain	Patient understands and uses four-step stress management skills training model
Stress management skills	Train the person in the use of cognitive imagery and muscle relaxation skills as the medium for reducing stress and pain	Patient learns effective use of cognitive coping skills and employs them in the control of anxiety, stress, and tension

specific therapeutic tasks, along with expected outcomes for dealing with death-related stress (see Table 10.2). Included in the model are behavioral, cognitive, and educational components. This approach may be appropriate for seniors in the modified abilities phase; for the loss of independence and dependent groups, however, this model assumes intellectual or social resource properties that are generally not available to these seniors. With their memory and physical activity levels at a reduced state, these later phased groups might have a difficult, if not impossible, task of understanding, processing, and adapting their cognitive imagery skills. The approach suggested in this chapter incorporates the special developmental needs of seniors. Their ability to deal with death's stress varies through the developmental phases; in the later stages, one's individual coping skills are limited.

This developmentally based process is the SLSDM. This model assesses seniors' individual developmental life stage, notes their unique strengths, and acknowledges their physical, psychological, social, and independence abilities and limitations. Seniors are not grouped together but separated by their developmentally phased abilities. As such, a senior who is functioning at a high physical, emotional, and social level with superior coping skills is not provided the same treatment as a senior who has a diminished capacity for cognitive comprehension or an inadequate cohort support network for attenuating the effects of a major stressor.

SENIOR LIFE SPAN DEVELOPMENTAL MODEL FOR TRAUMA REDUCTION

This trauma reduction model has five distinct steps that are epigenetic in nature and often sequential. When individuals believe that their environment, their coping systems, or their internal belief schema are challenged beyond their ability to adapt or comprehend, they either change or become overwhelmed. Seniors may become traumatized by a major stressor or multiple minor stressors. It is at this point that seniors are often dismissed as being senile or confused. As a result, they do not seek help from a friend or a therapist. They become depressed and are ignored. The process, of acknowledgment of a problem, acceptance of the need for assistance, and willingness to grow is disrupted.

The senior therapeutic process is developmental in nature, often cognitive-behavioral, and frequently involves a kinesthetic orientation. This approach is based on the assumption that the goal of therapy is to help the senior achieve developmentally appropriate social functioning (without trauma symptoms). Specifically, this model assists seniors in reacting to the symptom-producing components of a major stressor by helping them (a) move to a normative position in their respective developmental phase; (b) identify an optimal balance among their psychological, physiological, and social needs; (c) identify specific trauma symptoms and reactions that are disruptive, repetitive, and maladaptive; (d) develop alternative beliefs about the stressor and more beneficial problem-solving patterns that are developmentally functional; and (e) dislodge the internal beliefs/schemas that encourage or maintain the stressor-related maladaptive behavior patterns.

In working with individuals who have experienced a major stressor, it is important to remember their need for safety (Gentry & Schmidt, 1996). This need for safety is magnified with seniors. No other therapeutic work can possibly succeed if safety has not been adequately secured (Herman, 1992). We cannot guarantee that horrible experiences will never again occur. However, we can begin to address the real hazards and deficiencies in the lives of trauma survivors that continually leave them feeling vulnerable and terrified (Gentry & Schmidt, 1996).

After safety has been established, the therapy process moves into the assessment stage. During assessment, seniors are evaluated for symptoms related to the major stressor and for their developmental phase. Again, their developmental phase is a function of their physical health and mental health capabilities, environmental adaptability, size and nature of their social network, and degree of independence. Proper evaluation is critical. However, there are potential impediments to this approach, the most obvious being the therapist's ability to correctly identify the senior's stage of development. Examples of issues that could cloud or influence the therapist's judgment include (a) the therapist's ability to establish safety and trust with the senior, (b) changes in the therapist's assessment due to confounding variables, and (c) the therapist's degree of personal reactivity to a senior's personality, which may alter his or her perceptions of the senior's reaction to the major stressor.

After the assessment stage has been completed, the therapy process moves in differing directions depending on the senior's developmental phase. For those in the moderation of abilities phase, a cognitive-behavioral-based approach that emphasizes understanding and addressing the senior's schema is undertaken. This process encourages the senior to describe the major stressor and provides the therapist with a clear picture of how the stressor event is affecting the senior. Defense mechanisms and maladaptive behaviors that are a result of the stressor are identified and named. The therapy goals at this point are to disrupt the behavior patterns that maintain the distrusted perceptions of one another's characteristics and dirtectly challenge those dysfunctional interpersonal schematics (Seagraves, 1990). Seniors are provided materials to review regarding the impact of the stressor, and they are ancouraged fo discuss the event with their family and friends. As Figley (1989) notes, the process of listening and helping the affected individual make meaning of the recent trauma is empowering. With power or mastery of events, seniors are able to move on with their life and address necessary developmental issues.

Some gerontologists believe that seniors have experienced many satressful events in the course of their lives and are better able to put the current stressor into perspective (Hooyman & Kiyak, 1996). This belief has not been adequately researched, however. Therefore, if the stressor is still affecting the senior, then the use of eye movement desensitization and reprocessing (EMDR) or thought field therapy (TFT) techniques is suggested to assist in reducing the level of stress. These techniques involve the use of sensory processes and affect one's orienting reflex, which transmits anticipated symptom responses from the brain to the body (Denny, 1995). The resultant therapeutic process confuses the body and dissipates a memory's emotional charge. With a lowered level of anxiety, seniors are better able to manage their stressor's symptoms, address their stressor-related fears, and eliminate the stressor's negative feedback that reinforced the maladaptive coping mechanism.

Seniors in the loss of independence phase need both cognitive (re)processing and social support. Their need to establish mastery or control over their lives is their primary aim. Cognitive components addressed in the model help them develop insights into the stressor's impacts. This process is completed in a slow, methodical manner. Since seniors in this phase often process information at a reduced rate, it is important that the therapist allow them to integrate the meaning of the stressor in a comfortable process. Their thoughts are rational and systematic. Seniors will ask many many questions and frequently want feedback. Their goal is to gain a sense of control. To assist in this process, it is recommended this part of the therapy occur in a group or cohort setting. Validation of pain, acceptance of the trauma's symptoms, and a unified sense of control generally come more easily in this setting.

As with seniors in the moderation of abilities phase, if seniors in the loss of independence phase experience symptom anxiety that is so overwhelming that they are unable to address their feelings or discuss their thoughts regarding the stressor, then EMDR or TFT is recommended. The use of these techniques will likely occur sooner than with earlier phased seniors. These seniors experience confusion more easily and frequently rely on others for advice and information. If their anxiety is reduced, they may be more prepared to listen to others and share their concerns. This interactive process helps them interpret the stressor and make meaning of its consequences.

The dependent phase group involves a very different process. In many cases, these seniors do not have family near them and often reside in a nursing home or with other caretakers. Their reaction to a major stressor is more likely to be vicarious than symptomatic. Seniors in this phase are frequently bedridden and do not have the full range of cognitive or physiological abilities. As a result, their reaction to a stressor is closely correlated to their primary care provider's stress reactions.

Vicarious traumatization is an adjustment disorder that some people experience as a result of their involvement with an individual experiencing trauma or a major stressor (Figley, 1995). The symptoms are often identical to those of the person actually traumatized by the event. The primary difference is that the senior can recover from the effects of the stressor when the traumatized caregiver recovers. As a result, seniors and their caregivers are requested to complete a joint therapy process. As the caregiver improves, so does the senior.

TFT is strongly suggested for use in the initial therapeutic session. Dependent phase seniors operate on the basis of what they need for daily living. They often cannot think abstractly, care for themselves, or articulate their concerns. As a result, if they are suffering from a stressor, direct or vicarious, they may need to have their symptom anxiety reduced. After their anxiety has been reduced, they and their caregiver are encouraged to attend cohort meetings and discuss their feelings. Strong reassurances of positive progress are recommended. For the caregiver, a moderation of abilities phase stressor-reduction approach is recommended.

In each of the specific phases of the SLSDM, a good aftercare and follow-up program is recommended. In the case of seniors in the modified abilities phase, it is anticipated they will gain much from the therapy process as well as from conversations with family and friends. Six to 8 family sessions with a trained trauma therapist or 10 to 12 individual sessions that include some family members over a 4- to 6-month period should permit the senior to adequately address and ameliorate stressor symptoms.

For seniors in the loss of independence phase, a similar period of time is anticipated. These sessions, however, are group oriented. Social support and group assistance in making meaning of the event are accomplished in a three-step process: (a) acknowledgment of the need for others, (b) telling one's stressor story in a shared environment; and (c) using the resources of the group to help attenuate the stressor's impact and develop a meaning of the stressor event.

The dependent group treatment process is as much a function of the caregiver going for treatment as the senior him- or herself undergoing therapy. As stated earlier, both the caregiver and the senior attend therapy. If the senior's stressor symptoms are vicariously obtained, then the caregiver would also attend therapy separately (to address stressor reactions). The senior and the caregiver are encouraged to attend cohort meetings and stay for as long as they believe the meetings are useful or until the stressor symptoms have diminished.

CONCLUSION

Elders' decling functional abilities affect their individual coping abilities. As a result, ecosystemic support from family, friends, or other interactional microsystems can help the elder cope with the trauma of death or loss of life symptoms. With the developmental phases presented in this chapter, a basis for treating the trauma's symptoms is highlighted.

By focusing on functional abilities, the therapeutic process addresses an elder's declining coping abilities with the addition of appropriate amounts of ecosystemic support. This is critical, since previously noted research highlights that greater independence in activities of daily living and percieved control of events are more likely to modify the negative impacts of a trauma than the commonly held belief that the keys are self-esteem, coping, and general health (Roberts et al., 1994).

The SLSDM includes these issues as its focus. The model helps elders move to a normative position of functioning. The model is not age based but functional skill based. The goal is to utilize the elders coping abilities that are directly related to their functional level, and supplement it with ecosystemic support to maximize emotional well-being.

REFERENCES

Aarts, P. G., & Op den Velde, W. (1996). Prior traumatization and the process of aging: Theory and clinical applications. In B. Van der Kolk, A. McFarlane, & L. Weisaeth (Eds.), *Traumatic stress: The effects of overwhelming experience on mind, body, and society* (pp. 359–377). New York: Guilford Press.

Aguilera, D., & Messick, J. (1982). *Crisis intervention: Therapy for psychological emergencies.* New York: New American Library.

Aldwin, C. (1992). Aging, coping, and efficacy: Theoretical framework for examining coping in life-span developmental context. In M. Wykle, E. Kahana, & J. Kowal (Eds.), *Stress and health among the elderly* (pp. 96–113). New York: Springer.

Anderson, R., & Newman, J. (1973). Societal and individual determinants of medical care use in the United States. *Milbank Memorial Fund Quarterly, 51,* 95–124.

Billings, A. G., & Moos, R. H. (1982). Stressful life events and symptoms: A longitudinal model. *Health Psychology, 1,* 99–117.

Boss, P. (1988). *Family stress management.* Newbury Park, CA: Sage.

Burgess, A. W., & Baldwin, B. A. (1981). *Crisis intervention theory and practice: A clinical handbook.* Englewood Cliffs, NJ: Prentice Hall.

Butler, R. (1968). The life review: An interpretation of reminiscence in the aged. In B. Neugarten (Ed.), *Middle Age and Aging* (pp. 486–496). Chicago: University of Chicago Press.

Coleman, P. G. (1986). *Aging and reminiscence process: Social and clinical implications.* New York: Wiley.

Denny, N. R. (1995). An orienting reflex/external inhibition model of EMDR and thought field therapy. *Traumatology* [On-line], http://rdz.acor.org/lists/trauma//denny.html.

Department of Aging, Florida State Government. (1994). *Disaster planning for the elderly.* Tallahassee, FL: Author.

Dwyer, J. W., & Coward, R. T. (1992). Gender and family care of the elderly: Research gaps and opportunities. In J. Dwyer & R. Coward (Eds.), *Gender, families, and elder care* (pp. 151–162). Newbury Park, CA: Sage.

Erikson, E. (1965). *Childhood and society* (2nd ed.). Harmondsworth, England: Penguin Books.

Figley, C. (Ed.). (1978). *Stress disorders among Vietnam veterans: Theory, research and treatment.* New York: Bunner/Mazel.

Figley, C. R. (1982, January). *Traumatization and comfort: Close relations maybe hazardous to your health.* Invited lecture, Texas Tech University.

Figley, C. (1989). *Helping traumatized families.* San Francisco: Jossey-Bass.

Figley, C. (1995). Compassion fatigue as secondary traumatic stress disorder: An overview. In C. Figley (Ed.), *Compassion fatigue: Coping with secondary traumatic stress disorder in those who treat the traumatized* (pp. 1–21). New York: Brunnel/Mazel.

Figley, C., & McCubbin, H. (Eds.). (1983). *Stress and the family: Vol. 2. Coping with catastrophe.* New York: Brunner/Mazel.

Fozard, J. L., Vercruyssen, M., Reynolds, S. L., Hancock, P. A., & Quilter, R. E. (1994). Age differences and changes in reaction time: The Baltimore Longitudinal Study of Aging. *Journal of Gerontology: Psychological Sciences, 49,* P179–P189.

Freedy, J., Saladin, M., Kilpatrick, D., Resnick, H., & Saunders, B. (1994). Understanding acute psychological distress following a natural disaster. *Journal of Traumatic Stress, 7,* 257–274.

Gentry, J. E., & Schmidt, I. M. (1996). *Safety reconnaissance.* Paper presented at the Treating Traumatic Stress and Dissociation Conference, Morgantown, WV.

Golan, N. (1978). *Treatment in crisis intervention.* New York: Free Press.

Hagstrom, R. (1995). The acute psychological impact on survivors following a train accident. *Journal of Traumatic Stress, 8,* 391–402.

Hayward, M. D., Crimmins, E. M., & Wray, L. A. (1994). The relationship between retirement life cycle changes and older men's labor force participation rates. *Journal of Gerontology: Social Sciences, 49,* S219–S230.

Herman, J. L. (1992). *Trauma and recovery.* New York: Basic Books.

Hickey, T., Wolf, F. M., Robbins, L. S., Wagner, M. B., & Harik, W. (1995). Physical training activity for functional mobility in older persons. *Journal of Applied Gerontology, 14,* 357–371.

Hobfoll, S. (1989). Conservation of resources: A new attempt at conceptualizing stress. *American Psychologist, 44,* 513–524.

Holmes, T. H., & Rahe, R. (1967). The Social Readjustment Rating Scale. *Journal of Psychosomatic Research, 11,* 213–218.

Hooyman, N., & Kiyak, H. A. (1996). *Social gerontology: A multidisciplinary perspective.* Boston: Allyn & Bacon.

Horn, J. (1985). The theory of fluid and crystallized intelligence in relation to concepts of cognitive psychology and aging in adulthood. In F. Craik & S. Trehub (Eds.), *Aging and cognitive processes* (pp. 237–278). New York: Plenum.

Horowitz, M. (1976). *Stressful response syndrome.* New York: Aronson.

Jarvik, L. F., Lavretsky, E., & Neshkes, R. (1992). Dementia and delirium in old age. In J. C. Brock-elhurst, R. C. Tallis, & H. M. Fillet (Eds.), *Textbook of geriatric medicine and gerontology* (4th ed., pp. 326–344). London: Churchill Livingstone.

Kahana, B. (1992). Late-life adaptation in the aftermath of extreme stress. In M. Wykle, E. Kahana, & J. Kowal (Eds.), *Stress and health among the elderly*. New York: Springer.

Kahana, E. F. (1975). A congruence model of person-environment interaction. In M. P. Lawton (Ed.), *Theory development in environments and aging*. New York: Wiley.

Kini, M. M., Leibowitz, H. M., Colton, T., Nickerson, J., Ganley, J., & Dawber, T. R. (1978). Preva-lence of senile cataract, diabetic retinopathy, senile macular degeneration and open-angle glau-coma in the Framingham Eye Study. *American Journal of Ophthalmology, 85*, 28–34.

Kiyak, H. A., & Kahana, E. F. (1975). *Life events scaling by college students and the elderly*. Paper presented at the meeting of the American Psychological Association, New York.

Knight, B. G. (1992). *Older adults in psychotherapy: Case histories*. Newbury Park, CA: Sage.

Kubler-Ross, E. (1969). *On death and dying*. New York: Macmillan.

Lawton, M., & Nahemow, L. (1973). Ecology and the aging process. In C. Eisdorfer & M. Lawton (Eds.), *The psychology of adult development and aging* (pp. 619–674). Washington, DC: Amer-ican Psychological Association.

Levinson, D. J. (1986). A conception of adult development. *American Psychologist, 41*, 3–13.

Levitt, M., Antonucci, T., Clark, M., Rotton, J., & Finley, G. (1985). Social support and well-being: Preliminary indicators based on two samples of the elderly. *International Journal of Aging and Human Development, 21*, 61–77.

McGee, M. P. (1996a). *A preliminary ethnographic study: The culture of assisted living facilities*. Unpublished research report, Florida State University.

McGee, M. P. (1996b). *What is known and observed in our response to senior trauma*. Unpublished research report, Florida State University.

Miller, T. W., & Jay, L. L. (1989). Multifactorial stressors in life change events for the elderly patient. In T. W. Miller (Ed.), *Stressful life events* (pp. 729–747). Madison, WI: International Universities Press.

Nadler, A., & Ben-Shushan, D. (1989). Forty years later: Long-term consequences of massive trauma-tization as manifested by holocaust survivors from the city and kibbutz. *Journal of Consulting and Clinical Psychology, 57*, 287–293.

Nelson, G. M. (1995). The field of adult services. In G. Nelson, A. Eller, D. Streets, & M. Morse (Eds.), *The field of adult services: Social work practice and administration* (pp. 3–16). Washington, DC: NASW Press.

Newman, B. M., & Newman, P. R. (1995). *Development through life: A psychosocial approach*. Pacific Grove, CA: Brooks/Cole.

Ordy, J. M., Brizzee, K. R., Beavers, T., & Medhart, P. (1979). Age differences in the functional and structural organization of the auditory system in man. In J. Ordy & K. Brizzee (Eds.), *Sensory systems and communication in the elderly* (pp. 156–172). New York: Raven Press.

Parad, H. J., & Parad, L. (1990). Crisis intervention: an introductory overview. In H. Parad & L. Parad (Eds.), *Crisis intervention Book 2: The practitioner's source book for brief therapy* (pp. 3–66). Milwaukee, WI: Family Service of America.

Phifer, J. F. (1990). Psychological distress and somatic symptoms after natural disasters: Differential vulnerability among older adults. *Psychology and Aging, 5*, 412–420.

Riley, M. W., & Riley J. (1986). Longevity and social structure: The potential of adding years. In A. Pifer & L. Bronte (eds.), *Our Aging Society: Paradox and promise* (pp. 53–77). New York: Norton.

Roberts, B. L., Dunkle, R., & Haug, M. (1994). Physical, psychological, and social resources as mod-erators of the relationship of stress to mental health of the very old. *Journal of Gerontology: Social Sciences, 49*, S35–S43.

Rosow, I. (1967). *Social integration of the aged*. New York: Free Press.

Ross, M., & Wonders, J. (1993). An exploration of the characteristics of post traumatic stress disorder in reserve forces deployed during Desert Storm. *Archives of Psychiatric Nursing, 7*, 265–269.

Schmidt, A. H. (1991). The deficiency model: An exploration of current approaches to late-life disorders. *Psychiatry, 54*, 358–367.

Seagraves, R. (1990). Short-term marital therapy. In R. A. Wells & V. Giannetti (Eds.), *Handbook of the brief psychotherapies* (pp. 437–460). New York: Plenum.

Shaie, K. W. (1989a). Perceptual speed in adulthood: Cross-sectional and longitudinal studies. *Psychology and Aging, 4*, 443–453.

Shaie, K. W. (1989). The hazards of cognitive aging. *The Gerontologist, 29*, 484–493.

Smith, T. (1985). Rap groups and group therapy for Vietnam veterans. In S. Sonnenberg, A. Blank, & J. Talbott (Eds.), *The trauma of war: Stress and recovery in Vietnam veterans* (pp. 125–163). Washington, DC: American Psychiatric Press.

Solomon, Z. (1988). The effects of combat-related posttraumatic stress disorder on the family. *Psychiatry, 51*, 323–329.

Solomon, Z., Mikulincer, M., Fried, M., & Wosner, V. (1987). Family characteristics and post traumatic stress disorder: A follow-up of Israeli combat stress reaction casualties. *Family Process, 26*, 383–394.

Steinglass, P. (with Bennett, L., Wolin, S., & Reiss, D.). (1987). *The alcoholic family.* New York: Basic Books.

Steinglass, P., & Gerrity, E. (1990). Natural disasters and post traumatic stress disorder: Short-term versus long-term recovery in two disaster-affected communities. *Journal of Applied Psychology, 20*, 1746–1765.

U.S. Bureau of the Census. (1989). *State population and household estimates with age, sex and components of change: 1981–1988* (Current Population Reports, Special Studies P-25, No. 1044). Washington, DC: U.S. Department of Commerce.

U.S. Bureau of the Census. (1993). *Population projections of the U.S. by age, sex, and race: 1993 to 2050* (Current Population Reports, Series P-25, No. 1104). Washington, DC: U.S. Department of Commerce.

U.S. Senate, Special Committee on Aging. (1986). *Aging America: Trends and projections.* Washington, DC: U.S. Government Printing Office.

U.S. Senate, Special Committee on Aging. (1991). *Aging America: Trends and projections (1990–1991 edition).* Washington, DC: U.S. Government Printing Office.

Wister, A. (1992). Residential attitudes and knowledge, use, and future use of home support agencies. *Journal of Applied Gerontology, 11*, 84–100.

Zarit, S. H. (1980). *Aging and mental disorders.* New York: Free Press.

Chapter 11

Safety Reconnaissance for Grieving Trauma Survivors

J. Eric Gentry and Iris M. Schmidt

We have developed the Safety Reconnaissance to help clinicians who work with trauma survivors to establish an effective means of assessing and building stability in the lives of their clients in early treatment. While this procedure has been developed to work effectively with all trauma survivors, it is adapted for this chapter to focus on working with clients who have witnessed and/or experienced traumatic death.

Safety is of paramount importance in developing successful treatment with trauma survivors. Clinicians who work regularly with posttraumatic conditions endorse a triphasic model of trauma resolution in which safety is the critical first phase and essential to successful completion of treatment goals (Herman, 1992). The procedure described here offers the clinician a systematized multimodal technique of assessment, treatment planning, and interventions toward the goal of safety conspicuously absent from present literature. This strategic procedure is designed to circumnavigate survivors' recalcitrant defense systems (which often thwart conventional methods of assessment and intervention), providing both the clinician and survivor with a "blueprint" to begin this important therapeutic foundation. By combining tools of relaxation, imagery, voluntary dissociation, cognitive restructuring, and behavioral contracting, clinicians who use this technique, in addition to teaching their clients these skills, will construct a comprehensive treatment plan for addressing the chaos that can derail the early stages of recovery.

BACKGROUND

"The first task of recovery is to establish the survivor's safety... for no other therapeutic work can possibly succeed if safety has not been adequately secured" (Herman, 1992, p. 159).

Ultimately, safety is an illusion. We can offer no one the guarantee, especially survivors of fatal traumatic experiences, that these horrible experiences will never again occur. We can, however, begin to address the real hazards and deficiencies in the lives of these survivors that continually leave them feeling vulnerable and terrified. Many survivors report being exploited and overwhelmed by their environment and by the unmanageability of their lives following traumatic experiences. This compromised safety and stability can render them victimized, retraumatized, and, too often, paralyzed with hopelessness (Michenbaum, 1994). The retraumatizing nature of posttraumatic stress can lead the survivor down a spiraled path of even more desperate comfort-seeking behaviors that, instead of providing the sought-after comfort and protection, exacerbate danger and chaos.

With survivors of traumatic experiences that involve fatalities of loved ones, or even strangers, the dimension of traumatic grief resolution must be added to the tasks of recovery (Rando, 1992). With this added burden, it is imperative that the clinician take every possible measure to ensure that the survivor begins his or her recovery on sure footing with maximum environmental and intrinsic stability. By making the effort to ensure stability in early recovery, the clinician can expect to be rewarded with lessened crises and a more expedient recovery (Kluft, 1993).

What, then, is "safety" in the lives and treatment of trauma survivors? In our review of the literature we found little that clarifies the definition of "safety" in the treatment trajectory of survivors of traumatic experiences. For the purposes of this procedure, we have operationally and hierarchically defined safety in terms of three levels:

- Level 1: resolution of impending environmental and intrapersonal danger (i.e., victimizing relationships, active suicidality/homicidality, ambient violence, exploitation, perpetration)
- Level 2: amelioration of self-destructive patterns (i.e., suicidal/homicidal ideation/behavior, self-injurious behavior, eating disorders, persecutory alter ego states, addictions, trauma bonding, risk-taking behaviors, isolation)
- Level 3: restructuring victim mythology into a proactive survivor identity by development and habituation of life-affirming self-care skills (i.e., daily routines, relaxation skills, grounding/containment skills, assertiveness, secure provision of basic needs, self-parenting)

Identification of safety deficiencies and dangers in the lives of our clients is the first task in the establishment of these objectives, followed by treatment planning to resolve shortcomings. In addition to a comprehensive inventory of deficiencies and hazards, an inventory of the survivor's assets is also necessary if the clinician is to know when skills need to be developed and when skills need to be fortified.

In our review of the literature, we found many references as to the importance of establishing safety in the treatment of posttraumatic stress and dissociative disorders (Herman, 1992; Fine, 1991; Goodman, 1993; Kluft, 1993; Putnam, 1989; Braun, 1986; Ross, 1989; Torem, 1989; van der Hart, Steele, Boon, & Paul,

1993; Michenbaum, 1994), but we were unable to extract operational definitions of safety, access assessment tools, or identify procedures that adequately develop planning and interventions toward the goal of safety. If safety is indeed a priori in successful treatment with trauma survivors, then the need for a systematic and comprehensive method of assessment, planning, intervention, and monitoring of this goal seems to be emergent.

In the Safety Reconnaissance, the client and clinician complete these goals through a series of procedural steps involving several different modalities. Through techniques for relaxation, visualization, cognitive-behavioral therapy, and systems theory, a protocol for assessing safety deficiencies/resources, comprehensive treatment planning, and effective monitoring toward this most important goal is offered.

The Safety Reconnaissance offers the individual client, family, or groups who have experienced fatal trauma clear direction toward the goal of safety and stability in their lives. This six-phase treatment model is an efficacious and unique tool for assessing safety deficiencies/resources, developing comprehensive treatment planning, and maintaining effective monitoring toward this most important early treatment goal. Some of the benefits that the clinician can expect from using this procedure are as follows:

- Establishing and prioritizing treatment objectives toward the goal of safety with their clients
- Creating of a manageable, behaviorally specific treatment plan for increasing safety
- Developing an ongoing monitoring tool to assess movement toward the goal of safety

In addition to these benefits, clients will identify triggering situations, thoughts/feelings, objects, and people (S.T.O.P.) that can then be addressed with grounding, containment, and other cognitive-behavioral interventions. We have found no populations with which the Safety Reconnaissance is contraindicated; however, there may be some unwanted side effects, including accessing of disturbing material, uncomfortable feelings, or difficulty with the procedure. These side effects should be discussed with clients, and informed consent should be obtained before implementing the procedure. A documented verbal consent by the client should be sufficient for most clinicians; however, some may wish to create written consent forms.

PROCEDURE

The Safety Reconnaissance is separated into six procedural phases: (a) preparation; (b) orientation to the procedure; (c) relaxation induction, visualization and imagery; (d) scan and mapping; (e) closure and debriefing and (f) treatment planning.

Safety Map

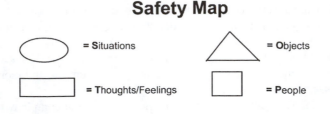

Figure 11.1 Safety Map template.

Phase 1: Preparation

The Safety Reconnaissance can be offered as a healing tool to grieving/traumatized individuals, families, or groups. It should be introduced as an assessment tool to assist the person in regaining a sense of safety, stability, and life continuity.

The clinician needs to allow 45–50 minutes for individuals and 75–80 minutes for groups or families to complete this procedure. The healing team will gather in a comfortable and quiet room where they are assured of uninterrupted time. The setting should offer physical comfort with an option to sit or lay down. The materials required are simple and inexpensive.

Needed are a pen/pencil for each person, individual copies of the Safety Map template and sample (see Figures 11.1 and 11.2), worksheet for hazards and resources (see Figures 11.3 and 11.4), and the treatment plan (see Figure 11.5) and conjoint contract for mastery (see Figure 11.6). Ambient music to facilitate relaxation is optional.

Phase 2: Orientation to the Procedure

The second phase starts with a brief overview of the procedure and an explanation of benefits and possible side effects. Side effects are rare but, as mentioned ear-

Safety Map

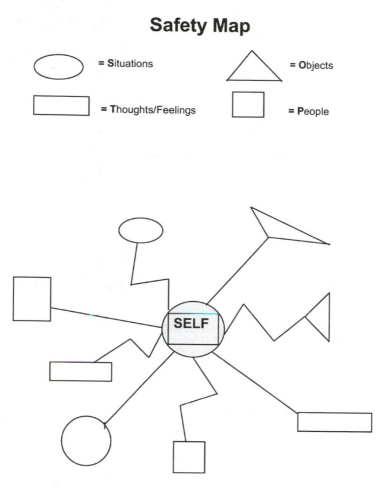

Figure 11.2   Safety Map sample.

lier, can include the possibility of accessing disturbing material, uncomfortable feelings, or difficulty with the procedure. A signal of "stop," such as the raising of a hand, allows the client to terminate the procedure at any time and maintain ultimate control.

The session begins with a solicitation from the clients of their definition of safety and a topical assessment of danger areas and safety hazards in their present-day lives. The clinician may choose to affirm and reframe the client's chronic hypervigiliance as an adaptive protection strategy and challenge this organization toward a more present-day utility (Michenbaum, 1994). This is also an excellent opportunity for the clinician to discuss the critical importance of the goal of safety/stability in the lives and treatment of trauma survivors.

SAFETY HAZARDS TARGET LIST Situations Thoughts Objects People	SUBJECTIVE UNITS OF DISTURBANCE (SUDS) Circle the number that best reflects the strength level for each safety hazard disturbance LOW————————————————HIGH
	0 1 2 3 4 5 6 7 8 9 10
	0 1 2 3 4 5 6 7 8 9 10
	0 1 2 3 4 5 6 7 8 9 10
	0 1 2 3 4 5 6 7 8 9 10
	0 1 2 3 4 5 6 7 8 9 10
	0 1 2 3 4 5 6 7 8 9 10
	0 1 2 3 4 5 6 7 8 9 10
	0 1 2 3 4 5 6 7 8 9 10
	0 1 2 3 4 5 6 7 8 9 10
	0 1 2 3 4 5 6 7 8 9 10
	0 1 2 3 4 5 6 7 8 9 10
	0 1 2 3 4 5 6 7 8 9 10
	0 1 2 3 4 5 6 7 8 9 10
	0 1 2 3 4 5 6 7 8 9 10
	0 1 2 3 4 5 6 7 8 9 10
	0 1 2 3 4 5 6 7 8 9 10
	0 1 2 3 4 5 6 7 8 9 10
	0 1 2 3 4 5 6 7 8 9 10
	0 1 2 3 4 5 6 7 8 9 10
	0 1 2 3 4 5 6 7 8 9 10
	0 1 2 3 4 5 6 7 8 9 10
	0 1 2 3 4 5 6 7 8 9 10
	0 1 2 3 4 5 6 7 8 9 10
	0 1 2 3 4 5 6 7 8 9 10
	0 1 2 3 4 5 6 7 8 9 10
	0 1 2 3 4 5 6 7 8 9 10
	0 1 2 3 4 5 6 7 8 9 10
	0 1 2 3 4 5 6 7 8 9 10
	0 1 2 3 4 5 6 7 8 9 10
	0 1 2 3 4 5 6 7 8 9 10

Figure 11.3   Safety Reconnaissance worksheet for hazards.

This discussion is followed by a brief exploration of the operational definition of safety according to the three levels described earlier.

Discussion with the client or lecture with the group on "What is safety?" should, finally, explore the difference between feeling safe and being safe. This is the clinician's opportunity to challenge the historically adaptive victim schema and emotional reasoning of the client that continually leave the client feeling vulnerable (i.e., the fact that clients are experiencing a flashback or other intrusive/arousal symptoms does not necessarily mean that they are physically in harm's way, even though they may *feel* very much like they are in danger). Such

SAFETY RESOURCE LIST Situations Thoughts Objects People	SUBJECTIVE UNITS OF STRENGTH (SUS) Circle the number that best reflects the strength level for each safety resource LOW————————————HIGH
	0 1 2 3 4 5 6 7 8 9 10
	0 1 2 3 4 5 6 7 8 9 10
	0 1 2 3 4 5 6 7 8 9 10
	0 1 2 3 4 5 6 7 8 9 10
	0 1 2 3 4 5 6 7 8 9 10
	0 1 2 3 4 5 6 7 8 9 10
	0 1 2 3 4 5 6 7 8 9 10
	0 1 2 3 4 5 6 7 8 9 10
	0 1 2 3 4 5 6 7 8 9 10
	0 1 2 3 4 5 6 7 8 9 10
	0 1 2 3 4 5 6 7 8 9 10
	0 1 2 3 4 5 6 7 8 9 10
	0 1 2 3 4 5 6 7 8 9 10
	0 1 2 3 4 5 6 7 8 9 10
	0 1 2 3 4 5 6 7 8 9 10
	0 1 2 3 4 5 6 7 8 9 10
	0 1 2 3 4 5 6 7 8 9 10
	0 1 2 3 4 5 6 7 8 9 10
	0 1 2 3 4 5 6 7 8 9 10
	0 1 2 3 4 5 6 7 8 9 10
	0 1 2 3 4 5 6 7 8 9 10
	0 1 2 3 4 5 6 7 8 9 10
	0 1 2 3 4 5 6 7 8 9 10
	0 1 2 3 4 5 6 7 8 9 10
	0 1 2 3 4 5 6 7 8 9 10
	0 1 2 3 4 5 6 7 8 9 10
	0 1 2 3 4 5 6 7 8 9 10
	0 1 2 3 4 5 6 7 8 9 10
	0 1 2 3 4 5 6 7 8 9 10
	0 1 2 3 4 5 6 7 8 9 10

Figure 11.4 Safety Reconnaissance worksheet for resources.

a challenge allows for rudimentary cognitive restructuring toward a new, more functional belief system and self-management strategies. This opening discussion sets the stage for the procedure while describing the concepts of safety and its importance in recovery from trauma.

Consent for relaxation and imagery techniques, as with any other procedure, is obtained from the client or group members by explaining the procedure along with its benefits and possible side effects. Some of the benefits that can be offered to clients are as follows:

HIERARCHY OF TREATMENT GOALS:
I.   Resolution of impending environmental and/or intrapersonal danger
II. Amelioration of self-destructive patterns
III. Restructuring victim mythology into a proactive survivor schema by
     development and habituation of life-affirming self-care skills

I. PROBLEM IDENTIFICATION:
   EXAMPLE: Client is experiencing impending environmental and/or
   intrapersonal danger as evidenced by...
   • _____
   • _____
   • _____
   • _____
   • _____

GOAL:
   Resolution of impending environmental and/or intrapersonal danger.

OBJECTIVES:
Identification and development of specific intervention:
   1. Victimizing relationships
   2. Ambient violence
   3. Exploitation
   4. Active suicidality
   5. _____
   6. _____

INTERVENTION STRATEGIES AND FREQUENCIES:

II.PROBLEM IDENTIFICATION:
   EXAMPLE: Client engages in self-destructive patterns of...
   • _____
   • _____
   • _____
   • _____
   • _____

Figure 11.5   Safety Reconnaissance master treatment plan (template).

1   Development of a personal experiential definition of safety.
2   Learning of relaxation skills.
3   Creation of an internal "safe place."
4   Practice using imagery as a tool for distancing from disturbing material.
5   Assessment of current "safety hazards" in present-day life.
6   Inventorying resources that can be better used toward enhancing a sense
of safety.
7   Establishing and prioritizing treatment objectives toward the goal of
safety.
8   Creation of a manageable, behaviorally specific treatment plan for increasing safety and stability.
9   Development of an ongoing monitoring tool to assess movement toward
this goal.

GOAL
Amelioration of self-destructive patterns

OBJECTIVES
Identification and development of specific intervention:
1. Suicidal/homicidal ideation/behavior
2. Self-injurious behavior
3. Eating disorders
4. Addictions
5. Trauma bonding
6. Risk-taking behaviors
7. Isolation
8. _____
9. _____
10. _____

INTERVENTION STRATEGIES AND FREQUENCIES:

_____
_____
_____
_____
_____
_____
_____
_____
_____
_____
_____
_____
_____
_____
_____
_____
_____
_____
_____

III. PROBLEM IDENTIFICATION
Client engages in pattern behaviors and cognitions which perpetuate victimization as evidenced by...

- _____
- _____
- _____
- _____
- _____

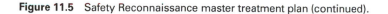

Figure 11.5 Safety Reconnaissance master treatment plan (continued).

GOAL
   Restructuring behavioral and cognitive victim mythology into proactive self-care skills.

OBJECTIVES
Development and habituation of life-affirming self-care skills:
   1. Secure provision of basic needs
   2. Daily routines relaxation training and other meditation techniques
   3. Safe place visualization
   4. Grounding and containment skills training
   5. Stress management
   6. Assertiveness training
   7. Self-parenting
   8. _____
   9. _____
   10. _____

INTERVENTION STRATEGIES AND FREQUENCIES:

Figure 11.5   Safety Reconnaissance master treatment plan (continued).

Phase 3: Relaxation Induction, Visualization and Imagery

   Relaxation Induction   Begin by asking clients to find a comfortable posture with their feet on the floor. We use the "1,000-mile stare induction," in which the participant is instructed to initially fixate and focus and then progressively soften the focus (Tinnin, 1995) with a progressive muscle relaxation script (Hammond, 1990) to elicit the relaxation response. We then employ a counting backward technique, from 30 to 1, during which the client is challenged to find a balance between "holding on" and "letting go," between tension and relaxation. Each number should be verbalized on the exhale breath of the client. It is important to communicate to clients that whatever balance they find, and whatever their relaxation level, it is "good enough" to complete this procedure successfully.

Contract for Mastery

Name: _____   Date: _____

Safety Goal Area: _____

I care about myself and my healing from the horrible things that have happened to me. I realize that to do this I have to make changes in my life and the way I live it. By making these changes, no matter how small, I am affirming my choice to become the person I want to be.

I want (to): _____

_____(my goal)

I will prove to myself that I am committed to becoming my best self by completing the following behavioral objectives (tiny steps):

1. _____

2. _____

3. _____

I will complete these affirmations of myself on or before: _____

_____   _____
signature   date

_____   _____
witness   date

Figure 11.6   Contract for mastery.

Visualization   With the completion of the relaxation script, the therapist can begin the process of imagery for a safe place (Poprajac & Block, 1995). If the client already has an internal safe place established it would be beneficial to integrate it here. We use a script that first focuses on visualization of the safe place and then explores all other sensory channels. Essential components of the safe place are boundaries, presence of safe objects, absence/removal of unsafe objects, and language to fully experience each sensory channel (i.e., sights, sounds, fragrances, textures, feelings in the body, etc.). The client is reminded that he or she can reenter this safe place at any time after the procedure.

Dissociative Imagery   When the safe place has been established and the client has experienced moving about in safety with "relaxed joyfulness" (Hendrix, 1989), it is time to begin to create a dissociative "observer mode" (Tinnin, 1994) while the client remains in the safe place. This is done by asking clients to take a step backward outside themselves so that they can see themselves from behind. Suggestions that they are able to see the back of their head, shoulders, hair, and so forth are helpful (note that this can be confirmed by ideomotor signaling or direct questioning). Next, "the observer" is instructed to view him- or herself from all four sides (with descriptions of clothing, posture, etc.). Then, taking care to time the suggestion with an inhalation breath, instruct "the observer" to "go up, up, up, ... so that you can look down upon yourself ... can see yourself moving with relaxed joyfulness in this safe place." A further suggestion that this "observer" can fly over the perimeter of the safe place, memorizing every detail, can also be helpful.

Phase 4: Scanning and Mapping

Hazards   The client is now in the position to access material that may otherwise be too threatening to acknowledge or to discuss in verbal therapy. Using the observer mode, clients are instructed to study themselves acting and interacting in their environment during the past month. They are first requested to identify situations in which the "person you are studying" is experiencing danger, fear, or any other disturbance. They are asked to pay close attention first to the environmental cues that trigger this disturbance and then to thoughts and/or feelings. S.T.O.P. is helpful in categorizing these observations. This suggestion can be repeated several times as they move through the previous month. A suggestion to "stay up above it all," or "remain safely above" is also helpful. When the client has completed this scan, the following instruction is provided:

> Open your eyes. Pick up your pen and using the S.T.O.P. symbols in the key of your Safety Map, make a jagged line which connects each hazard that you discovered to the circle "Self" (see Figure 11.2).

(Three to 5 minutes should be sufficient for the completion of this portion of the mapping process.) Clients are then requested to put down their pen and close their eyes for the second part of the mapping process.

Resources   This part of the mapping process focuses on a review that will identify safety resources that may formerly not have been fully recognized or not have been systematically used. The clinician can use any creative combinations of suggestions that enhance clients' ability to find experiences of safety in their lives, such as: "You can now begin to observe yourself having experiences of safety ... no matter how small, or brief ... pay attention to the ways in which the person that you are experiences safety, peace, comfort, serenity, joy, hope ... look and see what kindles these feelings ... in the environment ... in the mind ... how does your body behave when it feels safe?" Clients are reminded to "stay above," employing the observer mode while they are led through the 1-month environmental/internal scanning and consequent mapping of safety resources. Mapping instructions are similar to the safety hazard portion of the mapping procedure, with the exception that S.T.O.P. symbols are connected to the "self" with straight, instead of jagged, lines.

Phase 5: Closure and Debriefing

Closure   With the mapping completed, the "observer" is instructed to return to the safe place and reenter the body of the participant with suggestions to integrate all sensory channels (i.e., looking though the same eyes, hearing with the same ears, etc.). The client is invited to move about in the safe place, enjoying the sensations of safety for another moment. The client should be assured that she or he is safely "back together." A postprocedural suggestion similar to the following can also be offered:

> "Congratulations for completing some of the necessary groundwork to provide yourself with the gift of safety. You will find that as you resolve the hazards, using and developing more and more of the resources that you have identified here today, an ever-increasing sense of safety, peace, and hope will begin to replace the fear, isolation, and hopelessness that has been your struggle for so long."

Clients are then directed to begin noticing sounds in the room and sensations in their body and to reorient to here and now.

Debriefing   The client is given ample opportunity to process his or her experiences, insights, and difficulties with this procedure. The clinician should use this time to reiterate the necessity of creating safety and stability as the foundation to all subsequent therapeutic goals. A contract is negotiated with the client to complete the Safety Reconnaissance hazards and resources worksheets as homework prior to the next session, using the information obtained on the Safety Map. The client is also instructed in the use of subjective units of distress (Wolpe, 1991) and subjective units of strength (Gentry & Schmidt, 1996) to be identified for each hazard and resource, respectively. The client is informed that the next session will begin treatment planning toward the goal of safety. Clinicians may wish to gain permission to photocopy clients' Safety Map for their files. This concludes the procedural session and begins treatment planning and intervention toward the goal of safety.

Phase 6: Treatment Planning

The completion of the Safety Reconnaissance provides the clinician and the client with a "blueprint" to adequately identify treatment goals and objectives for the safety phase of posttraumatic treatment (Kluft, 1993). When the client returns for his or her next visit, the clinician should assist him or her in prioritizing the hazards that are to be addressed during this phase as well as which resources will be fortified to create effective and systematic therapeutic movement in pursuit of safety. A template for treatment planning is included (see Figure 11.5). Specific cognitive-behavioral interventions, such as grounding/containment strategies, stress-management techniques, and assertiveness training, should be included in treatment planning.

With the treatment plan completed, the client is then ready to begin contracting for change, growth, and mastery of the skills necessary to successfully navigate these early stages of treatment. The contract for mastery (see Figure 11.6) identifies three specific behavioral objectives toward the amelioration of safety hazards and/or the fortification of safety resources. Prioritization of objectives/issues, time frame, and specific procedures can be contracted individually or in groups.

DISCUSSION

This procedure crystallizes the essential role of establishing and maintaining safety as the foundation for all therapeutic work with trauma survivors, especially those who have experienced traumatic death. The Safety Reconnaissance, involving an eclectic fusion of techniques, provides clinicians and clients with an efficacious and circumspect approach toward completing the tasks of the first phase of trauma therapy.

The goal of safety is grouped into a manageable trilevel hierarchy of objectives and task. The Level 1 task of safety is the resolution of impending environmental danger. Level 2 tasks involve amelioration of the self-destructive patterns of trauma survivors. Level 3 focuses on the restructuring of victim mythology to develop life-affirming self-care skills. By factoring together clients' subjective units of distress ratings of safety hazards and the preceding prioritized hierarchy of safety tasks, clinicians can assist clients in creating a systematic approach to safety and help them confront cognitive and behavioral patterns that exacerbate traumatic stress in their lives. This gentle confrontation can create within clients a desire for change coupled with titrated and manageable tasks toward, once again, the goal of safety. It should be indicated to clients, in clear terms, that treatment cannot progress until they have created a reasonable level of stability and are practicing the skills necessary to develop and maintain safety. With this established, the clinician and client are ready to begin their journey into the resolution of traumatic material and traumatic grief.

In addition, treatment with trauma survivors can sometimes reach an impasse in which therapeutic movement is stymied. One possible explanation for such impasses is the reemergence of safety issues that need to be addressed before treatment can continue. Safety hazards can be reassessed and resolved thus allowing treatment to progress.

CONCLUSION

The Safety Reconnaissance provides the clinician and trauma survivor with a procedure that

1   Operationally and hierarchically defines safety.
2   Challenges victim mythology.
3   Teaches relaxation.
4   Creates an internal "safe place."
5   Teaches *voluntary* dissociative distancing.
6   Assesses current safety hazards.
7   Inventories current safety resources.
8   Establishes a safety treatment plan.
9   Prioritizes goals.
10   Provides a format to create specific behavioral objectives toward the goal of safety.
11   Provides a monitoring tool for ongoing therapeutic efforts in the first phases of treatment.
12   Provides a tool to navigate therapeutic impasses.

While no single procedure can generically assess and effectively plan for the development of safety in the lives and treatment of all posttraumatic clients, the Safety Reconnaissance is a procedure that can circumspectively address many of the needs of the first phase of therapy. With this accomplished, one moves toward the objectives of time-efficient and efficacious treatment. Expedient and effective securing of safety will minimize treatment length, lessen health care costs, and ultimately diminish the suffering of the trauma survivor.

REFERENCES

Braun, B. G. (1986). Issues in the psychotherapy of multiple personality disorder. In B. G. Braun (Ed.), *Treatment of multiple personality disorder*. Washington, DC: American Psychiatry Press.

Fine, C. G. (1991). Treatment stabilization and crisis prevention: Pacing the therapy of the multiple personality disordered patient. *Psychiatric Clinics of North America, 14*, 661–676.

Gentry, I. E., & Schmidt, I. M. (1996). *Safety in treating trauma survivors*. Paper presented at the Sixth Annual Conference for Treating Trauma and Dissociation, West Virginia University School of Medicine, Morgantown, WV.

Goodman, J. (1993). Sadistic abuse: Definition, recognition and treatment. *Dissociation, 6*, 181–184.

Hammond, C. (1990). Progressive relaxation induction or deepening technique. In *Handbook of hypnotic suggestions and metaphors*. New York: Norton.

Hendrix, H. (1993). *Getting the love you want*. New York: Imago.

Herman, J. L. (1992). *Trauma and recovery*. New York: Basic Books.

Kluft, R. P. (1993). The initial stages of psychotherapy in the treatment of multiple personality disorder patients. *Dissociation, 6*, 145–161.

Michenbaum, D. (1994). *A clinical handbook/practical therapist manual for assessing and treating adults with post-traumatic stress disorder.* Toronto, Ontario, Canada: Institute Press.

Poprajac, T., & Block, D. (1995). Minimizing crisis with dissociative disorder patients: Techniques for stabilization. Paper presented at the ISTSS conference, Boston, MA.

Putnam, F. W. (1989). *The diagnosis and treatment of multiple personality disorder.* New York: Guilford Press.

Rando, T. A. (1992). The increasing prevalence of complicated mourning: The onslaught is just the beginning. *Omega, 26,* 43–59.

Ross, C. A. (1989). *Multiple personality disorder, diagnosis, clinical features, and treatment.* New York: Wiley.

Tinnin, L. (1994). *Time-limited trauma therapy for dissociative disorders.* Bruceton Mills, WV: Gargoyle Press.

Tinnin, L. (1995). *One thousand mile stare.* Unpublished manuscript.

Torem, M. (1989). Regression and management of dissociative regressions. *Hypnosis, 16,* 4.

van der Hart, O., Steele, K., Boon, S., & Paul, B. (1993). The treatment of traumatic memories: Synthesis, realization, and integration. *Dissociation, 6,* 162–178.

Wolpe, J. (1991). Post-traumatic stress disorder overcome by eye movement desensitization: A case report. *Journal of Behavior Therapy and Experimental Psychiatry, 22,* 39–43.

Name Index

Aarts, P.G., 186
Abakoumkin, G., 40
Abraham, K., 110
Adler, T., xix, 57, 110, 111
Affleck, G., 137
Agger, I., 24
Aguilera, D., 190
Aiken, L.R., 3
Albeck, J., 15
Albrecht, W., 136
Aldwin, C., 186, 188
Allen-Byrd, L., 178
Alvarez, M.A., 39
Alverez, W., 28, 74
Amick-McMullen, A., 54, 58, 71, 112
Anderson, B., 135
Anderson, R., 185
Antonovsky, A., 139
Antonucci, T., 185
Applebaum, D.R., 14, 54
Aquilino, W.S., 97
Arata, C.M., 60
Archer, T., 167
Armone, H.C., 71
Aron, A., 23, 71
Asai, M., 100
Asendorpf, J.B., 41, 94

Bacon, 138
Baer, B.A., 46
Bagge, R.W., 38, 133, 134, 142, 143
Baldwin, A., 114
Baldwin, B.A., 185
Baldwin, C.P., 114
Bandura, A., 139
Bard, M., 56, 71

Barrett, K.C., 92
Barrionuevo, G., 156
Baruch, R., 139
Baumeister, R.F., 44, 138
Beardslee, W.R., 139
Beavers, T., 187
Beck, A.T., 39
Becker, D., 24
Becker, L.A., 156, 178
Beighle, K., 23
Belenky, G.L., 72
Belestos, G., 24
Belitsky, R., 42, 90
Bem, D.J., 93
Ben-Shushan, D., 185
Benzaquim, P., 110
Berkman, L., 40, 89
Blazer, D.G., 25, 56
Bleich, A., 134
Block, D., 211
Bluck, S., 137
Bickman, L., 79
Bieber, S.L., 6, 7, 8, 10, 15, 24, 26, 28
Billings, A.G., 189
Bisbey, L.B., 170, 179
Boccellari, A., 43, 44, 89
Bolger, N., 40
Boman, B., 72
Bonafacio, P., 72
Bonanno, G.A., xvii–xix, 38, 39, 40, 41, 43, 44,
    45, 46, 89, 90, 91, 92, 93, 94, 95, 96, 97,
    98, 135
Bond, M., 42
Boon, S., 202
Bornemann, T., 13
Bornstein, P.E., 39, 43, 93
Boss, P., 185
Botempo, R., 100

Boudewyns, P., 136
Bowen, D.J., 23
Bower, G.H., 167
Bowlby, J., 9, 42, 43, 45, 55, 89, 90, 92
Bracken, P.J., 24
Brand, E.F., 25
Brandsma, J.M., xx, 38, 133, 134, 141, 142, 144
Brandt, R.B., 99
Braun, B.L., 202
Bremer, D., 157
Bremner, J.D., 113
Brennan, A.M.W., 54
Brent, D.A., 25
Breslau, N., 15
Bride, B.E., 25, 53
Bridge, J., 25
Brigham, D., 138
Brizzee, K.R., 187
Bromet, E., 3, 7
Brown, J.D., 93
Brown, L.L., 41
Brown, P., 56, 134
Buckingham, W., 56
Bugen, L.A., 57
Bullman, T.A., 25
Bumpus, L.L., 97
Burgess, A.G., 185
Burgess, A.W., 56
Burnett, P., 4, 9, 78
Burns, G.L., 14, 54
Buskirk, J.R., 42, 90
Butler, R., 188

Calhoun, L.G., 133, 137, 140, 143
Campos, J.J., 92
Canobbio, R., 25
Carlson, E.B., 24
Carscadden, L., 23
Carver, C.S., 139
Cashman, L., 136
Caspi, A., 93
Casserta, M.S., 40
Castonguay, L.G., 92
Catherall, D.R., 5
Ceci, S.J., 167
Cerney, M.W., 42, 90
Charney, D.S., 5, 113
Chesney, M., 43, 44, 89
Chopra, D., 159
Christian, J., 42
Cigar, N., 24
Claiborn, J.M., 120
Clark, L.A., 93

Clark, M., 185
Clarke, G.N., 24
Clayton, P.J., 39, 43, 93
Cobb, S., 110
Cohen, S., 72, 74
Coleman, P.G., 186
Collette, L., 43, 44, 89
Colton, T., 187
Contrada, R.J., 41, 94
Cook, A., 134, 135
Cook, J.D., 79
Cooke, M., 43, 44, 89
Corne, S., 23
Corr, C.A., 6, 99
Corr, D.M., 99
Costa, P.T., 42
Coughlin, W.E., 155, 179
Coward, R.T., 185
Cowen, E.L., 114
Coyne, J.C., 95
Crawford, C.B., 39, 40
Creamer, M., 56
Crimmins, E.M., 187
Crofton, C.V., 95
Crocker, J., 13

Danieli, Y., 15, 24, 53
Danto, B.L., 72
Darko, D.F., 38
Darwin, C., 92
Davidson, J.R., 25, 41, 94, 96
Davidson, J.T., 56
Davidson, M.N., 44
Davidson, R.J., 41
Davis, C.G., 137
Davis, G.C., 15
Davis, P.J., 41
Davis, R., 139
Dawber, T.R., 187
de Jong, J.B., 120
de Jong, J.T., 13
Delongis, A., 137
Demi, A.S., 25
Denny, N.R., 195
Derogatis, L.R., 60, 74, 75
Descilo, T., xx, 158, 166
Deutch, A.Y., 5
Deutsch, H., 43, 90, 110
Devaul, R.D., 38
Dickson, K.A., 100
Dimond, M.F., 40
Dodge, K.A., 93
Doka, K.J., 25
Domittner, G., 113

Drabek, T., 76
Dua, J.K., 92
Dubrow, N., 13, 24
Dunkle, R., 188, 192, 197
Dunne, M., 4, 9, 78
Dworkin, D., 134, 135
Dwyer, J.W., 185
Dyer, K., 6

Eagley, A., 13
Easson, W., 14
Eastin, D.L., 146
Eddins, C., 40, 97
Edwards, K., 93
Egendorf, A., 79
Eggan, F., 99, 100
Ekblad, S., 13
Ekman, P., 92, 94
Elder, G.H., 93
Ellard, J.H., 137
Ellenberger, H.F., 100
Elliot, A.J., 25
Ellsworth, P.C., 93
Enright, R.D., 147
Enright, R.E., 146
Epstein, S., 131, 133, 138
Erickson, E., 72, 134, 186
Eth, S., 4, 14, 54, 56
Everstine, D., 155
Everstine, L., 155

Fabrega, H., 13
Fairbank, J., 79
Fairbanks, L., 4, 112
Farber, E.W., 25
Farberow, N.L., 25
Farley, M., 13, 24
Faschingbauer, T.R., 38, 39, 60
Field, N., 38, 44
Figley, C.R., 6, 15, 23, 24, 25, 53, 54, 72, 79, 153,
    154, 185, 195, 196
Fine, C.G., 202
Finley, G., 185
Finister, S.R., 72
Fisher, R.A., 39
Fisler, R., 132, 133, 136
Fleming, I., 23
Fleming, S., 138, 142, 143
Florian, V., 54
Folkman, S., 6, 43, 44, 89, 91, 92
Foa, E.B., 136
Ford, J., 147
Forgue, D.F., 120

Fossati, A., 134
Fouke, C.J., 24
Fozard, J.L., 187
Frank, E., 135
Frankl, V., 112
Freedman, S., 146
Freedman-Letofski, K., 128
Freedy, J., 184
Freeman, S.J.J., 43, 93, 128
Frederick, C.J., 4, 74, 77, 112
Freud, S., 37, 45, 89, 110
Fried, M., 185
Friedman, L., 56
Friedman, M.J., 4, 5, 7, 23
Friesen, W.V., 95
Fulcher, G., 178
Fursland, A., 23

Gallagher, D., 40
Gallagher-Thomson, D., 138
Ganley, J., 187
Ganz, F., 138
Garb, R., 134
Garbarino, J., 13, 24
Gardner, S.T., 42
Garnets, L., 13
Geiger, S.P., 72
Gendlin, E., 138
Gentry, J.E., xxi, 194, 213
Geoffrey, R., xix
George, L.K., 25, 56
Gerbode, F.A., 155, 158, 165, 166, 167
Gergen, K.J., 98
Gergen, M.M., 98
Gerrity, E., 23, 188
Gershman, K., 137
Getzel, G.S., 56
Ghaziuddin, N., 25
Gifford, R.K., 71, 72
Gilberg, A.L., 16
Gilbert, L., 23
Gill, A.G., 25
Giller, J.E., 24
Glaser, G.C., 71
Glick, I., 4
Goetz, R., 3, 14
Golan, N., 190
Gold, D.N., 81
Golden, S., 146
Goleman, D., 166
Gonzalez-Crussi, F., 99
Goodman, J., 202
Goodwin, D.W., 157

Gorman, J.M., 3, 14
Gottlieb, B.H., 95
Gottman, J.M., 93
Grace, M.C., 56, 71, 72, 113
Grainger, R.K., 178
Green, B.L., 14, 15, 71, 72, 113
Green, F., 42, 90, 98
Greenberg, H.S., 54, 97
Greenberg, L.S., 138
Greene, B., 185
Grego, B.C., 56
Gribble, P.A., 114
Grigsby, J.P., 120
Gruler, A.M., 83
Guastello, S.J., 42
Guidano, V.F., 138
Gunzerath, L., 41, 45

Hagman, G., 131
Hagstrom, R., 185
Halikas, J.A., 39, 43
Hamera, E.K., 137
Hamilton, D.L., 13
Hammond, C., 210
Hancock, P.A., 187
Hansen, C.H., 41
Hansen, F., 40, 89
Hansen, R.D., 41
Hansson, R.O., 39
Harber, K.D., 95, 158, 168
Harik, W., 187
Hartman, S., 24
Hartsough, D.M., 60, 61, 74
Haug, M., 188, 192, 197
Hayward, M.D., 187
Hebl, J.H., 147
Hendrix, H., 212
Herbert, S.E., 25
Herceg, M.S., 24
Herman, D.S., 60, 66, 133, 142
Herman, J., 160, 162, 166, 168
Herman, J.L., 14, 16, 194, 201, 202
Hickey, T., 187
Higson-Smith, C., 24
Him, C., 24
Hoberman, H., 72, 74
Hobfoll, S.E., 15, 185
Hodde-Vargas, J., 112
Hodgkinson, P.E., 14, 15, 16, 25
Hoine, H., 157
Holen, A., 38, 39, 40, 41, 43, 44, 45, 89, 90, 92, 94, 98, 135
Holloway, D.R., 72

Holmes, T., 37, 39, 54, 183
Hooyman, N., 183, 184, 188, 195
Horn, J., 71, 187
Horowitz, M.J., 14, 28, 38, 39, 40, 41, 43, 44, 45, 46, 73, 89, 90, 92, 94, 96, 98, 112, 128, 135, 142, 185
Hoyt, M.F., 137
Hughes, D., 56
Hughes, D.C., 25
Hughes, M., 3, 7
Hurrel, J.J., 71
Huska, J.A., 60
Hyer, L., xx, 132, 133, 134, 136, 138, 141, 142

Irwin, M., 38
Izard, C.E., 92

Jacobs, S., 4, 6, 7, 9, 14, 15, 40, 42, 57, 65, 89, 90, 111, 113, 127, 135
James, B., 153, 169
Jang, K.L., 39, 40
Janoff-Bulman, R., 5, 6, 7, 8, 14, 16, 44, 138, 155
Jaranson, J.M., 7, 23
Jarvik, L.F., 187
Jay, L.L., 192
Johnson, D.R., 113
Jones, A.R., 72
Joseph, S.A., 25, 136
Jung, C.G., 140

Kadushin, C., 79
Kahana, B., 188
Kahana, E.F., 183, 186, 190
Kalin, N.H., 41
Kalish, R.A., 99, 100
Kaltreider, N., 74, 142
Kamarck, T., 72, 74
Kang, H.K., 25
Kaplan, K.J., 45
Kaprio, J., 55
Kardiner, A., 110
Kasl, S., 40, 89, 135
Kastenbaum, R.J., 14, 100
Kazak, A.E., 72
Keane, T.M., 60, 79
Kehle, T.J., 13
Kellner, R., 120
Kelly, A.E., 97
Keltner, D., 38, 39, 40, 41, 43, 44, 45, 91, 92, 93, 94, 95, 96
Kessler, R.C., 3, 7, 38, 45, 90
Khoury, E.L., 25
Kilpatrick, D.G., 54, 58, 60, 71, 112, 184

Kim, K., 40, 89, 113, 135
King, C.A., 25
Kini, M.M., 187
Kinney, R., 24
Kirschner, E., 71
Kiyak, H.A., 183, 184, 188, 195
Klass, D., 56
Klein, M., 110
Kluft, R.P., 7, 202, 214
Knight, B.G., 187
Kobasa, S.C., 139
Koskenvico, M., 55
Kostelny, K., 13, 24
Kowalskis, J.M., 116
Kozak, M.J., 136
Krakow, B., 120
Kramer, R., 13, 24
Kreamer, H.C., 60
Kroes, W.H., 71
Krupnick, J., 142
Krystal, H., 114
Kubany, E., 146
Kubler-Ross, E., 184

Lancee, W.J., 43, 93
Larson, J., 156
Laub, D., 24
Laufer, R., 79
Lavinge, J., 15
Lavretsky, E., 187
Lawton, M., 185, 188, 190
Lazare, A., 42, 90
Lazarus, R.S., 6, 91, 92
Leakey, R.E., 98
Lehman, D.R., 39, 45, 54, 137
Leibowitz, H.M., 187
Leicht, L., 54
Leichtman, M.D., 167
Lemerise, E.A., 93
Leonard, A.C., 113
Lepore, S., 139
Lerer, B., 134
Lerner, H.G., 13
Levenson, R.W., 93, 95
Levin, C., 178
Levinson, D.J., 188
Levitt, M., 185
Lewinsohn, P., 24
Lifton, R.J., 7, 14, 15, 16, 112, 134
Light, S.C., 72
Lin, N., 72
Lindeman, E., xix, 26, 45, 55, 78, 110, 111
Lindy, J.D., 14, 56, 72, 113

Lingiardi, V., 134
Litz, B.T., 60
Loosen, P.T., 41
Lopata, H.Z., 137
Loya, F., 112
Lucca, N., 100
Lund, D.A., 40
Lundin, T., 39
Lyall, W.A., 43, 93, 128
Lynch, G., 156
Lyons, J.A., 57

MacIan, P., 8
Maddison, D.C., 39, 57, 58
Madeddu, F., 134
Maffei, C., 134
Malatesta, C.Z., 93
Malinak, D.P., 137
Mandel, D.R., 137
Mandelbaum, D.G., 99
Margolis, B.L., 71
Marks, I.M., 91
Marmar, C.R., 40, 128, 142
Marsella, A.J., 13, 23, 100
Martinek, N., 4, 9, 16, 26, 31, 40, 55, 78, 89, 90
Martinson, I., 6
Marwit, S., 134
Mas, C., 8
Mason, P.T., 42
Masters, R., 56
Masuda, M., 54
Matsakis, A., 72
Mawson, D., 91
Mazza, N., 25, 53
Maurice, W.L., 39, 43, 93
McAdams, D.P., 140
McCammon, S.M., 5
McCann, I.L., 5, 7, 8, 13, 14, 15, 16, 53
McCaughey, B.G., 13
McCool, R.E., 113
McCrae, R.R., 42
McCranie, E.W., 136
McCreery, J.M., 38, 54, 61, 71, 82, 112, 115
McCubin, H., 185
McCullough, M.E., 147
McFarlane, A.C., 116
McGree, M., xx, 188, 189
McGlashan, T., 24
McKay, G., 74
McKilltop, K.J., 97
McNeil, J.S., 56, 60
McSharry, S., 24
Medhart, P., 187
Melamed, B.G., 24

Melges, F.T., 133, 142, 144
Merleau-Ponty, M., 142
Mermelstein, R., 72, 74
Messick, J., 190
Metuh, I.E., 98
Michenbaum, D., 202, 205
Middleton, W., 40, 54, 78, 89, 90
Mikulincer, M., 54, 185
Milbrath, C., 92
Miles, M.S., 25
Miller, T.W., 192
Millon, T., 139
Misso, V., 40, 89, 90
Mitchell, J.T., 73
Moffitt, T., 93
Molnar, C., 136
Monrovia, 24
Moore, J., 99, 100
Moore, T., 131
Moore, R.H., 155, 158
Moos, R.H., 139, 189
Moritz, G., 25
Moylan, A., 4, 9, 78
Munczek, D., 13, 24

Nabe, C.M., 99
Nader, K., 4, 14, 112
Nadler, A., 185
Nahemow, L., 185, 188, 190
Nambi, J., 153
Nathan, P., 15
Naylor, M., 25
Nelson, C., 3, 7
Nelson, G.M., 187
Nelson, J.C., 127
Nemiroff, D., 71
Neshkes, R., 187
Ness, D., 112
Neugebauer, R., 3, 14
Newman, B.M., 186
Newman, L.S., 44
Newman, J., 185
Newman, P.R., 186
Newmann, D., 8
Newton, T.L., 41, 94
Nickerson, J., 187
Niederhoffer, A., 72
Niederhoffer, E., 72
Niedhart, J., 120
Nilsson, L.G., 167
Nisbett, R.E., 100
Nolen-Hoeksema, S., 43, 93
Norris, F.H., 58, 69

North, C.S., 112, 113
Notarius, C., 45
Nutini, H., 13

Ochberg, 79, 112
Olson, E., 25
Op den Velde, W., 186
Opoku, K.A., 98, 100
Ordy, J.M., 187
Orley, J., 13
Ornstein, P.A., 167
Orr, S.P., 120
Orth, D.N., 41
Osterweis, M., 42, 90, 98
Ostfield, A., 40, 89
Ottenberg, D.J., 72

Pages, K.P., 25, 54
Parad, H.J., 189
Parad, L., 190
Parere, N., 25
Paris, J., 42
Parker, G.R., 114
Parkes, C.M., 4, 9, 14, 39, 40, 45, 55, 56, 71, 81,
        89, 90, 112, 113, 141, 142
Parsons, J.P., 13
Pasternak, R.E, 127
Pathak, D., 120
Paton, D., 79
Patterson, V., 137
Pattison, P., 56
Paul, B., 202
Paulay, D., 92
Paulhus, D.L., 41, 96
Paz, O., 99
Pearlman, L.A., 5, 7, 8, 13, 14, 15, 16, 53
Pennebaker, J.W., 93, 95, 97, 158, 168
Perper, J.A., 25
Perry, B.D., 5
Pfeffer, C., 112
Phifer, J.F., 183
Pickett, M., 54
Pitman, R.K., 120
Pleck, J.H., 13
Podorefsky, D., 139
Poprajac, T., 211
Potocky, M., 154
Poussaint, A.F., 56
Powell, B., 157
Pregrad, J., 24
Price, R., 100, 140
Price, S., 100
Prigerson, H., 135

Putnam, F.W., 202
Puig, C., 25
Pynoos, R.S., 4, 14, 54, 56, 112

Quilter, R.E., 187

Rabkin, J.G., 3, 14
Rahe, R., 37, 39, 183
Ramm, L., 91
Rando, T.A., xi, 4, 6, 14, 16, 25, 29, 53, 54, 154, 177, 202
Raoof, A., 114
Raphael, B., 4, 9, 14, 16, 26, 31, 40, 45, 54, 55, 77, 90, 112, 127
Raymond, C.A., 71
Redmund, L., 14
Reimer, R.H., 3, 14
Reiser, M., 72
Resnick, H., 184
Reviere, S.L., 25
Reynolds, C.F., 127, 135
Reynolds, D.K., 99, 100
Reynolds, S., 187
Riley, J., 183
Riley, M.W., 183
Rinear, E.E., 53, 54, 56, 58, 112
Rita, H., 55
Roberts, B.L., 188, 192, 197
Robins, E., 39, 43, 93
Robbins, J., 24
Robbins, L.S., 187
Robinson, P., 138, 142, 143
Rodman, J., 138
Rodriguez, A.L., 72
Rogers, J., 43, 93, 128
Rorty, A.Q., 131
Rosen, E., 14
Rosen, H., 14
Rosen, M., 14
Rosenberg, S.E., 46
Rosenblatt, P., 98
Rosenheck, R., 15
Rosenthal, J., 66
Rosovsky, K., 38
Rosow, I., 186
Ross, C.A., 202
Ross, L., 100
Rosser-Hogan, R., 24
Rothbart, G., 79
Rotter, J.B., 139
Rotton, J., 185
Roy-Byrne, P.P., 25
Rozee, P.D., 24

Ruback, R.B., 58, 69
Rudolph, J.M., 6, 7, 10, 15, 26, 28
Rusch, K.M., 42
Russo, J., 25
Ryan, M., 15
Rynearson, E.K., xix, 38, 54, 56, 61, 64, 71, 82, 112, 115, 116, 120, 122, 128

Saakvitne, K.W., 8, 14
Sack, W.H., 24
Safran, J.D., 138
Sahin, J.I., 114
Saladin, M., 184
Salisbury, H., 134
Salovey, P., 138
Salter, B.E., 39, 40
Samalou, D., 24
Sameroff, A.J., 114
Sandberg, C.T., 6, 10, 16
Sanders, C.M., 39, 40, 43, 45, 60, 89, 90, 98
Sangrey, D., 56
Sarinopoulos, S., 146
Saunders, B., 184
Sawyer, S., 77
Schaefer, J.A., 139
Schafer, R., 122
Schaie, K.W., 187
Scheier, M.F., 139
Scherer, K.R., 41, 94
Schlernitzauer, M., 127
Schmidt, A.H., 186
Schmidt, I.M., 194, 213
Schneider, D., 40
Schnurr, P.P., 7
Schottler, F., 156
Schuster, S.R., 4, 14, 38, 40, 43, 89, 90, 91, 92, 93, 95
Schut, H., 40, 91
Schwarz, E.D., 116
Schwarz, N., 93
Schwartz, G.E., 41, 94, 96
Scott, W.A., 45
Scurfield, 23
Seagraves, R., 195
Sechrest, 179
Seeley, J.R., 24
Segal, S.A., 24, 42
Seifer, R.S., 114
Shapiro, F., 138, 141, 156, 157, 158, 177, 178
Shaw, 73
Shay, J., 13, 134
Shea, J.M., 113
Sheikh, A.A., 120

Shelder, 94
Sheldon, A.R., 43, 93
Sherman, E., 134, 135, 141
Shonkwiller, M., 15
Shontz, F.C., 137
Siddique, H., 41, 46, 91, 92, 94, 96
Siegel, B., 92
Siegel, D.J., 136
Silver, R.C., 5, 6, 38, 43, 45, 90, 93, 95, 98, 139
Simpson, M.A., 24
Singer, J.A., 138
Singer, J.L., 41, 96
Sinnema, C.S., 122
Sledge, P., 38
Sloan, L., 79
Smith, B., 24
Smith, E.M., 112, 113
Smith, S., 54, 58, 71, 112
Smith, T., 186
Solomon, F., 42, 90, 98
Solomon, R., 178
Solomon, Z., 54, 71, 185
Sonnega, A., 3, 7
Southwick, S.M., 113
Spanier, G.B., 46
Spiegel, D., 7
Spitznagel, E., 112
Sprang, V.M., 56, 60
Ssekiwanuka, J.K., 24
Stamm, B.H., xvi, xvii, 4, 5, 6, 7, 8, 10, 13, 15, 16, 24, 26, 28, 54
Stamm, H.E., 13, 24
Steele, K., 202
Steer, R.A., 39
Steinberg, H.R., 7, 60
Steinglass, P., 186, 188
Stern, H., 157
Stern, L.S., 91
Stevens-Guille, M.E., xvii, 14, 66
Stillman, F.A., 73, 74, 77, 78, 79, 84
Stinson, C.H., 92
Stone, A., 97
Strickland, B.R., 139
Stroebe, M.S., 7, 9, 14, 16, 37, 39, 40, 41, 42, 43, 55, 58, 89, 90, 91, 92, 98, 113
Stroebe, W., 7, 9, 14, 16, 37, 39, 40, 41, 42, 43, 55, 58, 89, 90, 91, 92, 98, 113
Stouthamer-Loeber, M., 93
Stutman, S., 139
Suris, J., 25

Tangney, J.P., 146
Tarrier, N., 120

Taylor, S.E., 13, 93
Tedeschi, R.G., 133, 137, 140, 143
Tennen, H., 137
Terr, L., 7
Terry, M.J., 5, 13
Thompson, M.P., 58, 69
Tierra Blanca, 23
Tinker, R.H., 156, 178
Tinnin, L., 210, 212
Titchener, J.D., 56
Titiev, M., 99
Tomarken, A.J., 41
Torem, M., 202
Triandis, H.C., 100
Trice, A.D., 4
Trolly, B.C., 4
Turco, R.M., 56, 134
Turnbull, R., 4, 6, 7, 9, 10, 16, 29, 55
Tyler, M.P., 71, 72
Tyson, G.A., 24

Ureno, G., 46
Ursano, R.C., 72

Vachon, M.L., 43, 93, 128
Valentine, P.V., 155, 178
Vargas, L.A., 112
Varra, E.M., 6, 7, 10, 16, 28
Van Boemel, G.B., 24
van den Bout, J., 91
Van der Hart, O., 56, 112, 134, 202
Van der Kolk, B.A., 78, 79, 112, 132, 133, 136
van Schaik, M.M., 13
Vaughan, K., 120
Vega, W.A., 25
Vercruyssen, M., 187
Veronen, L.J., 54, 58, 71, 112
Villereal, G., 134, 135
Villareal, M.J., 100
Villasenor, V.S., 46
Violanti, J.M., xviii, 71
Vojvoda, D., 24

Wagner, M.B., 187
Walker, W.L., 39, 57, 58
Wallerstein, R., 142
Wannon, M., 114
Warheit, G.J., 25
Warwick, M., 4, 9
Watson, D., 93
Weathers, F.W., 60
Weil, A., 156
Weinberger, D.A., 41, 44, 96

Weine, S.M., 13, 24
Weisaeth, L., 24
Weiss, D.S., 128
Weiss, R.S., 4, 9, 39, 45, 89, 90, 94, 141
Widdison, H., 134
Widiger, T.A., 42
Williams, A.F., 39, 45, 54
Williams, C., 72
Williams, G., 83
Williams, J.B., 3, 14
Williams, P., 38, 44
Williams, R.M., 25, 136
Wilner, N., 28, 74, 142
Wilson, J.P., 14, 71, 72
Wilson, L.G., 25
Wilson, S.A., 156, 178
Windholz, M.J., 40
Wister, A., 186
Woelfel, M.W., 72
Wojcik, E.H.S., 74
Wolf, F.M., 187
Wolpe, J., 213
Woods, M., 136
Worden, J.W., 53, 82, 98, 134, 135, 142, 143

Work, W.S., 114
Worrell, J.D., 54
Worthington, E.L., 147
Wortman, C.B., 5, 6, 38, 39, 40, 43, 45, 54, 90, 93, 95, 98, 137, 139
Wosner, V., 185
Wray, L.A., 187
Wright, R., 56, 60
Wyman, P.A., 114

Yeaton, 179
Yehuda, R., 113
Young, M.B., 72
Yule, W., 25, 136

Zarit, S.H., 189
Zelwer, B., 23
Zimmerman, R.S., 25
Zisook, S., 4, 14, 38, 40, 43, 89, 90, 91, 92, 93, 95, 127
Znoj, H., 46, 94
Zubenko, G., 135
Zweig-Frank, H., 42

Subject Index

AIDS, 15
Abrogation of Expected Reality Scale, 30

Bereavement
  assessment, 119
  normal, 26–27
  traumatic, 26–27
  (*See also* Grief)
Bureau of Justice Assistance, 84

Case Histories
  of grief for homicides, 122–127
Causal Directions (CD), 166
Closeness to victim
  coefficients for multiple regression, (table) 63
  risk factor for pathology, 64
Constructivist self-development theory, 8–9
Coping mechanisms, xix

Death
  African view, 98, 100
  difficulties, 14
  duty related, 71–85
  Hopi Indian view, 99
  Mexican Day of the Dead, 99
  nonnormal, (table) 29
  non-war, 24–25
  of police officer, 71–85
  poverty, 23–24
  risk factor, 23
  Saramaka of Suriname, 99–100
  by suicide, 32
  distribution of, (table) 29
  survivors, 72–85
  Uganda, 153
  violent, 32
  war, 23–24

Depression
  commingling with grief, 131
Details of Death Scale, 30
Disease
  prevention, 127–128
Dissociative
  Dissociative Experience Scale (DES), 116,
      (table) 117
  imagery, 212
Distress
  levels, global, 75
  psychological, 74
  women at greater risk, 57
Drills
  acknowledgement, 162–163
  attitude adjustment, 161–162
  closure, 163–165
  focusing, 159–161
Dyadic Adjustment Scale, 46

Elderly
  assessment models, 189–190
  death related stress, 183
  consequences of, 185
  demographics, 187
  developmental activities, 186–188, (table) 191
  differences in, 183–184
  interventions, current, 189
  life structures, 188
  phases of reactions to death, 184
  six factors of energetic lifestyles, 187
  stress management model, (table) 193
  theories of, 185–186
Emotion
  dissociation, 93–97
  experience and expression, 42–43
  self-deception, 93–97
  social-functional account, 92–93
  verbal-autonomic response dissociation, 94

Environment
  contextual, 13
Eye Movement Desensitization and Reprocessing
    (EMDR)
  in drills, 165–166
  in interventions, 154
  relieving trauma and stress, 156–159
  role of emotions in, 168–169
  with seniors, 195–197
  treatment procedures of, xx, 174–181

Facial Action Coding System (FACS), 95
Feminine Situational Adaptation Scale, 29
Forgiveness
  ego skills necessary, (table) 147

General Severity Index (GSI), 60
General Symptom Inventory (GSI), 76–78
Gender
  differences in experiencing grief, 65–66
  women at risk for greater distress, 57
Grief
  adjustment during, 45–46
  appraisal, 43–44
  avoidance of reminders, 91
  confrontation, 91
  coping process, 43–44
  depression, 135–136
  dimensional pattern, 9–10
  distraction, 91
  emotional control, 91
  grief work approach, xvii, xviii, 90–91
  stages in, 142–148
  growth in, 136–142
  interactionist stress perspective, 92
  measuring, 37–39
  nondisclosure, 91
  perceived social support, 40
  phases of, 55
  self-blame, 44, 81–82
  severity, 41–44
  stressful event, 55
  suppression, 91
  tenets of, 137–142
  unfinished business, 82
  (See also Loss)

Homicide
  Canadian incidence of, 57–58
  Coconut Grove, 110–111
  western Canada families study, 58–66

comparison of results and scale norms,
    (table) 62
dependent measures intercorrelations,
    (table) 61
gender differences, 65–66
General Severity Index, 60
method, 59
PPTDS, 61
respondent characteristics, 59–60
results, 62–63
  SCL 90-R, 60–61
  TRIG, 60–61
history, 109–112
images of, 56, (table) 117
peculiarities, 112
resiliency, 114–115, 117–118
pacification, 114, 120–121
partition, 115, 120–121
perspective, 115
searching behavior, 56
secondary traumatization, 54
Support Project for Unnatural Dying (1990),
    115–119
traumatic grief of, 53–54
goals of, 121
seeking versus refusing, (table) 116
vulnerability
  risk factors, (table) 113–114

Impact of Events Scale, 28, 31–32, (table) 31
Inventory of Interpersonal Problems, 46

Loss
  adaptation, 89
  demographic variables, 40
  denial, maladaptive, 42–43
  effective loss accommodation, 37
  emotional dissociation, 89
  forewarning, 39
  level of adjustment with previous loss, 40
  meaning of, 44–45
  self-deception, 89
  type of, 39–40
  (See also Grief)

Military, 72
Minnesota Multiphasic Personality Inventory
    (MMPI), 176
Mourning process, 9

Numbness, 9

Person
  resources of, 10
Person in Event Scale, 30
Personality
  borderline personality disorder, 41–42
  predictors of grief severity, 41–42
  repressor, 41
  self-deceptive enhancement dimensions, 41
Police Officers
  Concerns of Police Survivors (C.O.P.S), 79–80
  death notification, 80
  liaison officers, 80
  surviving children, 83
  work culture, 71–72
Post Traumatic Stress Disorder (PTSD)
  commingling with giref, 131
  description of, xv–xvi, 3–7, 154
  and grief, xx–xxi
    definition, 134–135
    depression, 135–136
  of homicide, 53–54
  among police spouses, 77
  positive symptoms of, 156
  in self theory, 133
  seven stressors, 14–16
  seven symptoms, 136
  treatment model, 142–148
Protection within the Collective Scale, 30
Psychotherapy
  group, 121–122
  preliminary thoughts, 120
Public Coping/Private Pain Scale, 29
Purdue Post-Traumatic Disorder Scale
  (PPTDS), 61

Relationship
  ambivalent, 45–46
  centrality of, 57
  conflicted, 45–46
  with deceased, 45–46
Recovery, 9
Relaxation induction, 210
Resources
  psychosocial, 29
Revised Impact of Events Score (RIES), 116,
  (table) 117
Rynearson
  Three V's model, 112

Safety
  closure, 213
  levels, 202
  hazards, (illus.) 206, 212

  map, (illus.) 204, 205
  resources, (illus.) 207, 212–213
  treatment plan, (illus.) 208–210
Safety Reconnaissance, xxi, 201, 203–215
Self-Deceptive Enhancement (SDE), 96–97
Self-theory
  definition of, 132
  in context of trauma, 131, 132–134
Semantic Representations of Others Scale
  (SROS), 45–46
Senior Life Span Development Model (SLSDM),
  184, 192, 193–194
  for trauma reduction, 194–197
  goal, 194
Separation
  distress, 9
  responses, 111
Social interaction
  changes in, 74–75
Social Support
  risk factor for pathology, 63–65
  role of, 56–57
Stress
  stressful experience, 6
  classification of, 28
  distributiuon of, (table) 28
  system stress, 13
Structural Assessment of Stessful Experiences
  (SASE), 25–26, 28
Structural Conceptualization of Stressful Experiences (SCSE), 7, 10, 25–26
Symptom Checklist 90-Revised (SCL-90-R),
  75–78
  Canada study, 60–61

Texas Revised Grief Inventory (TRIG), 60–61,
  116, (table) 117
Therapist
  five elements of, 147
Thought Field Therapy (TFT)
  with seniors, 195–197
Trauma
  description of, 131
  group level intervention, 79–81
  individual treatment, 81–83
  clinical rules, 158–159
  communication skills, 159
  role of emotions, 168–169
Trauma Reaction Index, 74, 76–78
Traumatic Incident Reduction (TIR)
  assumptions of, 158–159
  description of, 154–155
  in drills, 165–166

methodology, 168–178
    treatment procedures of, xx
Traumatic distress, 9–10
Traumatic stress
    conceptualization, (illus.) 5
    disorder, 6
    reaction, 6, 111

Visualization, 211–212

War
    shell shock, 110
World assumption theory, 7–8